Acoustic Guitars

And Other Fretted Instruments

◆ ◆ ◆

A PHOTOGRAPHIC HISTORY

Acoustic Guitars

And Other Fretted Instruments

A PHOTOGRAPHIC HISTORY

◆ ◆ ◆ ◆ ◆

George Gruhn & Walter Carter

GPI Books

Miller Freeman Inc.

San Francisco

◆ ◆ ◆

GPI Books
Miller Freeman, Inc.
600 Harrison Street, San Francisco, CA 94107

Library of Congress Cataloging-in-Publication Data
Gruhn, George
    Acoustic guitars and other fretted instuments:
a photographic history / [text by] George Gruhn
& Walter Carter.
      p.   cm.
    Includes bibliographical references (p.).
    ISBN 0-87930-240-2
    1. Guitar—United States—Pictorial works.
2. Banjo—Pictorial works. 3. Mandolin—Pictorial
works. I. Carter, Walter. II. Title.
ML1015.G9G76 1993
787.87' 1973—dc20   92-44435

Designed by Brad Greene, Greene Design
Production Editor: Linda Jupiter

Printed in Hong Kong

98 97 96 95 94 93   5 4 3 2 1

TABLE OF CONTENTS
♦ ♦ ♦

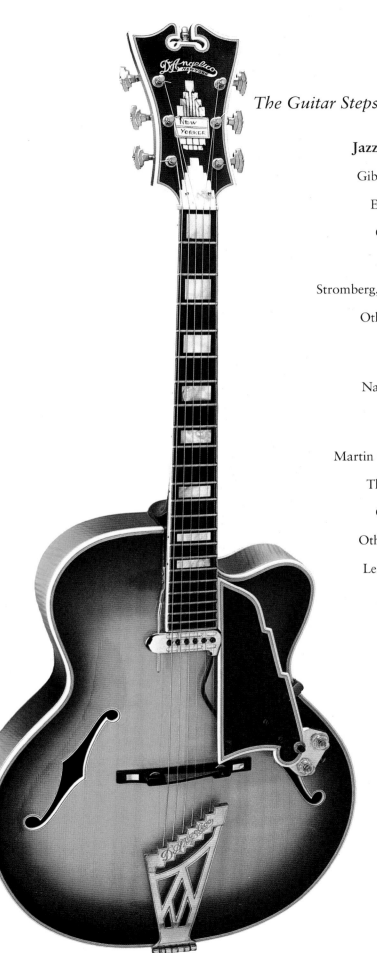

PART TWO
The Guitar Steps Forward, 1930s to Current Times

INTRODUCTION

♦ ♦ ♦

In March 1988 we hired Dan Loftin, a professional photographer and banjo buff, to go to a Nashville guitar show with us and photograph instruments for an entity we called Gruhn Publications. We meant to start a vintage instrument magazine, but when we looked at that first set of transparencies, we got a touch of collector's fever. We held these photos carefully in our hands, almost as if they had been the actual instruments. As the photo files grew, they became not just material for a book, not just an often-used reference, but a prized collection. After all, no one—not even the richest instrument collector in the world—can own everything. The vast majority of instrument lovers may never have the opportunity to even lay eyes on, much less touch or play, a D'Angelico New Yorker or a prewar Martin D-45 or a complete family of Gibson Style 5 models signed by Lloyd Loar. We cannot play music on photographs, of course, but we can look at them whenever we want, and a collection of hundreds of photos takes up less space than the smallest guitar.

So before the idea to do a book, there was the idea to collect and preserve these instruments on film. Long after we had acquired enough photos to fill several books, we continued to shoot. In addition to Dan Loftin, Billy Mitchell of San Antonio helped us cover guitar shows. We eventually set up a photo booth in Gruhn Guitars so that instruments that were only visiting at our store would not escape our camera. Several collectors who are also excellent photographers provided photos of their instruments.

Our plan with this book was to *show* a lot of interesting instruments—some pretty, some historically important. By grouping them according to type and period, we could show the evolution of American fretted instruments. From an evolutionary perspective, these instruments break into two basic categories—acoustic and electric—and it quickly became obvious that to avoid creating a ponderous, cumbersome tome, we should break our work along the same lines, with one book devoted to acoustic instruments and one to electrics.

We had hoped to let the pictures speak for themselves, using only enough text to put each instrument in the proper historical perspective. That sounded easy but was surprisingly difficult. From the very beginning—a section on the European ancestors of the modern American guitar—even the most innocuous statement of fact proved troublesome. We could not even use the word *guitar* without some qualification. To illustrate, the *guitarra moresca* of the 1200s was probably a lute, while the *viola* and *demi-luth* of the late 1400s were probably guitars. In other words, a guitar by any other name may still be a guitar, but a guitar by its own name may not be a guitar at all.

Other obstacles to brevity arose in crediting innovations. More often than not, innovators or inventors could be described more accurately as establishers or perfecters. They established or perfected someone else's design so that it became the industry standard. Luthier/historian Richard Bruné summed up the situation with the comment: "In guitar history, somebody is always reinventing the wheel." Indeed, almost every innovation—C. F. Martin's X-pattern bracing, Orville Gibson's three-point scroll-body mandolin, the Larson brothers' metal support rod—warranted some discussion, if not outright qualification. It was certainly not our intent to trample on the legends and lore of the American guitar, and in fact, most of the accepted innovators were the first to incorporate their design into a *successful* instrument. The one who generally deserves the credit is not necessarily the one who thinks it up, but rather the one who makes it work.

Part of the intrigue of old instruments comes from the curious nature of companies and the fascinating array of personalities behind them. We found some stories simply irresistible:

♦ The Martin company has made one thing exceedingly well for over 150 years—flat top guitars—and has been not only a successful company but one whose innovations have become industry standards. Gibson, by contrast, is an equally successful company but one that changed its focus several times— from mandolins to banjos and finally to guitars. After its initial innovations in the mandolin and archtop guitar field, Gibson often had to play catch-up to other manufacturers, achieving success by perfecting some else's innovation with greater innovations, adding its own distinctive flair, and then outmarketing its competitors.

♦ Many of the great manufacturers' names are now unfamiliar or known for different products. Lyon and Healy, one of the giants of fretted instrument and piano manufacturing at the turn of the century, survives today only as a harp manufacturer. Many five-string banjo makers were unable to make the easy adjustment to the tenor banjo. Later, when tenor banjos gave way to guitars, the only major banjo makers to make a successful switch were Gretsch, Gibson (both of which were already diversified and remained so after the rise of the guitar), and Epiphone.

♦ National and Dobro went into business just before the Depression and, despite an inordinate amount of management infighting, were successful with highly innovative instruments. Then they switched their focus to cheaper electrics with innovations that were more gimmicky than effective.

Historical summation and encapsulation can be deceiving. Eras and trends are typically marked by historians with beginning and end points, but in reality, they fade and merge into and out of each other. For example, to say the tenor banjo began to overshadow the mandolin does not mean one day the land was full of mandolin orchestras and the next day all the chairs were filled by tenor banjo fanatics. The tenor banjo drove the mandolin out of style, to be sure, but not out of existence. To read a copy of *The Crescendo*, a mandolin-oriented magazine that was published into the mid-1930s, one would never know that the tenor banjo had even arrived, much less departed to be replaced by the guitar, or that the Depression had hit. The same magazine's ever-shrinking size, however, did provide evidence of the mandolin's decline.

Already, the text is running longer than we intended, and no amount of text can accurately describe the instruments represented in these photographs. They are presented here for you to enjoy and appreciate.

George Gruhn
Walter Carter
Nashville, 1992

ACKNOWLEDGMENTS

◆ ◆ ◆

Sources of information for this book were by no means limited to those books and magazines listed in the bibliography. We picked up bits and pieces of information everywhere—from articles, conversations, company literature, catalogs, and so on. Friends with special expertise provided valuable information, and we thank them. For European guitars: Richard E. Bruné; pre-1900 American guitars: Michael Holmes and Mark Silber; Washburns: Michael Holmes; five-string banjos: Jim Bollman and Calvin Minner; Orville Gibson and Lloyd Loar: Roger Siminoff; acoustic Hawaiian instruments: Bob Brozman and Mike Newton; Oscar Schmidt, Stella, and Lead Belly: Michael Holmes, Kip Lornell, Jon Lundberg, and Ralph Rinzler.

Michael I. Holmes deserves a special thanks. We showed up on his phone line, as he put it, "like a bad penny" that would not go away. He freely gave up information that he has spent the past 11 years researching. His upcoming book, *The Encyclopedia of American Musical Instruments: Fretted Instruments and Their Makers,* will cover 1,100 makers and an equal number of patents, and its publication should free up his telephone.

Thanks to the many collectors and dealers who let us photograph their instruments. Ownership credit refers to the time when the photo was taken, although instruments may have changed hands since then. The photographers are Walter Carter, Dean Dixon, Steve Evans, Jonathan Levin, Dan Loftin, and Billy Mitchell. Their initials follow the ownership credits.

PART ONE

◆ ◆ ◆

A Time for Every Instrument,
1800s to 1920s

For the majority of Americans—those born after World War II—the guitar has been the dominant instrument in popular music for their whole lives. But it was not always that way. From the founding of the United States up until the late 1920s, the guitar played second fiddle, so to speak, to a variety of other instruments. Many still remember the saxophone as the key instrument in the evolution of big band music into modern jazz or the trumpet as the power of the first jazz bands of the 1920s. Beyond living memory now is the turn-of-the-century ragtime piano, which caught the public's fancy with a combination of popular rhythms and classical structure. These instruments dominated the guitar in their time. Even within its own family of fretted instruments, the guitar played a secondary role through most of its history. Its European forerunners were overshadowed by the lute during the Middle Ages and Renaissance. In America, the guitar was dominated first by the five-string banjo, then the mandolin, and finally the tenor banjo.

One of the monumental events in the history of American fretted instruments, the emergence of a distinctively American guitar, occurred around 1850, but it actually represented the grande finale—not a beginning—of a rapid evolution that had begun in Europe in the late 1700s. The guitar was by no means an obscure instrument in nineteenth-century America, but it rested on an evolutionary plateau. The period from the late 1700s to the 1920s belonged to the minstrel banjo, the classical banjo, the mandolin, and the tenor banjo.

♦ *Unlabeled, early 1800s.
(See page 11.)*

EARLY GUITARS
♦ ♦ ♦

European Ancestors

Guitar-shaped instruments appear in stone *bas-relief* sculptures of the Hittites in northern Syria and Asia Minor from as far back as 1350 B.C. The word "guitar" also has origins in the Middle and Far East, deriving from *guit,* the Arabic word for four, and *tar,* the Sanskrit word for string. The earliest European guitars did, in fact, have four "courses" or groups of gut strings (usually in pairs), but these instruments seem to have been called anything but guitars. The term *guitarra* appears in Spanish literature of the 1300s, but it probably refers to lutelike instruments. A writer in 1487 described an instrument with curved-in sides, but this was called a *demi-luth* by the French (literally, a "half-lute") and a *viola* by Italians and Spaniards (*viola* was a generic term in Italian for all stringed instruments; *vihuela* was the generic term in Spanish). By whatever name, these early guitars were distinguished from lutes by body sides that curved inward to form a waist and by four courses of

strings. In addition, some, though not all, early guitars had a flat back, while lutes always had a rounded back.

Culturally, the guitar was not the dominant fretted instrument during the Middle Ages and Renaissance. That honor belonged to the lute, except in Spain, where the lute's Arabic origins kept it out of favor. In addition to physical differences that distinguished it from the guitar—pear-shaped body (no waist), rounded back, and five or more courses of strings—the lute was generally regarded as a higher class of instrument.

Despite the guitar's status as an instrument of the common people, it had gained enough respect and popularity by 1546 to merit publication of a book of guitar music. By that time, five-course guitars were coming into vogue, and modern tuning had been introduced. Chord positions were the same as they are today (without the lowest string), but a guitar of the mid 1500s would hardly feel familiar to the hands of a twentieth-century musician. Frets were made of gut and tied around the neck, and accurate placement of frets was so tricky that manuals were published on the subject. The neck was shorter than that of a modern guitar, joining the body at the 10th or 11th fret rather than the 14th of a modern steel-string acoustic or the 12th of a modern classical guitar. The fingerboard stopped short of the body, and the spruce top of the instrument extended several frets up the neck. Upper frets made of metal or ivory were mounted directly onto the top.

If one had to choose an instrument of the Middle Ages that would evolve into the modern guitar, the favorite might well have been the cittern. In the 1500s the cittern was considered an instrument of the common people and it was second only to the lute in popularity. Despite having a pear-shaped body and a unique tuning, it was much more like a modern guitar than were the guitars of its day. It had metal strings, fixed frets, a fingerboard that extended onto the top, a flat back, and a movable bridge with strings anchored by a tailpiece; and it was played with a quill or plectrum. From a twentieth-century perspective, the cittern seems to have been far ahead of its time, but it was actually behind the times. The plectrum style was considered old-timey by the late 1500s, having been replaced by fingerpicking. For this and other reasons, including perhaps the expense or scarcity of metal strings, the cittern proved to be an evolutionary false start, disappearing by the late 1600s.

Through the 1600s and the mid-1700s, guitar design changed very little, although interest in it increased among luthiers. An Italian style emerged, developed by German immigrants and characterized by a lutelike rounded back made from multiple pieces or "ribs." Some Italian guitars were highly orna-mented and made with such exotic materials as ebony, ivory, mother-of-pearl, and tortoiseshell. The French style, by contrast, usually featured a flat back and simpler trim. Still, the guitar remained in the lute's shadow.

In the 1770s the first guitars with six single strings appeared, blowing the evolutionary lid off the instrument. Within a few decades, numerous inno-vations followed: body waists became narrower and body bouts changed shape, becoming circular in northern Europe and more oval shaped in southern Europe. Inlaid frets of brass or ivory replaced the tied-on gut frets and the neck was extended to leave a full octave (12 frets) clear of the body. Metal tuners with "worm gear" machine heads began to replace friction pegs, and strings were anchored by bridge pins, replacing the old method of tying strings to the bridge. By the 1820s most guitars had a fingerboard extending all the way to the soundhole and a bridge saddle set into the bridge. Spain, where the modern classical and flamenco guitars evolved, was the exception; Spanish makers used saddleless bridges into the 1840s, and modern classical and flamenco guitars still have strings tied to the bridge.

As rapidly as the guitar changed, so did its acceptance. By 1800 the lute had all but disappeared, taking with it the rounded-back guitars. The cause of the guitar's sudden surge in popularity is a matter for speculation. Certainly it was easier to play than the lute, but that had been true for over 200 years. One factor may have been a change in musical tastes and the playing public's tendency to follow a new fad. Some writers have ascribed the guitar's rise to a fad that swept across Europe in the late 1700s for all things Spanish, including the Spanish version of the lute—the *vihuela*. But although the vihuela may have had the body shape of a guitar, (the lone surviving vihuela is of questionable authenticity, according to historian Richard E. Bruné), it had courses of strings rather than six single strings. In fact, the typical Spanish-made guitar was dou-ble-strung long after the rest of Europe had switched to six single strings. The overriding factor may have been simply that the six-string guitar was easier to tune than the double-strung lute.

One of the best-known makers of this new-style guitar was Johann Georg Staufer of Vienna, whose earliest instruments date to about 1800. Two innovations credited to Staufer came as a result of a license granted to him and Johann Ertel in 1822 to improve construction of guitars. Staufer and Ertel de-signed a fingerboard raised off the top of the guitar, and they experimented

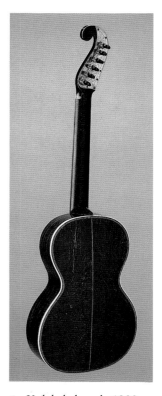

◆ *Unlabeled, early 1800s. Though unlabeled, this guitar (shown in detail on page 9) has some distinct Staufer characteristics. The scroll peghead is typical of Staufer and other German makers. This example has straight-through tuners (nonoriginal) without the long shafts typical of Stau-fer's six-on-a-side tuner configuration. Floral inlay was available from German suppliers in precut form, and it appears on many guitars of this period. Her-ringbone trim is associated with Staufer's most famous protégé, C. F. Martin. Bra-zilian rosewood would also be Martin's choice for backs and sides. Pyramid/BM*

with fret materials, settling on an alloy of brass, copper, silver, and arsenic, which was commonly used at the time for clothing buttons.

The first half of the nineteenth century was a time of great experimentation for the guitar. Many innovations credited to the twentieth century were tried with varying degrees of success a century earlier. A few examples:

◆ *Peghead with all six tuners on one side and scroll shape at the top.* In the late 1940s country guitarist Merle Travis drew such a peghead on a napkin as he described a solidbody electric guitar to luthier Paul Bigsby. A similar design, without the suggestion of a scroll, topped Leo Fender's first solidbody electric models, the Esquire and Broadcaster (soon to be Telecaster) of 1950, and the scroll profile showed up on the peghead of Fender's 1954 Stratocaster and almost all later Fender models. Travis admitted that he had seen the scroll on European guitars, and it was, in fact, a distinguishing mark of instruments made by Staufer and other German makers in the early 1800s. It has been in style on some instrument, somewhere in the world, ever since—on many minstrel banjos of the mid 1800s, on zithers of the late 1800s, and on tamburitza family instruments of eastern Europe from the 1880s to now.

◆ *Detachable neck.* Rickenbacker's Bakelite-body guitar of the 1930s, the first solidbody electric model, had a detachable, bolt-on neck designed for easy adjustment or replacement. The concept was perfected on electric guitars by Fender and eventually adopted by some acoustic guitar makers as well. A bolt-on neck, adjustable by a clock-key mechanism, was patented by C.F. Hautman for the Martin company in 1893, but the idea was hardly fresh, even then. Martin had been using the clock-key mechanism for 60 years, and ironically, the concept had been almost completely phased out by the time of Hautman's patent. Furthermore, it did not originate with Martin but with Johann Staufer. Hautman did show some creativity, however, in his patent application. He listed portability foremost among the innovative aspects of his design.

◆ *Raised fingerboard.* In 1922, Gibson took great pride in introducing a fingerboard that did not touch the top of the guitar. The same concept was a product of the license granted to Staufer and Ertel exactly 100 years earlier.

◆ *Body support rod.* The Larson brothers of Chicago fitted their Prairie State flat tops of the 1930s with a metal support rod inside the body, extending from neck block to endpin. In the 1960s Fender also put a support tube in its larger flat top models. The support rod of wood or steel was one of Staufer's less successful innovations.

Before canonizing Staufer as the guitar world's most prolific and profound innovator, it should be noted that the scroll peghead design was common among German and Austrian makers and was probably borrowed from the zither. Staufer's raised fingerboard may have been the idea of Italian guitar virtuoso Luigi Legnani. In addition, Staufer had his share of design follies. His *guitarre d'amour* of 1821 was a bowed guitar whose name was no doubt inspired by the way it was held—between the legs. Then as now, it was probably more interesting for its sexual innuendo than for its place in the history of guitar design, although a similar bowed cellolike guitar has been revived by several modern makers. Staufer eventually turned to violin making, where his double-bottom violin and his elongated narrow-bodied violin were both unsuccessful. He died in the poorhouse in 1853.

♦ *Scalloped fingerboard.* Fender's Yngwie Malmsteen signature model Stratocaster, introduced in 1988, featured a scalloped fingerboard, but Parisian luthier René Lacôte had experimented with the concept in the first half of the 1800s.

♦ *Moustache bridge.* In 1937 Gibson's fancy new flat top, the Super Jumbo (SJ-200), sported a bridge that turned upward at the ends to resemble a moustache. Gibson's idea of a moustache was a large, full walrus type, but thinner moustache bridges—more like handlebars, some of them very ornate—had appeared on many guitars from the 1580s to the 1850s.

♦ *Cutaway body shape.* In the 1920s, Italian musician and luthier Mario Maccaferri and his teacher Luigi Mozzani designed guitars with the upper treble bout "cut away" to make the upper frets easier to reach. The Selmer company of France introduced Maccaferri-designed cutaway models in the early 1930s, and Gibson led the way for major American makers with cutaway archtops in 1939. Fender's 1951 Precision bass took the concept a step further with a double-cutaway design that provided access to the higher frets on both sides of the neck. One of the earliest cutaways, however, was a double-cutaway guitar made by a luthier named Beau in Mirecourt, France, about 1840. His guitar had a symmetrical body shape with pointed horns, a shape very similar to Gibson's Les Paul Jr. and Les Paul Special solidbody electric models of 1959.

♦ *Untempered fingerboard.* The tempered scale, with its even, half-tone intervals, makes some notes of the standard guitar fingerboard out of tune. The Novatone company set out to correct the problem in the early 1980s with a series of interchangeable fingerboards that had frets fragmented and positioned to achieve a truer tonality. Back in 1822 General T. Peronet Thompson, an

♦ *Unlabeled, circa 1650. Though unlabeled, this guitar is attributed to Matteo Sellas of Venice. A typical Renaissance guitar, it has five courses of strings, gut frets, a relatively narrow body, a top extending several frets up the fingerboard, strings tied to the bridge, and no separate bridge saddle. The ornamentation in the soundhole is made of parchment and known as the "rose." Although the rose has disappeared from modern guitar design, the term lives on in the name for the ornamentation around the soundhole—the rosette. The rose and peghead of this guitar are original-style reproductions. Metropolitan Museum of Art/© R. E. Bruné*

Englishman, invented the "enharmonic" guitar, which tackled the same problem by means of movable frets that resembled small croquet wickets, with six frets for each fret position. René Lacôte also took a stab at an untempered fingerboard in 1852 with sliding frets.

◆ *Slanted frets.* In 1964 Gretsch introduced a partially "tempered" fret configuration ("compensating" would be more accurate than "tempered"). In the "T-zone" above the 12th fret, frets were mounted at a slight slant in order to alleviate intonation problems on the bass strings. A guitar made in 1898 in Mittenwald, Germany, by Kaspar Brandner, an apprentice to a violin maker, used the same principle over the entire fingerboard, with the nut mounted at an angle so that the bass strings were longer than the treble strings. A more recent design by luthier Ralph Novak slants the frets both ways. Frets near the nut are slanted so that the bass end of the fret is farther away from the bridge than the treble end. The fret-string angle graduates to a right angle at about the 12th fret, and the graduation continues so that in the upper register the bass side of the fret is higher up the fingerboard than the treble side. The nut and bridge are also angled. Gretsch patented the T-zone fingerboard in 1967 and Novak patented his design in 1989. The concept, however, goes back at least as far as 1561, when John Rose, an Englishman, invented an offshoot of the cittern called the *bandora.* Both the bandora (a bass accompaniment instrument) and its smaller, higher-pitched relative, the *orpharion,* had frets, nut, and bridge angled in a fan arrangement similar to Novak's design. (Novak's guitars, marketed under the name Novax, use fan-pattern frets for a second application—to create better tonal balance.)

◆ *Artist endorsement models.* In the twentieth century, a measure of success among guitarists has been the endorsement agreement, resulting in a Les Paul model or a Chet Atkins model, to name the two most successful endorsers. The name value of a guitar star was also well known to the earliest six-string guitar makers. In the 1820s Johann Staufer marketed a model with Italian virtuoso Luigi Legnani's name on the label, and some historians have suggested that Staufer's raised fingerboard was Legnani's idea. In London, Louis Panormo, the luthier who made General Thompson's enharmonic guitar, was quite successful with models designed in collaboration with renowned Spanish-born guitarist Fernando Sor.

♦ Benedid, 1787 (opposite, upper left, and above). This guitar shows some of the innovations taking place in the late 1700s: six (rather than five) courses of strings, fixed frets, and a more pronounced waist. Even though the label clearly identifies the maker (complete with his address on the bottom line) and the date of this instrument, labels in old guitars are no more reliable than labels in old violins. The workmanship authenticates the instrument, and this guitar does appear to have been made by Joseph Benedid of Cádiz in southern Spain. The maple back is flat, like that of a modern guitar, but it still has the ribbed construction of Renaissance guitars and lutes. Metropolitan Museum of Art/© R. E. Bruné

♦ Lacôte, circa 1820 (center). René Lacôte of Paris was the best-known French guitar maker of the early 1800s. This instrument shows most of the major evolutionary features of the nineteenth-century European guitar, including six single strings, 12 frets clear of the body, bridge pins, a separate saddle, and metal tuning gears. The Brazilian rosewood back (lower left) shows that guitar buyers, then as now, valued a highly figured piece of wood. The back of this guitar has been refinished. Metropolitan Museum of Art/ © R. E. Bruné

♦ *Martin and Coupa,
circa 1840. (See page 18.)*

EARLY GUITARS

♦ ♦ ♦

Martin: The American Guitar

Although Johann Staufer's name turns up often in the history of the modern guitar, his fame derives not so much from his own work as from the accomplishments of his former shop foreman. Staufer's protégé carried on the Staufer tradition of experimentation and improvement until he came up with the American flat top guitar we know today. He was a German by birth, but his name is synonymous with the highest standards of American guitar making: C. F. Martin.

Christian Friedrich Martin grew up in a period when the six-string guitar was a new and evolving instrument. He was born January 31, 1796, in Mark Neukirchen, Saxony, a city that was a center for both guitar and violin makers, and he learned the art of guitar making from his father, Johann Georg Martin.

At some point, probably in the early 1820s, C. F. Martin was a foreman in Johann Staufer's shop in Vienna, but by 1826 he was back in Mark Neukirchen. That year he was named along with his father in a legal document pertaining to a dispute between the violin makers guild, some of whom made guitars, and the cabinetmakers guild, to which the Martins and many other guitar makers belonged. As early as 1807, the violin makers had argued that they were true artisans while the guitar/cabinetmakers were mere mechanics who should not be allowed to make musical instruments. Presumably as a result of more than 20 years of squabbling, several guitar makers left Mark Neukirchen for New York City. Heinrich (Henry) Anton Schatz, who was mentioned in the same document with the Martins, arrived in 1831. Schatz's friend C. F. Martin arrived in late 1833 and opened a full-line music store at 196 Hudson Street. In addition to making and selling guitars, C. Frederick Martin (as he spelled his name after arriving in New York) sold strings, sheet music, and wind instruments and repaired wind and stringed instruments.

In 1835 Henry Schatz left the city for the homier German-settled area of Milford, Pennsylvania. In 1839, Martin again followed Schatz's example and set up shop in Nazareth, Pennsylvania, less than 100 miles—but a world away—from New York. Because Martin retained business and distribution associations in New York, the brands on Martin instruments would not reflect the move until 1898.

C. F. Martin was not the first guitar maker in America. Colonial Williamsburg had one, and a half-dozen others have been documented earlier than Martin. However, none was as influential. In fact, it is no exaggeration to say that no other nineteenth-century American guitar maker was influential *but* C. F. Martin. (Orville Gibson's work in the 1890s would qualify him as a nineteenth-century maker, but his influence would not be fully realized until the twentieth century.) The numerous Martin guitars from the 1800s that survive today in good playing condition testify to the quality of Martin's craftsmanship and design. Although the Lyon and Healy company sold many more guitars than Martin in the 1800s, there are probably more Martins still around today than Washburns (Lyon and Healy's brand) and all other nineteenth-century brands combined.

♦ *Martin and Coupa, circa 1840 (above and opposite). C. F. Martin had early business associations with John Coupa, Henry Schatz, and Charles Bruno, and their names appear with Martin's on the labels of some instruments. Staufer's influence is still evident in the peghead and tuners (the peg closest to the nut tunes the high-E string—the opposite of the six-on-a-side tuner arrangement popularized in the 1950s on Fender electrics), but Martin was well on his way to establishing the American guitar with this example. The body shape, with upper bouts narrower than lower bouts, is his design. The wood grain visible through the soundhole is not that of the highly figured Brazilian rosewood back but of an inner sheathing of spruce, which is not uncommon on Martins of this period. Roy Acuff Museum, Opryland USA/WC*

C. F. Martin did not arrive in America with plans for a new style of guitar rolled up under his arm. His guitar evolved from a Staufer style to his own style over a period of 15 or 20 years. Most Staufer features were gone by 1850, but the clock-key neck adjustment showed up on the occasional Martin guitar into the 1890s. The characteristics that would set Martin apart from earlier makers—body shape with upper bouts noticeably smaller than lower bouts, squared-off slotted peghead, X-braced top, and tasteful, reserved ornamentation—all appeared by 1850. With these features, a new American guitar was born. Over the next 100 years, more changes were in store for the standard flat top guitar: an ever-increasing body size, a one-piece neck and peghead (replacing the spliced-on peghead design), a 14-fret neck, and heavier construction to withstand the tension of steel strings. But the flat top guitar as we know it today is basically the same one established by C. F. Martin in the 1850s.

One of Martin's most important innovations was the X-braced top. Most European guitars of the 1800s were built with straight-across lateral or "ladder" bracing. (The exception, as usual, was Spain, where luthiers developed fan-pattern bracing that was finally standardized, along with most other characteristics of the modern classical guitar, by Antonio de Torres in the 1850s.) In America, Martin developed a new pattern based around two diagonal braces that cross below the soundhole. The great majority of Martins from 1850 onward have some form of X-bracing. The placement of secondary braces and the distance of the X from the soundhole have varied right up through present production, but the X-pattern has remained the standard, not just for Martin but for the great majority of flat top guitar makers today.

Martin's invention of X-bracing is one of the least debatable innovations in the history of fretted instruments, although there are a few other makers who warrant footnotes. The most intriguing of these are D. and A. Roudhloff, Russian natives who built violins and guitars in London from 1830 to 1850. Two X-braced Roudhloff guitars survive. Martin's friend Henry Schatz made an X-braced guitar in Boston sometime between 1845 and 1851. And an X-braced guitar with the Schmidt and Maul label was made in New York sometime between 1839 and 1858. Guitar historian Mark Silber has been collecting instruments for 30 years, and these four examples are the only X-braced non-Martin guitars he has seen from that time period. Martins with X-bracing definitely appear in the 1840 to 1845 period, so the best argument a Martin skeptic can mount is that the X-bracing concept was in the air in the

1840s and may have occurred to several makers simultaneously. There is no concrete evidence to deny Martin his place as the inventor of X-bracing, and he is indisputably the one who made it a success.

By 1852 Martin had standardized his designs to the point where he offered guitars in four different sizes. By the end of the decade, he had also standardized his styles of wood and ornamentation. Martins from the 1850s and after are typically plainer than most of the earlier guitars (by Martin as well as by European makers) that survive today. Whatever Martin's purpose—to distinguish his guitars from European instruments or simply to keep prices down—tastefully understated ornamentation became a Martin company tradition.

C. F. Martin died on February 16, 1873, but his innovations remained the industry standard for more than 50 years after his death. In the late 1920s and early 1930s, when guitar design took off in many directions, including archtop, resonator, and electric designs, the Martin company introduced several important innovations to ensure its continuing status as the standard bearer of the acoustic flat top guitar. C. F. Martin and Company is still located in Nazareth, and C. F. Martin's descendants maintain the founder's tradition of fine craftsmanship. C. F. (Chris) Martin IV, great-great-great grandson of the founder, is the chief executive officer and chairman of the board.

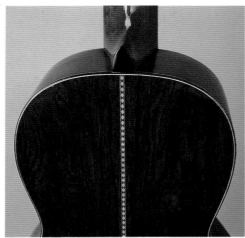

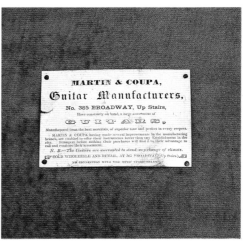

◆ *Martin and Coupa, circa 1845 (upper left and right, and lower left). Martin's association with John Coupa had begun by 1840 and continued through at least 1845. From outward appearances, this guitar has all the characteristics of a typical Martin guitar of the second half of the 19th century. On the inside, however, Martin's move from European-style ladder bracing to his famous X-bracing is in progress, with a lateral top brace just below the soundhole, plus two braces that cross to form an X. Martin abandoned the ornate Staufer-style peghead in favor of another European design—a plain, slotted peghead spliced onto the neck. The Martin and Coupa label is usually found in the guitar, but this one is affixed to the case. Chet Atkins/WC*

◆ *Martin, circa 1840s (lower right and opposite page). In shape and ornamentation, this guitar is highly unusual, especially for a Martin. The long, narrow body suggests a Renaissance guitar, but the decidedly smaller upper bouts are a nineteenth-century feature. The small "shoulders" where the neck joins the body are unusual for any maker of any period. The spectacular abalone pearl fingerboard and multiple soundhole rings run counter to Martin's reputation for conservative, tasteful ornamentation. The edge trim, however, is not a great deal fancier than that of some later models. The detachable neck with clock-key adjustment bolt is a feature of Johann Staufer's guitars and most of C. F. Martin's early instruments. The side marquetry of fancy wood is unusual. A strip of wood marquetry in various patterns inlaid down the center of the back would be a distinguishing feature of many later Martin models of Style 21 and higher. Gruhn Guitars/DD*

♦ Martin, 1840s (below). This guitar may not make as big a visual splash as one with an abalone pearl fingerboard, but it is quite an exotic creation nevertheless. The entire fingerboard is elephant ivory and the peghead is ebony with ivory binding. The tuning pegs are ivory with silver sleeves and the nut is aluminum. The herringbone and rope-pattern purfling patterns are standard Martin features, but the small, diamond-shaped pearl inlays around the soundhole are not. The purfling around the middle of the sides was brought to the United States by C. F. Martin and used only on presentation-grade instruments. It does not appear on instruments made after 1850. The case for this instrument is appropriately fancy. It is made of rosewood and has inlaid purfling. Mandolin Brothers/© John Peden

♦ Martin 5-18, 1937. Martin model numbers denote a body size and a style number. The higher the body size, the smaller the instrument; the higher the style number, the fancier. Size 5, at 11¼ inches wide, was the smallest in the Martin line when it was introduced in 1854. In the 1800s small guitars such as Martin sizes 5, 4, and 3 were sometimes known as terz guitars and were tuned a minor third (three frets) higher than standard tuning. In the 1920s the Size 5 body was used for four-string tenor guitars. In the 1960s and 1970s, Size 5 guitars continued to be popular thanks in part to their association with country entertainer Marty Robbins. Paul Gillette/DL

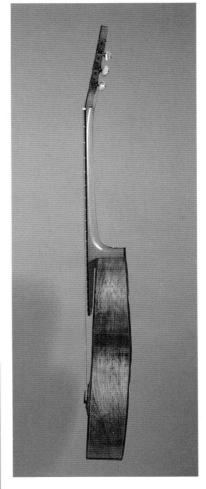

♦ *Martin, 1898 (left). This odd instrument was made in Nazareth, Pennsylvania, in 1898, but it belongs conceptually to Germany in the first half of the century. The raised fingerboard and clock-key neck adjustment are trademarks of C.F. Martin's former boss, Johann Staufer of Vienna. (This may be the latest appearance of the clock-key neck adjustment on a Martin guitar.) The large circular body bouts and the negative neckset angle, with the neck angling to the front of the guitar, are associated with another Staufer pupil, Johann Scherzer. Staufer, Martin, and Scherzer had all been dead for over 25 years when this guitar was made. Perhaps this was ordered by a traditional German guitarist who could not find or could not afford to import an old-style German guitar. A negative neckset angle—at a more severe angle than on this example—is a key feature of the Millennium model guitar patented in 1987 by luthier Tom Humphrey, who considers this a harplike feature. Gruhn Guitars/WC*

◆ *Martin 2-24, late 1880s (right). At 12 inches wide, Size 2 was one of Martin's most popular sizes in the nineteenth century. No recent Martin styles feature edge purfling of colored wood, but it was common in the 1800s. Style 24 is one of several obscure styles between the popular 21 and 28 for which little information and very few examples survive. Walter Carter/WC*

◆ *Martin 3-17, circa 1870 (below). Size 3 is the smallest of the standard body sizes first recorded by C. F. Martin in 1852. It is the same width as Size 5 (introduced in 1854) but slightly longer, and it has a longer scale. Martin's body lines lie somewhere between the Germanic circular shapes and the elongated ovals of southern Europe. Whereas the typical European guitar from this period has an upper bout almost as wide as the lower, the upper bout on a Martin is noticeably smaller. Until the introduction of Style 15 in 1940, Style 17 carried the plainest of Martin's appointments. All styles, including Style 17, had rosewood back and sides in the 1800s. Style 17 went to mahogany back and sides in 1909 and to a mahogany top in 1922. The wood "coffin" case carries a label with the model. Jim Colclasure/BM*

◆ *Martin 2½-40, circa 1860. Size 2½ is 11⅝ inches wide (3/8 inch wider than Size 3). Style 40, with abalone soundhole ring and top border, was the second-fanciest Martin in the catalog at the time this guitar was made, topped only by Style 42 (which has an extra bit of pearl bordering the fingerboard between the soundhole and the edge of the top). The bridge and body binding are of elephant ivory. Ivory bridges, which appear on Styles 34 and higher, and ivory bindings were phased out completely in 1918, replaced by wood bridges and ivoroid (ivory-grained celluloid) binding. Ivory nuts and bridge saddles were phased out much later, with the last ivory nut appearing on a 1980 guitar. Henry Wynn/DL*

♦ *Martin 2-34, late 1800s. Until the introduction of Style 35 in 1965, Martin styles in the 30-series (and, inexplicably, Style 27) had wood purfling around the top and a pearl soundhole ring. They act as a bridge between the wood-purfled 20-series and the abalone-bordered 40-series. Style 34, available from 1870 to 1907, is distinguishable from the lower abalone-ring models by its ivory bridge. From 1921, when Style 30 was last made, to 1965, Martin made no models with style numbers in the 30s. Owner unknown/WC*

♦ *Martin 1-26, late 1800s. Size 1, at 12 ¾ inches wide, is the largest of C. F. Martin's 1852 models. Style 26 differs from Style 28 primarily in top trim—rope-pattern or "half-herringbone" on Style 26 versus herringbone on Style 28. The solid peghead and ivory friction pegs are not rare features on nineteenth-century Martins but are not nearly as common as the slotted peghead with geared tuners. The solid peghead would resurface more than 30 years later (with geared banjo-style tuners) as a standard feature of Martin's 14-fret models. The strap button is original. Unlike Style 28, which remains one of Martin's most popular styles, Style 26 did not make it into the twentieth century. Barter Guitars/BM*

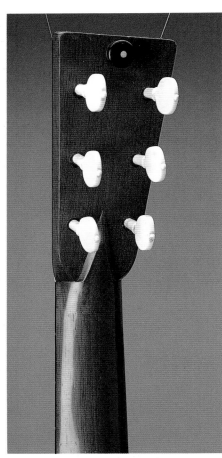

♦ *Martin 2-44, 1930. Style 44 is an exception to the Martin numbering system. It really belongs in the group of models made by Martin for other companies or, in this case, for guitar player and teacher Vahdah Olcott-Bickford. Martin historian Mike Longworth learned from C. F. Martin III that Ms. Olcott-Bickford, a renowned classical guitarist, wanted a guitar of Style 45 quality but without the pearl trim—thus the Style 44 designation. Some Olcott-Bickford examples have "Soloist" inlaid on the peghead. The plain black-and-white celluloid binding was unique in the Martin line at the time, although it would appear on some Martin archtops and would eventually replace the herringbone purfling on Style 28. About 32 examples of Style 44, ranging in size from 2 to 000, were made between 1913 and 1939. Gruhn Guitars/WC*

♦ *Martin 0-28, 1899 (center and upper left). Style 28 is one of Martin's classic styles. As on a current Style 28, the body is rosewood and the soundhole rings are grouped in a 5-9-5 arrangement. The herringbone inlay around the top edge was discontinued in early 1947 and revived (designated in model names by an H prefix) in 1976. This zigzag-pattern backstripe was replaced in early 1947 by a chainlike pattern, which was replaced the next year by a wider chainlike pattern. Size 0, at 13½ inches wide, was the largest when it was introduced in 1854 and the next to largest when this guitar was made. Aside from the tiny size 5, it is the smallest size available today, and then only by special order. Gruhn Guitars/DL*

♦ *Martin 00-42, 1927 (lower left). Martin added Size 00, 14 1/8 inches wide, in 1877. The abalone pearl ornamentation of Style 42 is surpassed only by Style 45. Real Guitars/BM*

◆ *Martin 000-45, 1929. Size 000, at 15 inches wide, first appeared as a special order item in 1902 and became a standard catalog size in 1911. The first Style 45s, in 1902 and 1903, were actually Style 42s special-ordered with abalone pearl borders around the back and sides. In 1904, Style 45 became a standard style, available in Sizes 1, 0, and 00. This example has two modern features—the "belly" bridge and the pick-guard—both introduced in 1929. Model 000-45 was the fanciest style and largest size at the time this one was made. Size 000 is now the smallest cataloged size, except for special orders. Beginning in the mid 1970s, Martin assigned higher numbers to some styles, but Style 45 is still the top of the line. Gruhn Guitars/DL*

◆ *Biehl, circa 1900.*
(See pages 32 and 33.)

EARLY GUITARS
◆ ◆ ◆

Lyon and Healy and Others

For design and quality, Martin was the dominant American guitar manufacturer throughout the latter half of the 1800s. In marketing and sales volume, however, no company came close to Lyon and Healy and its Washburn brand guitars. In 1889, 25 years after the founding of the company, Lyon and Healy boasted of nearly 20,000 Washburn guitars, mandolins, and

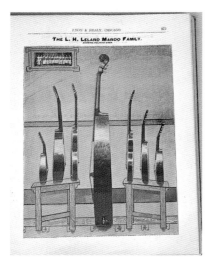

♦ *Lyon and Healy catalog, 1912. The L. H. Leland mando family represents an attempt to cash in on the mandolin craze with, among other things, a guitar that is only 2 inches deep—even thinner than the mandolins. The best that could be said about this model is that it appeared about 40 years too soon. Thinbodies—electric archtop thinbodies—did become popular after Gibson introduced them in the 1950s, and thinbodied acoustic-electric flat tops came into vogue in the late 1980s. Gruhn Guitars/WC*

zithers in use—an average yearly production of 800 instruments. By 1897 the company was making the astonishing claim of an annual production of over 100,000 Washburns.

By comparison, Martin's annual output in the 65 years since C. F. Martin opened shop averaged about 123 guitars. Martin's annual guitar production would not even top 1,000 until 1919, and the cumulative number of guitars produced (as indicated by serial numbers) would not reach 100,000 until 1947. In only two years, 1971 and 1973, would Martin ever produce more than 20,000 instruments. Gibson, usually perceived as one of the biggest guitar makers, is also dwarfed by the Lyon and Healy claims. Gibson averaged only about 10,000 instruments per year from its founding in 1902 to World War II and about 25,000 per year in the 1950s. Only in 1965 did Gibson produce more than 100,000 instruments, and that total includes instruments made under the Epiphone brand. By the 1970s Gibson's production had fallen back to about half the record figure. Even if Lyon and Healy had exaggerated by 50 or even 100 percent, its production figures at the turn of the century were phenomenal.

Lyon and Healy was unlike any other important American guitar manufacturer. Whereas Martin, the Larson brothers, Gibson, National, Rickenbacker, and Fender originated in a small shop or in the vision of a single person, Lyon and Healy began life as a large company. It was founded in 1864 to be the Chicago distributor for Oliver Ditson, a leading Boston instrument dealer and music publisher, and named for Ditson associates George Washburn Lyon and Patrick Joseph Healy.

Lyon's middle name identified the stringed instrument line, and the brands on Washburn instruments read "George Washburn." Washburn guitars were actually designed by George Durkee, an acoustical and mechanical engineer who authored a number of patents, most of them assigned to Lyon and Healy, and eventually became the company's factory superintendent.

The company started out in a large four-story structure with signs advertising sheet music and Steinway pianos. A larger building was destroyed by a fire in 1870, and yet another building was lost in the famous Chicago fire of 1871. The company was well insured and continued to prosper. In 1893 Lyon and Healy's exhibit at the World's Columbian Exposition in Chicago comprised over a thousand instruments displayed at three different pavilions, the largest of which was an ornate two-story structure with an upper veranda.

Lyon and Healy garnered 12 awards at the exposition, and company literature left no doubt as to the importance of the honors: "the highest honor bestowed upon any instrument of their class. . . This attesting in trumpet tones their no-longer-to-be-disputed right to be considered the STANDARD INSTRUMENTS of the world."

A year later, at the International Exposition in Antwerp, Belgium, Lyon and Healy won a Diploma of Honor and a Gold Medal. Again, the company did not miss the opportunity to capitalize in its promotional literature: "No competing house (of any nation whatsoever) received as high honors, our triumph was final and complete." Despite these honors, collectors today generally do not regard Washburn guitars as highly as Martins.

In addition to fretted instruments, Lyon and Healy sold band instruments, accordions, harps, harmonicas, violins, and accessories—and sold them aggressively. According to historian Michael Holmes, "George Washburn Lyon brought advertising to the industry. He is the P. T. Barnum of the musical instrument industry." Lyon retired in 1889; Healy continued with the company until his death in 1905.

Lyon and Healy was one of the first makers to recognize the value, or perhaps the profit potential, of mahogany for guitar bodies. In the 1889 Washburn catalog, under the heading "Rosewood vs. Mahogany," the company pointed out rosewood's tendency to crack, to resist absorbing a finish, and to deteriorate in appearance continually from the day it is finished. Mahogany, on the other hand, was described as "an honest wood, so reliable in a changing climate and so trustworthy in finishing that at even a higher price than Rosewood, purchasers could well afford to pay the difference." This last statement seems odd in light of the fact that throughout the twentieth century mahogany has been cheaper than rosewood. The point was rendered moot by the guitars in the catalog, all of which were rosewood. Mahogany was offered as an option, presumably at additional cost.

Into the early 1900s Lyon and Healy made a great many guitar models under several brands, ranging in price from under $10 to over $200. By 1913 the Lyon and Healy brand was inaugurated on a budget line. Other lines included Lakeside, Leland, and American Conservatory. Among the company's claims in the early 1900s were the invention of the tenor guitar and the introduction to America of the tiple, a 10-string, four-course ukulele-type instrument popular in Brazil.

♦ *Lyon and Healy catalog, 1913. In 1913 L. H. Leland's thinbody guitars were out, as Lyon and Healy apparently switched to a bigger-is-better philosophy. The biggest of them all was 22 1/4 inches wide and called the Conservatory Monster. Gruhn Guitars/WC*

In the winter of 1928 Lyon and Healy trimmed its instrument production down to harps and pianos only. The Washburn name, along with the patents and manufacturing equipment for all fretted instruments, was sold to the J. R. Stewart company. Stewart then made Washburns exclusively for distribution by Tonk Bros. of Chicago, which had already been distributing Washburns and had also absorbed some of the management personnel after Lyon and Healy's cutback. Stewart went bankrupt in 1930 and Tonk acquired the former Lyon and Healy brands. Tonk was apparently interested only in distribution and sold the Washburn manufacturing facility to Regal (later acquired by Harmony and Slingerland).

After World War II the Washburn name went unused until 1962, when the Roland company of Los Angeles revived it for a line of guitars made in Asia. In 1975 Roland sold the rights to the Washburn name, along with some inventory, to a new Washburn company based in the Chicago area that introduced lines of guitars, mandolins, and banjos made in Asia. An American-made solidbody electric Washburn was introduced in 1991, and the company announced plans at that time to introduce an American-made acoustic line as well.

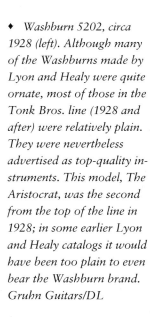

♦ *Washburn 5202, circa 1928 (left). Although many of the Washburns made by Lyon and Healy were quite ornate, most of those in the Tonk Bros. line (1928 and after) were relatively plain. They were nevertheless advertised as top-quality instruments. This model, The Aristocrat, was the second from the top of the line in 1928; in some earlier Lyon and Healy catalogs it would have been too plain to even bear the Washburn brand. Gruhn Guitars/DL*

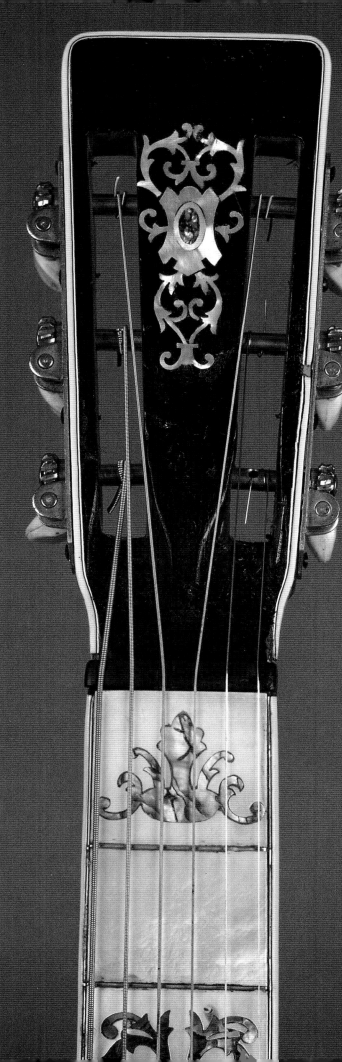

♦ *Biehl, circa 1900 (this page and opposite lower right). Tony Biehl of Davenport, Iowa, was a musician and teacher. His career as a maker of guitars and mandolins lasted from 1884 to 1904, when he embarked with his family on a fairly successful career as an entertainer. The extensive top ornamentation (above) is of no practical use, unless one wants to risk damaging the pearl butterfly pickguard inlays. The iridescent abalone fingerboard inlays create a dazzling visual effect. With a lower bout measurement of 19¼ inches, this would be considered a huge guitar in any era. The bridge (above) is true to the period but not original. Roy Acuff Museum, Opryland USA/WC*

♦ *Washburn 308, circa 1889. Like Martin, the Washburn line initially had an organized model-numbering system based on size and ornamentation. Model 101 is a plain guitar in standard size; model 201 is the same but in concert size; model 301 is the grand concert version. Models 102, 202, and 302 are more ornamented. This example features Style 8 ornamentation, the fanciest in the line at the time, on a grand concert (Size 3) guitar. Later model numbers are keyed to the instrument's price. The extra spacing between the third and fourth strings is a common feature of many guitars from this period. Tony Klassen/WC*

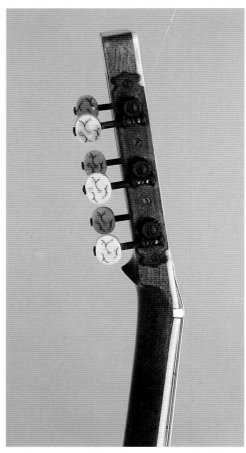

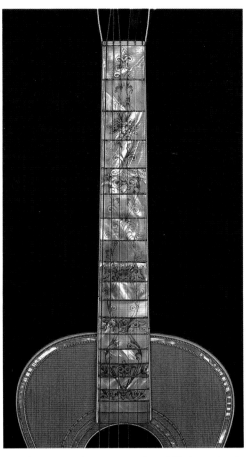

◆ *Washburn G380, circa 1912. The G380 is the second-fanciest model in the Washburn line of 1912. The mother-of-pearl fingerboard (upper left) is so highly reflective of light that only a close look can appreciate the degree of ornamental engraving. If one's eyes are not blinded by all the pearl, then the brain can be dazzled by the awards listed on the label (lower left). The price of the G380 jumped from $80 to $138.75 in 1913, and that, coupled with the profusion of budget brands in the Lyon and Healy catalog, signaled a short future for such ornate guitars. Roy Acuff Museum, Opryland USA/WC*

◆ *Washburn, circa 1900. This guitar is unlabeled but has the look of a custom-ordered Washburn. Mother-of-pearl inlaid directly on the top is quite unusual, and the delicate figures contrast with the heavy pearl pieces around the borders and soundhole. The floral pattern on the fingerboard is bolder than that of most ornate instruments of this period. The side purfling curling into an ornamental figure is a feature of the most expensive Washburn catalog model. The large inlays at the ends of the bridge are not original. Roy Acuff Museum, Opryland USA/WC*

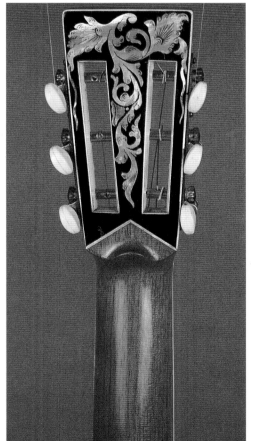

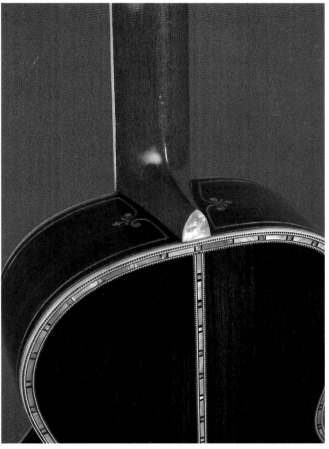

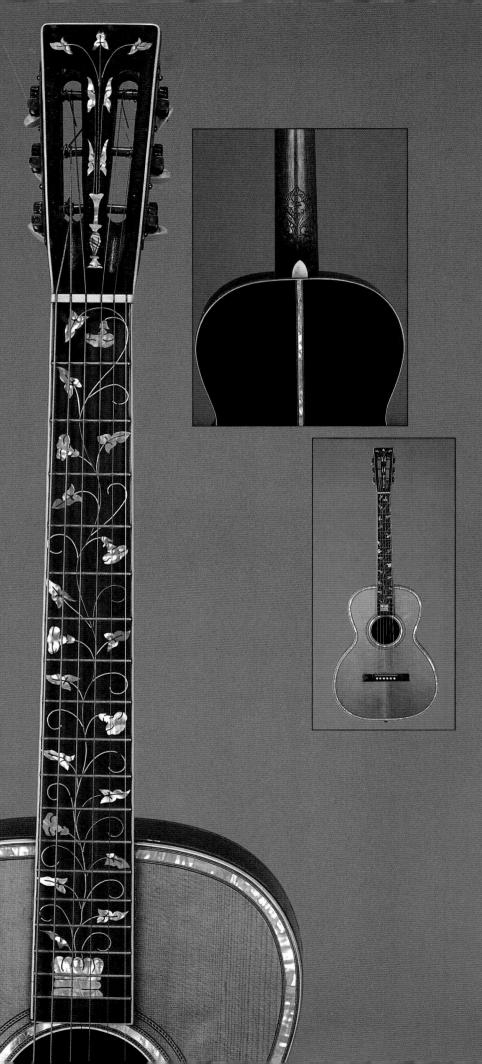

♦ *Stewart and Bauer, circa 1900. Though unlabeled, this guitar has pearl work and carving similar to mandolins made by Philadelphia maker George Bauer and sold through banjo maker S. S. Stewart under the Bauer or Bauer and Stewart brand. The bright pearl trim gives it the appearance of being illuminated. The floral pattern of the fingerboard inlay is more delicate than the tree-of-life found on high-end Washburns of the period. The heel carving is the same as that on many S. S. Stewart banjos. An ornamental backstripe is common on expensive guitars, but a mother-of-pearl backstripe is highly unusual. Gruhn Guitars/DL*

♦ Waldo, circa 1900. Waldo was a well-known banjo player and teacher, and Waldo banjos are more common than Waldo guitars. This instrument features a tree-of-life fingerboard inlay pattern similar to that of many fancy banjos of the period. The top trim is quite elaborate, with small gem-shaped pearl inlays bordered by lines of checkered purfling. Even the small area of the bridge between the saddle and pins has pearl inlays. The pearl and purfling motif continues on the back in a wide backstripe but is overshadowed by the spectacular pattern of the six-piece rosewood back. Gruhn Guitars/WC

FIVE-STRING BANJOS

◆ ◆ ◆

Minstrel to Bluegrass

The banjo is often singled out as the only native American instrument. However, the earliest reference to a banjo comes not from the United States but the Caribbean, in a piece of legislation passed by the French government of Martinique in 1678. It noted that the *banza* was played by blacks, and in the British colonies, too, these instruments were made and played by black slaves.

Early banjos had a gourd body, a head of animal skin, three strings of equal length, and no frets. The "fifth string"—the short drone string or *chanterelle* that distinguishes the banjo from virtually all other American instruments—appeared in the 1700s. Since most banjos had only three long strings at that time, the added short string was technically the fourth string rather than the fifth.

As early as 1769 white banjo players were performing in blackface. By the 1830s solo blackface artists were among the nation's most popular entertainers. The depression of 1842 put some of those performers out of work, but it also provided the impetus that sent blackface entertainment—and with it the banjo—to even greater popularity. In January 1843 in New York City, a group of unemployed actors and musicians led by Ohio native Dan Emmett pooled their talents and put on a blackface show at a local pool hall, billing themselves as the Virginia Minstrels. This was the first documented minstrel show and it quickly became the dominant showcase for popular music, producing such well-known songs as Stephen Foster's "Old Folks at Home" ("Swanee River") in 1851 and Dan Emmett's "Dixie" in 1859. Minstrelsy was still popular in America and on the rise in Europe in 1879, when James A. Bland, a black, college-educated minstrel from New York state, introduced two more songs that would become popular music standards, "Carry Me Back to Old Virginny" and "Oh Dem Golden Slippers."

Stephen Foster's "Oh Susanna" was the unofficial theme song of the California gold rush of 1849, and many gold miners literally went off, as the song says, "with my banjo on my knee." In response to a growing demand, professional banjo makers opened shops in the East and in California. Then as now, musicians wanted looks as well as playability, and by the 1850s banjo makers were outfitting their instruments with fancy ornamented fingerboards.

Banjo evolution in the mid 1800s resembled guitar evolution in Europe a few decades earlier, with a deluge of innovations and varying degrees of acceptance. In banjo lore, the most important figure of the period was minstrel Joel Walker Sweeney (1813–1860), who has often been credited with adding the fifth string to the banjo. Technically, he may have done that, but the string would have been the fourth—one of the long strings—of a five-string banjo. The short "fifth string" had been around longer than Sweeney had. During Sweeney's time, the construction of the banjo was modernized, with a wood rim replacing the old gourd body, and hooks, nuts, and a tension hoop added as a means of tightening the head.

Other innovations dating back to the mid-1800s were not accepted un-

♦ *Double-gourd banjo, 1876. This unusual gourd-shaped (though not actually made of a gourd) banjo is engraved "1876" at the end of the fingerboard and may have been made for the Philadelphia Centennial Exposition of that year. Frets were still taboo, but the faint lines of fret markers, inlaid flush with the fingerboard, are visible. Experiments with closed-back banjo design were taking place by 1876, but this example was undoubtedly made to be seen rather than played. Jim Bollman/WC*

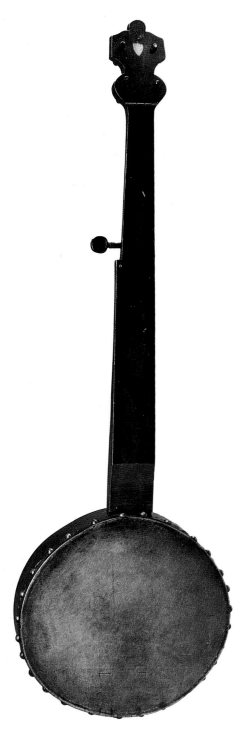

til many years later. In 1859 Stephen Van Hagen patented a seven-string banjo (six for normal guitar tuning, plus a short string) with a teardrop body shape and frets. Not even the frets caught on. Banjoists of the day looked upon frets much as a violinist or upright bass player would—as a crutch for those who could not play in tune. After a controversial transitional period, during which some players had fret markers inlaid flush with the fingerboard, frets became standard. Henry Dobson, a New York distributor, introduced fretted banjos in 1878, and he—not Van Hagen—is the one who generally receives the credit. Ironically, Dobson may not have actually made any banjos whatsoever, only distributed them under his brand.

Van Hagen's seven-string guitar banjo concept reappeared 20 years later, again with little success, as a banjo ensemble instrument. The "guitar-neck" banjo with six equal-length strings also made its first appearance at that time, but its small degree of success came later, in the banjo orchestras of the tenor banjo era.

Henry Dobson is also credited with marketing, though not inventing, the first closed-back banjo and the first top-tension adjustment with head-tightening nuts on the top rather than the back. These innovations would take almost 50 years to find a market, and like Van Hagen's guitar banjo, they would be associated with the tenor banjo rather than the five-string era.

With advances in design came advances in technique and repertoire. By 1865, the last year of the Civil War, the "stroke" or strummed style was giving way to the "guitar" or fingerpicking style. Toward the end of the century, the banjo ascended into high society, an ironic move in light of both its roots in slavery and blackface music and its modern association with earthier, less sophisticated styles such as bluegrass, Appalachian, or folk music. In the last years of the nineteenth century, the banjo reflected the opulence and good times of the Gay Nineties with elaborate pearl inlays, fancy carving, and prices to match. A presentation-grade S. S. Stewart model listed at $195 in 1895; by comparison, the fanciest Martin guitar listed for only $98.

The repertoire of the banjo evolved to include more serious music and some novelty tunes. Music written for banjo ensembles prompted the invention of a banjo family of instruments, all with five strings. S. S. Stewart of Philadelphia claimed credit for inventing the banjeaurine, with a standard banjo head size but a shorter scale, tuned a fourth or fifth above standard, in 1885. Stewart's 1896 catalog proclaimed that the banjeaurine was "the violin of a banjo orchestra, and music for such organizations cannot be properly rendered, unless the club contains, at least, one of these instruments." Stewart also claimed credit for creating the first banjo club. He acknowledged the help of banjo teacher and composer Thomas Armstrong, and Armstrong is generally credited by banjo historians with organizing the first banjo orchestra. His 16-banjo group, the American Banjo Club, made its concert debut in December 1887.

To fill out a banjo orchestra, a wide range of banjo-family instruments evolved. Lyon and Healy offered a piccolo banjo with a 7-inch head diameter, a small ladies' size with a 9-inch head, a regular ladies' size with a 10-inch head, a standard size with an 11-inch head, and a concert size with a 12-inch head. Among Stewart's offerings were a piccolo banjo with a 7-inch head, tuned an octave above standard; a pony banjo with an 8-inch head, tuned a fifth or sixth above standard; a specialty banjo with a 10½-inch head, tuned one whole step above standard; and a five-string bass banjo with a 16-inch head diameter but with a standard scale length, tuned an octave below standard. (The turn-of-the-century bass banjo should not be confused with the huge four-string bass banjo of the tenor banjo era, which was the banjo equivalent of an upright bass.)

With serious music came serious issues in the banjo world. In the September 1908 issue of *The Crescendo* magazine, an article by one Percy M. Jaques addressed two of the biggest controversies of the day: notation and picks. With so many different banjo models, each pitched differently, traditional notation had become a nightmare. A system called "A" notation came into use, under which a written A would correspond to the lowest string of the banjo, no matter if the banjo were a piccolo, pony, banjeaurine, special, standard, or bass model. Thus, in A notation, a written note or chord would be fingered in the same position on any banjo and a player could switch from one banjo to another without having to constantly transpose the music or relearn fingering positions. The actual pitch would vary, of course. On a banjeaurine it would come out a fourth or fifth higher than on a standard banjo; on the bass banjo it would be an octave lower. This A notation is the same system used for almost all woodwind and brass instruments. The alternative is "C" or "concert" notation, under which the written note corresponds to actual pitch. (The "C" in this case does not stand for "concert" but rather denotes the actual pitch of the lowest string of a standard banjo. Standard classical tuning for the four long strings is, from lowest to highest, C-G-B-D, rather than the modern bluegrass D-G-B-D tuning.)

◆ *Tack-head banjo, circa 1850s (opposite). Before banjo makers developed hoops and brackets to tighten the head, they used what appear to be upholstery tacks. The craftsmanship of this unknown maker is fairly crude, but the banjo does have a distinct peghead design and an inlaid peghead ornament. Country Music Hall of Fame Collection/BM*

Author Jaques saw nothing wrong with learning to read C notation, but he was dead set against using a pick. "The banjo has an original style of music that cannot be duplicated by any other instrument," he wrote, "and to secure the true typical banjo tone, players should pick with their fingers and play music born on the banjo." He also pointed out that the tremolo technique that was so effective on a double-strung instrument like the mandolin did not work well on the single strings of the banjo.

The controversy over picks raged stronger in the November 1916 issue of the magazine. George L. Lansing, a noted performer and, as *The Crescendo* described him, "eminent authority on matters banjoistic," voiced his opinion of picks in no uncertain terms: "Of late most stage players use either a plectrum or thimble with the result that audiences hear more noise than music."

Notation and picks were minor issues, however, considering that the very survival of the five-string banjo was in jeopardy. The opening paragraph of the 1908 Percy Jaques article stated that he was "as much surprised as pleased to find that good banjo music was still in demand... I had read so much about the banjo losing its popularity, and that it was a 'gone-by.'..."

The five-string banjo was indeed slipping, and the mandolin was on the rise. The mandolin would eventually wipe out the five-string, not alone but in combination with a mandolin-inspired instrument—the tenor banjo. The tenor borrowed the mandolin's tuning, with four single strings (rather than four pairs) tuned in fifths. Like the mandolin, the tenor had metal strings, rather than the gut of the five-string, and it was played with a plectrum. A mandolinist could now easily double on banjo. In addition, the plectrum style worked better with the new dance bands—so well, in fact, that the early tenor banjo was first called the "tango banjo" after the dance craze of 1910. By the end of World War I, the five-string banjo was, just as Percy Jaques had feared, a "gone-by."

The five-string literally took to the woods from World War I until the 1930s. Aside from a few diehard classical players, it was seldom heard outside of Appalachian or country music. In the rural South, musicians did adopt steel strings, and the five-string banjo became a vital part of early country and string-band music. Banjoist Charlie Poole was a popular recording artist of the 1920s. Uncle Dave Macon, who was over 50 years old when he started his career in the early 1920s, was the most popular five-string banjo player from the 1930s well into the 1940s.

The five-string experienced a resurgence in the 1940s that in one respect was similar to the tenor's rise 30 years earlier. As the tenor had gained a foothold through its association with the tango, the five-string aligned itself with a hot new style of music—bluegrass. Bill Monroe, a mandolin player, introduced his supercharged version of traditional string-band music on the Grand Ole Opry in 1939. In 1941 he added a banjo to his Blue Grass Boys. Dave Ackeman, who would later achieve fame as the country comedian String-bean, played five-string in a two-fingered style that was a new version of the old mountain "claw hammer" style. In 1945 Earl Scruggs replaced Ackeman in the Blue Grass Boys, bringing with him a rolling three-fingered style from his home area of western North Carolina. Scruggs' instrument was a far cry from the turn-of-the-century classical banjo or the homemade open-back Appalachian instruments. Innovations such as the resonator, tone ring, and steel strings, which had given the tenor banjo greater volume and a biting attack, made the five-string in Scruggs's hands a powerful, driving musical force. Scruggs was so influential that his banjo style—as much as Monroe's singing or mandolin playing—came to be the identifying sound of bluegrass, and he is largely responsible for the continued popularity of the five-string banjo today.

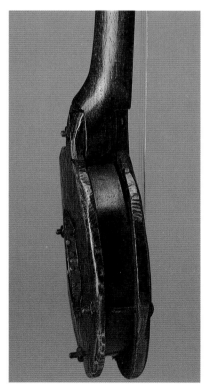

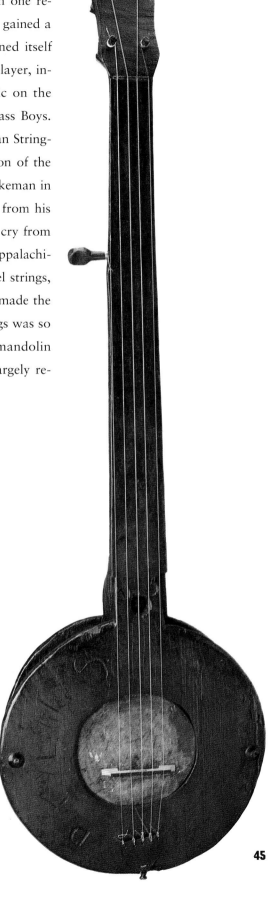

♦ *Dixie can banjo, circa 1850s. This five-string could represent a pioneering attempt to invent a resonator instrument, or it could have been made by someone who simply was unable to find a skin head. The maker used materials at hand. Large bolts fasten the back plate to the rim, and the bridge sits on a tin can that extends through a hole in the back plate and is fastened by nails. Country Music Hall of Fame Collection/BM*

♦ Double-head banjo, circa 1850s (upper left). This minstrel-era banjo looks from the front like a typical transitional example, with the scrolled peghead style of many early banjos and the tension hoop-and-brackets system of later models. The back (lower left) reveals an experiment in closed-back design, with a second head stretched across the back of the rim. Jim Bollman/WC

♦ Carved-peghead banjo, circa 1860s (center and opposite bottom left and right). With the increasing popularity of minstrel music, the level of banjo craftsmanship also rose. The lack of fingerboard inlay on this highly carved example may indicate that it was a player's instrument. It may indicate, however, simply that the maker's specialty was carving and not inlay work. The man's head on the peghead (opposite lower right) is a common feature of French violins but unusual on a banjo. Art Rosenbaum/BM

◆ Dobson, 1880s (upper left and right). The term "presentation grade" is used for the most highly ornamented instruments. Apparently, this one was literally presented—by "C. S. to C. S.," according to the peghead plate. It is not typical of Dobson banjos, but these have so much variation that most banjo collectors say there is no such thing as a typical Dobson. Many Dobsons appear to be the work of James H. Buckbee of New York, who made banjos from 1863 until his company was bought by Rettberg and Lange in 1897. Dobson was the first to successfully market banjos with a closed-back design, and the wood back of this example provided an opportunity for some fancy ornamentation. The wood floral-pattern fingerboard inlay is a simplified version of the pearl tree-of-life that graces the fingerboards of many later high-end guitars and banjos. Jim Bollman/WC

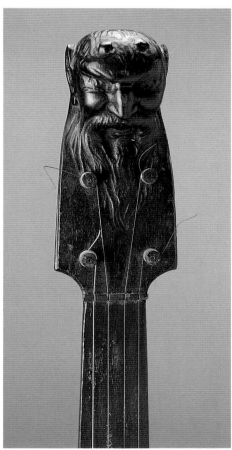

♦ *Teed six-string, circa 1860s (upper left). George Teed of New York added a sixth string, with the tuner in the middle of the peghead, as early as the 1860s. This example has a closed-back design. Country Music Hall of Fame Collection/BM*

♦ *Teed six-string, circa 1880s (upper right and lower left and right). After two decades of making six-string banjos, Teed remained true to his original basic design, including the curved-in fingerboard just above the short-string tuning peg. Teed's craftsmanship has improved noticeably from his earlier effort, as evidenced by the finely carved tuners. Jim Bollman/WC*

S. S. Stewart fretless, 1890s. Samuel Swaim Stewart (1855–1898) of Philadelphia first made banjos in 1878. He apparently made this presentation-grade instrument for someone with the initials "V. A." Stewart was a master of marketing in the aggressive style of Lyon and Healy. He published what were probably the first banjo catalogs, plus a banjo journal, discourses on proper construction, and sheet music. The inlays on the fingerboard and neck heel include star and crescent figures, which are also commonly seen on mandolins and guitars made by one of Stewart's contemporaries, Orville Gibson. Gruhn Guitars/DL

♦ *S. S. Stewart fretless six-string, circa 1895. Stewart viewed the six-string banjo not as an improved five-string but rather as an ensemble instrument. Stewart's 1896 catalog notes that the six-string has the advantage of "two bass strings instead of one.... This enables the performer, in playing accompaniments to the music performed on the five-string Banjo to have access to full chords that are not possible on the five-string Banjo, and to use the fundamental notes of many chords also, that are not possible to get on the ordinary Banjo." By the time this banjo was made, all of the models shown in the Stewart catalog had frets. However, about half of the musicians pictured in the catalog still played fretless banjos. The fingerboard inlay is rather reserved by Stewart standards, but the intricately engraved peghead cover indicates that this is a presentation-grade instrument. The catalog description of the standard six-string model includes the caution, "Wire strings are on no account to be used on these instruments." Jay Levin/WC*

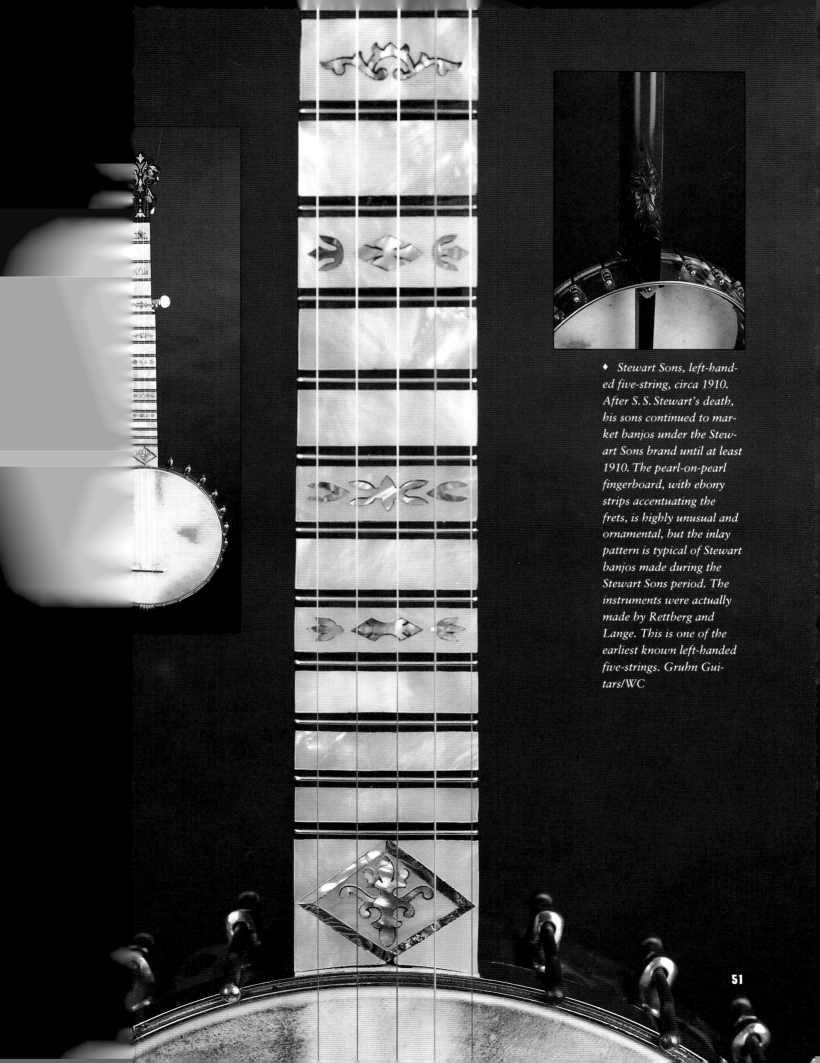

♦ Stewart Sons, left-hand-ed five-string, circa 1910. After S. S. Stewart's death, his sons continued to market banjos under the Stewart Sons brand until at least 1910. The pearl-on-pearl fingerboard, with ebony strips accentuating the frets, is highly unusual and ornamental, but the inlay pattern is typical of Stewart banjos made during the Stewart Sons period. The instruments were actually made by Rettberg and Lange. This is one of the earliest known left-handed five-strings. Gruhn Guitars/WC

♦ Pollman Ultra Artist mandoline-banjo, circa 1895. August Pollman of New York distributed his own line and also Stewart banjos. This model, labeled "W. J. D. B. The Favorite," combines a five-string banjo setup with a mandolin body. The concept did not catch on, but the reverse combination—mandolin setup (four strings tuned in fifths) with banjo body— would be highly successful as the tenor banjo. Jim Bollman/WC

♦ Fairbanks and Cole, circa 1884. Albert Conant Fairbanks (1852-1919) began building banjos about 1875 in Boston and joined in partnership with Boston music teacher William A. Cole about 1880. They split in 1890 and continued making banjos separately. In 1894, Fairbanks sold his banjo company and started a bicycle company. Fairbanks was a player as well as a craftsman, and this model reflects the preference of older players for a fretless fingerboard. Jim Bollman/WC

♦ Cole Eclipse, circa 1892. Boston maker W. A. Cole split with A.C. Fairbanks in 1890 and started his own line (even though Fairbanks continued to use the Fairbanks and Cole brand on some instruments). Cole died in 1909, and the company continued under his brother Frank's leadership until 1919. Cole's Eclipse model features some of the more imaginative inlay patterns of any maker. This banjo shows evidence of the general acceptance of frets by the 1890s. Jim Bollman/WC

♦ Cole Eclipse banjeaurine, mid-1890s (lower left). This example bears a patent date of 1894. The inlay is less fancy, but by no means less imaginative, than on some of Cole's other Eclipse models. Jay Levin/BM

♦ Cole Eclipse, circa 1898 (lower right). The butterfly inlay at the fifth fret is a memorable feature of this banjo. The peghead of this presentation-grade model is inlaid with what may be the original owner's monogram: CLF. Jim Bollman/WC

• Fairbanks Electric, circa 1896 (upper left and right and lower right). In the 1890s, the Electric was the top model of the Fairbanks line. It was not electrically amplified; rather, all models with Fairbanks' patented, wavy-shaped tone ring were labeled "Electric." Practically every available area is inlaid, including the back of the peghead. Jim Bollman/WC

• Fairbanks Whyte Laydie #2 piccolo, circa 1908 (lower left). The piccolo banjo is even smaller than the banjeaurine, but like all classical banjo-family instruments, it has five strings. Jim Bollman/WC

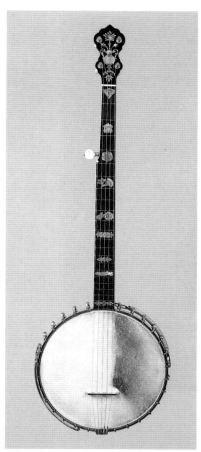

♦ *Fairbanks-Vega Whyte Laydie #7, 1921. David L. Day, later to become the D of the Bacon company's B&D brand, joined the Fairbanks company in 1883 and took over after the departure of A. C. Fairbanks in 1894. He oversaw the introduction of the Whyte Laydie (named for its white holly neck and rim) in 1901 and the Tuba-phone in 1909. After a factory fire in 1904, the company was sold to Julius and Carl Nelson, owners of the Vega instrument company in Boston, for $925 plus $1 each for the rights to four patents. Vega continued to make high-quality Fairbanks five-strings years after the instrument had become passé. This 1921 version of the Whyte Laydie has engraved pearl on the peghead as well as the fingerboard. Earlier models have larger fernlike patterns. The carving on the neck heel goes farther up the neck on the 1921 model than on earlier versions. Calvin Minner/DL*

◆ *Fairbanks-Vega Tu-ba-phone Deluxe, circa 1909 (upper left). The Tu-ba-phone and Whyte Laydie could be considered equals as Fairbanks-Vega's top lines, but the Tu-ba-phone Deluxe is the fanciest of any model in either line. The fingerboard features an unusual custom-ordered double-vine inlay pattern (upper right). Also custom-ordered is the heel carving design. The abalone pearl inlay around the back of the rim is standard on the Deluxe. Jim Bollman/WC*

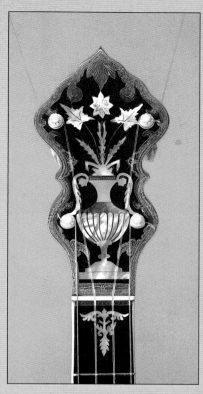

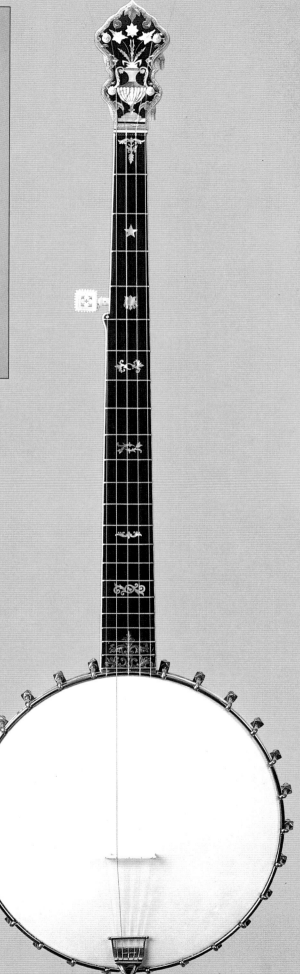

♦ *Waldo, 1894 (center). Waldo was a performer and teacher whose banjos were made by the Burrowes company of Saginaw, Michigan. In addition to the fine inlay, the peghead (above) features an engraved silver overlay around the border. Even the tips of the ivory tuners are carved (opposite lower right). According to the heelcap (opposite lower left), this presentation-grade instrument was delivered to C. Norman Burke in December 1894. The rim is engraved on the inside as well as the outside. Calvin Minner/DL*

♦ *Washburn Presentation, 1890s (above). Lyon and Healy made several Washburn guitar models fancier than this banjo and some mandolins with an abalone pearl fingerboard, but this fretless model is the fanciest catalog banjo model. Gruhn Guitars/DL*

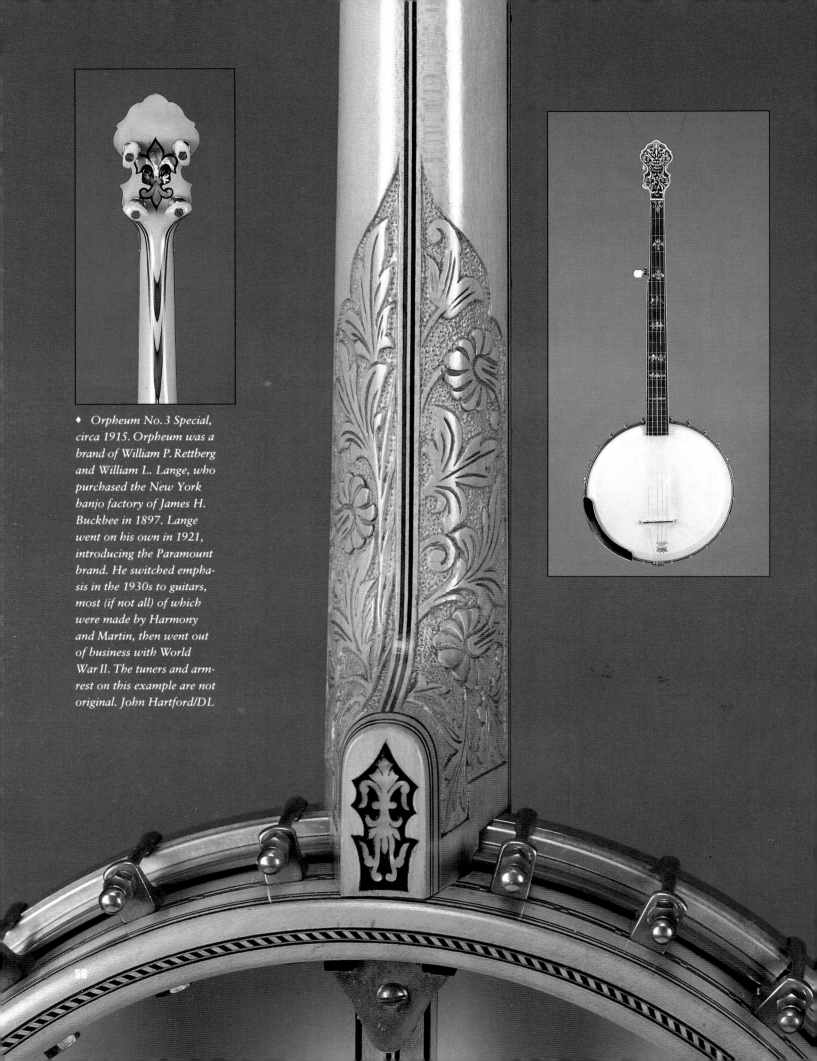

♦ Orpheum No. 3 Special, circa 1915. Orpheum was a brand of William P. Rettberg and William L. Lange, who purchased the New York banjo factory of James H. Buckbee in 1897. Lange went on his own in 1921, introducing the Paramount brand. He switched emphasis in the 1930s to guitars, most (if not all) of which were made by Harmony and Martin, then went out of business with World War II. The tuners and armrest on this example are not original. John Hartford/DL

♦ Bay State, circa 1898. Bay State was a brand name of the John C. Haynes Co. of Boston. This floral inlay is not so fancy but perhaps more tasteful than the inlay extravaganzas found on some other Bay State models or on some banjos made by Bay State's Boston competitors, Fairbanks and Cole. Jim Bollman/WC

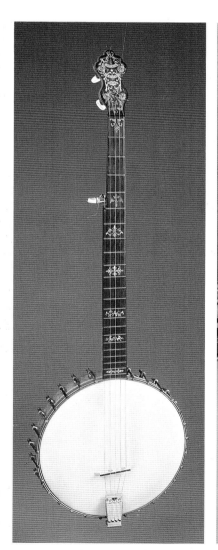

♦ Farland Artists Grand, early 1900s. A. A. Farland, a New York teacher and musician, marketed banjos beginning about 1890. Many of them were made by James H. Buckbee until 1897 and possibly by William Lange after 1897. Farlands typically have a beveled wood rim. The Farland design was favored by John Hartford, the folk-singer/songwriter who rose to fame in the late 1960s, and Hartford models made by the Stelling and Deering companies incorporated some Farland characteristics. The tuners and tailpiece on this example are not original. John Hartford/DL

♦ *Van Eps Recording, 1920s.* The resonator is usually regarded as an innovation of the tenor banjo era, although minstrel-era makers experimented with closed-back designs. One of the early resonator designs of the tenor era was developed by classical (five-string) banjo virtuoso Fred Van Eps in 1920. According to company literature, Van Eps discovered the secret to tone projection by holding a tin pan behind a banjo. He believed "the tone should be thrown outward and forward rather than backward," and to that end he put a metal bowl directly under the head and then cut a hole in the head. The metal bowl necessitated a curved support rod. Van Eps banjos were made through the late 1920s by Van Eps-Burr Corp. in Plainfield, New Jersey, and distributed by Lyon and Healy. Van Eps himself continued to make banjos for two more decades. *Gruhn Guitars/WC*

♦ *Van Eps, 1949.* Fred Van Eps was an old man when he made this banjo, and only about 50 of this type were made. Players consider these relatively plain models to be the ultimate in a classical banjo. He abandoned the metal bowl resonator of his Recording models and returned to an open-back design. The tone ring is in an unusual place—about an inch inside the rim rather than sitting on the rim itself, but it has the same shape as the metal bowl resonator of the Recording models. The fingerboard is highly unusual. Although it is fretted, it is scalloped so that the frets are flush. It feels almost like a fretless fingerboard but provides the precision of a fretted banjo. The scale length of 28 $^{1}/_{2}$ inches and head diameter of 12 inches are old-time dimensions, and this banjo belongs to an era that ended 50 years earlier. *Gruhn Guitars/WC*

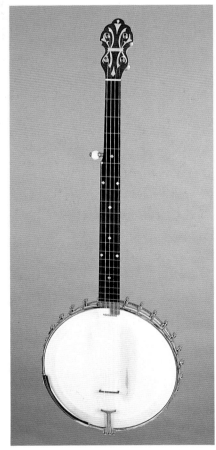

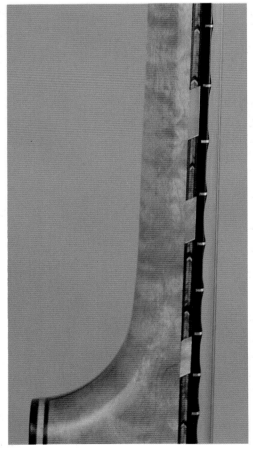

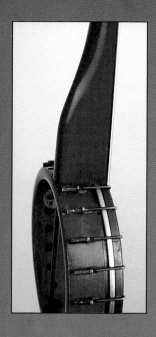

♦ *Gibson custom fretless, late 1920s (upper left). The tenor banjo era was peaking when Gibson made this mysterious fretless five-string. The open back is an old-timey design, and the tone ring (not visible) is unusual for a Gibson. The shoes to which the tension hooks attach are a very early style that had been upgraded on all but lowest-end Gibsons by the late 1920s. The neck heel shape is unique for a Gibson and resembles pre-1890 designs. And the unplated brass parts are unheard-of on a Gibson banjo. With no fingerboard inlay whatso-ever, this banjo was probably custom-made for a serious but economy-minded player of the late 1800s minstrel style. Gruhn Guitars/WC*

♦ *Gibson custom, 1940 (right), owned and played by Uncle Dave Macon. Uncle Dave was 70 years old and entering the last decade of a 30-year career when this banjo was made. Like most country performers, Macon played resonator models during his heyday, but the open-back design was ap-propriate for two reasons. First, it allowed him to grasp the support rod and twirl the instrument for a novel effect in his stage act. Second, the Scruggs blue-grass style was just around the corner, and once it hit, Macon's playing style would be as old-timey as this open-back banjo. Gruhn Guitars/DL*

♦ *Gibson Granada RB, 1932. In the 1920s and 1930s, Gibson made very few RB ("regular banjo" or five-string) models. Most of the five-strings in use today from the 1920s and 1930s started out as tenors and have been converted to five-string with a new neck. This example is a rare original five-string. DeWitt "Snuffy" Jenkins, an early proponent of the three-fingered picking style, owned a Granada when he bought the Gibson RB-4 that he played until his death in 1990. He sold the Granada to Don Reno, who would also become an influential bluegrass musician. Reno then traded it to Earl Scruggs, who went on to make the Granada model famous. Despite the Granada's engraved gold-plated metal parts, it is not a fancy banjo by the standards of the day. This example has a "flat-head" tone ring (available as an option but not standard on any model until 1937) and a one-piece flange—the combination of equipment most highly sought by bluegrass banjo players. "Made in the U.S.A." impressed into the back of the peghead denotes an exported model, and this instrument was sold in Scotland. Anonymous collector/DL*

♦ Gibson RB-4, circa 1934 (center), owned and played by Snuffy Jenkins. Gibson's Mastertone line in the early 1930s comprised Styles 3, 4, Granada, 6, Florentine, and All American. Styles 3, 4, and Granada have a one-piece flange (introduced in late 1929), while those above the Granada have a two-piece flange. The one-piece flange (with flat-head tone ring) is so highly regarded by bluegrass players today that a plain Style 3 from 1934, which listed new for $100, will bring more than the much fancier Florentine, which listed for $450. Snuffy Jenkins bought this banjo in a pawn shop for $40. The pickguard is standard on high-end Gibsons of this period. It may protect the head from players who use a plectrum, but finger-style players generally have no use for it. Jenkins was no exception. In a 1989 interview he explained: "I don't know why it was on there. I just never did take it off." Snuffy Jenkins/BM

♦ Gibson Earl Scruggs, 1991 (above). Although Scruggs endorsed Vega banjos in the 1960s, he continued to record with a Gibson Granada. In 1984 Gibson introduced the Earl Scruggs model, essentially a Granada with chrome-plated metal parts and an ebony fingerboard with two additional inlays. In 1987 Gibson reintroduced the Granada with hearts-and-flowers inlay or optional "flying eagle" inlay pattern. To further confuse the model delineation, two additional Scruggs models later appeared: the Earl Scruggs Classic with "bow tie" inlays and the gold-plated Earl Scruggs Deluxe. The Scruggs model is fitted with what are commonly known as "Scruggs" tuners. Earl Scruggs installed a pair of cams on his banjo head so that he could retune the second and third strings quickly and accurately, allowing him to change on the fly from G to D tuning and back. Bill Keith, one of Scruggs' successors in the Blue Grass Boys, refined the design by integrating the cam stops into an enclosed tuner assembly, and this banjo is fitted with Keith tuners. Gruhn Guitars/WC

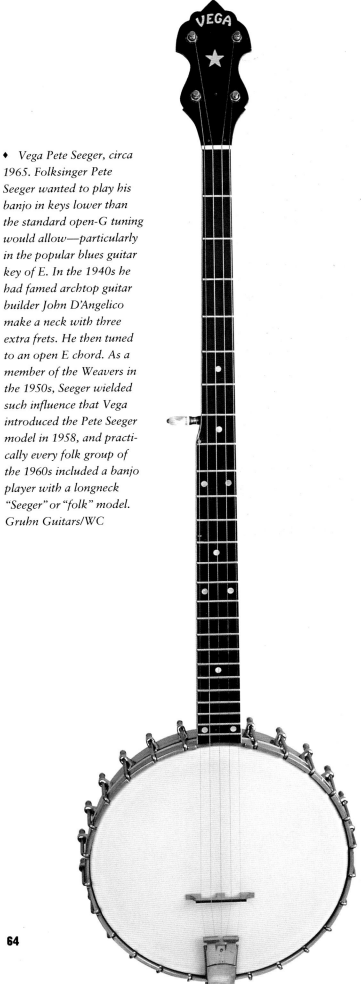

♦ *Vega Pete Seeger, circa 1965. Folksinger Pete Seeger wanted to play his banjo in keys lower than the standard open-G tuning would allow—particularly in the popular blues guitar key of E. In the 1940s he had famed archtop guitar builder John D'Angelico make a neck with three extra frets. He then tuned to an open E chord. As a member of the Weavers in the 1950s, Seeger wielded such influence that Vega introduced the Pete Seeger model in 1958, and practically every folk group of the 1960s included a banjo player with a longneck "Seeger" or "folk" model. Gruhn Guitars/WC*

◆ *Washburn 1125, circa 1897. (See page 66.)*

MANDOLINS

◆   ◆   ◆

Italian-Style Mandolins

The mandolin's family tree goes back even farther than the guitar's—at least as far back as the 1100s. The ancestor of the modern mandolin was the mandora, essentially a small lute. The term *mandora* was used for a variety of instruments: with single strings or courses of strings, with gut or metal strings, played with a plectrum or with the fingers. At one point the term was even used for instruments that were larger than the lute. The term *mandola* came into use by the 1600s for instruments that were smaller than a lute but larger than a mandolin.

The Lombardy region of northern Italy became a center of mandolin production, and the Lombardy-style mandolin, like the lute, had a flat top and

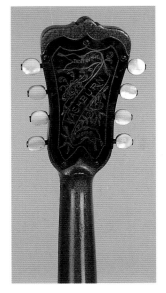

♦ *Washburn 1125, circa 1897. The highly ornate Model 1125 was one of the new Washburn models of 1897 and remained at the top of the line for almost 20 years. The top features rope-pattern binding of alternating pearl and ebony with an additional pearl border. The pickguard inlay is an exquisite cecropia moth of golden-hued mother-of-pearl (described in the Lyon and Healy catalog as "gold fish pearl") and multi-hued abalone pearl. The black headstock sets off the gold pearl of the peghead inlay and the white "Sydney" pearl of the tuner buttons and fingerboard. The back has 42 ribs. Roy Acuff Museum, Opryland USA/WC*

a bowl-shaped back. The back was formed by multiple pieces of wood or "ribs;" the more expensive the instruments the greater the number of ribs. Eight metal strings were arranged in pairs and tuned in fifths. In the 1700s a new style emerged, centered around the Vinaccia family of Naples in southern Italy. An Italian history of the mandolin published in 1923 described the Lombardy body as resembling half an egg and the Neapolitan, half a pear. More important than the shape, however, were differences in the neck and top. Whereas the Lombardy style typically had a neck-body joint at the seventh fret, the Neapolitan style had a full octave (12 frets) clear of the body. The Neapolitan also had a top that was bent near the line of the bridge, rather than the flat top of the Lombardy. The bent-top Neapolitan style would become dominant through the 1800s.

The scale length and tuning of the mandolin were the same as those for the violin, and this close relationship to the violin influenced the mandolin's cultural status as an instrument for classical or serious music. In 1787 Mozart put a mandolin onstage in his opera *Don Giovanni*, although the part was played in the pit orchestra by a pizzicato (plucked) violin. In 1887, Verdi's orchestration for the opera *Otello* included a part for mandolin.

By the late 1800s mandolin clubs and orchestras were springing up in the United States. The typical American mandolin of that time was a Neapolitan bowlback or "taterbug" model, with bent top and ribbed back. With the instrument's rising popularity, however, revolutionary innovations were soon to come. By 1910 bowlbacks would be pushed aside, and the company that made the new mandolins—Gibson—would go on to be the most pervasive force in the American fretted instrument industry in the twentieth century.

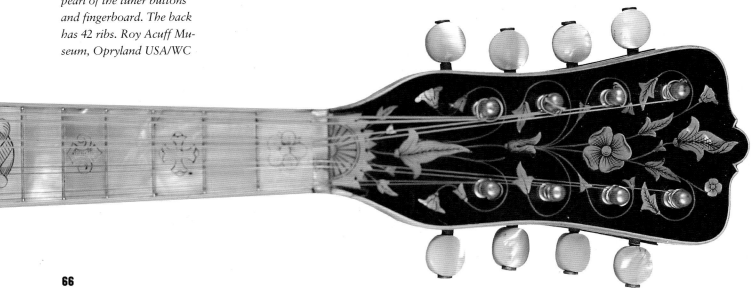

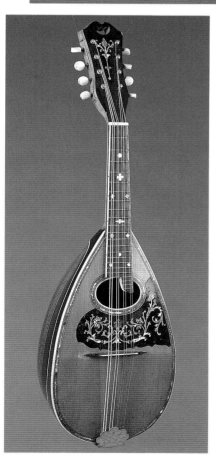

♦ Merrill, early 1900s. From the front, this mandolin looks like a typical fancy Neapolitan instrument from the turn of the century, with abalone pearl fingerboard, inlaid tuner buttons, pickguard inlay, and pearl inlays in the edge trim. From the back, however, it is a different animal. Instead of wood ribs, the back is a single piece of aluminum with fancy engraving. New York maker Neil Merrill patented aluminum-back instruments in 1896. Later experiments with materials other than wood, such as National's metal bodies of the late 1920s and 1930s or Ovation's fiberglass bowl-back guitars from the late 1960s on, have been much more successful commercially. Ross Music/BM

♦ Stahl, circa 1915 (lower left). The Larson brothers of Chicago made this instrument for distribution by the Wm. C. Stahl company of Milwaukee. It is fairly ornate, but the extension of the pickguard all the way to the edge shows that it was intended to be a functional instrument. Gruhn Guitars/DL

♦ D'Angelico, early 1930s (lower right). Even without the maker's name on the peghead, the cutout and button at the top of the peghead—more formally, the broken-scroll pediment framing the ornamental cupola—identify this as the work of John D'Angelico. D'Angelico is best known as the premier maker of acoustic archtop guitars, but in the 1930s he made many mandolins—virtually all with modern carved-top design. This Neapolitan bent-top model is a rare exception. Gordon's Guitars/WC

♦ Vinaccia, 1896 (upper left and right). The Vinaccia family was a prime force in the development of the modern Neapolitan mandolin in the 1700s, and the Vinaccia name was still one of the most respected in the mandolin world when this example was made. The label is signed "Fratelli [Brothers] Vinaccia." Although this mandolin is rather fancy by today's standards, among its contemporaries it falls somewhere in the middle range of ornamentation. Classic Neapolitan mandolins of the nineteenth century have between 17 and 33 ribs, and this instrument's 23 ribs further indicate its midline status. Owner unknown/WC

♦ Washburn 275, circa 1910 (above and center). The fancy pearl-ornamented Model 275 is second in the Washburn mandolin line behind the 1125, but it has 44 ribs—2 more than the higher model. Walter Carter/WC

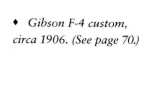

♦ *Gibson F-4 custom, circa 1906. (See page 70.)*

MANDOLINS

♦ ♦ ♦

Orville Gibson and Company

The man who revolutionized mandolin design is one of the most enigmatic figures in the history of fretted instruments. His only patented design was not at all successful; his most important design, which quickly became and remains the industry standard, was appropriated directly from the violin. Since 1902 his name, and for a few years even his picture, has been affixed to hundreds of thousands of mandolins and guitars made by the largest American manufacturer of high-quality stringed instruments, yet he never owned a single share of stock in the company that bears his name—Gibson.

♦ *Gibson F-4 custom, circa 1906 (above). This instrument was probably custom-ordered, as no models this fancy appear in Gibson literature. The Gibson company decreased the size of the F models from Orville Gibson's standards. This transitional example has the modern thin depth but is still as wide as earlier models. The ornate double-flowerpot peghead inlay (opposite) was standard on F-4s up until about 1911, when a simpler double flowerpot was adopted. Like other high-end models of this period, this mandolin has nicely figured maple back and sides (opposite right). The maple neck is not standard on any Gibson mandolin until the F-5 of 1922. Gruhn Guitars/WC*

Orville H. Gibson, the son of English immigrants, was born in Chateaugay, New York, in 1856. As a young man, he moved to Kalamazoo, Michigan, where city directories listed him as a clerk in various businesses. He began making instruments sometime in the 1880s, and he was first listed as a manufacturer of musical instruments in 1896.

Gibson had some wild ideas about instrument construction, some of them valid and some arguable. Like all instrument makers, he believed that aged, dry wood was superior to newly cut wood, and he was known for seeking old furniture as a source of seasoned wood. He achieved some notoriety in France and Italy for a violin he made of wood from the old Town Hall of Boston. The most famous of his experimental instruments, which appeared with his picture on instrument labels, had the body lines of an ancient lyre and was called a lyre-mandolin. His instruments were typically ornate.

Orville Gibson was not the only one experimenting with instrument design. Back in 1851 one of the exhibits at the Great Exposition in London was a double-neck instrument that combined a zither, guitar, and bass into one bizarre piece called a *guitarpa*. This instrument would be an obscure footnote in guitar history but for its body shape. The body had two points—one on the treble side and one on the bass side, both at about the same level as the soundhole. On the bass side where the four-string bass neck met the body, the body formed a scroll. The scroll circled outward rather than toward the neck, but the general body lines may well have provided the inspiration for Orville Gibson's scroll-body F-style mandolin, the style that would become the industry standard.

Gibson borrowed an element from violin design and carved the top of his instruments into an arched shape. It seems odd that he did not carry the violin concept one step farther and fit his mandolins with *f*-holes, but he stayed with the traditional oval hole of the Neapolitan style. He also carved out the inside of the back but left the largest area of the outer side of the back flat.

Orville Gibson's one and only patent, granted in 1898, was not for the carved-top design that would revolutionize the mandolin and eventually the guitar. The patent was for an equally radical concept: the sides and neck are carved out of a single piece of wood, and the neck is carved partially hollow in order to increase the volume of air in the body. The one-piece neck and sides concept was based on Gibson's belief that to achieve the best sound, wood should be put under as little stress as possible.

Whether the no-stress concept has merit is still debatable. The Larson brothers, who started making flat top guitars at about the same time, produced some fine instruments with the exact opposite approach, glueing the braces to the top of a guitar while the top was bent slightly. One of their claims to superior instruments was that their guitars were "built under tension."

Ironically, the no-stress concept may have been a mistake in Gibson's attempt to copy violin design. The Gibson company's Catalog F of 1908 made a prosaic case for the superiority of the Gibson mandolin's violinlike, tension-free top, but in reality only cheap violins have a tension-free top. In the construction of quality violins, the bass-side tone bar (brace) is shaped so that the top must be placed under tension for the tone bar to be glued into place. Thus, fine violins are built under tension. Only cheap violins, with a tone bar as an integral part of the top, are built tension-free.

In addition to their carved design, Orville Gibson's instruments were unique in size—wider and deeper than today's standard model. They had a 15-inch scale, 2 inches longer that of the violin or the mandolins of most other makers. In the age of parlor guitars, when a guitar 14 inches wide would be considered quite large, his archtop guitars were behemoths spanning 17 inches or more across the lower bout. One of the early Gibson company's harp guitars—which combined a standard guitar with a rack of non-fretted sub-bass strings—might measure 21 inches across the body.

Orville Gibson probably made no more than a dozen instruments a year, but he achieved enough notoriety to interest a group of Kalamazoo investors. On November 11, 1902, they formed the Gibson Mandolin-Guitar Mfg. Co.,Ltd., soon to be simply the Gibson Mandolin-Guitar Co. Orville Gibson assigned his patent to the company and worked initially as a consultant.

♦ *Orville Gibson 10-string mandolin-guitar, 1894 (above and opposite center). According to Gibson historian Julius Bellson, this unusual instrument was tuned to the highest five strings of a guitar, with the paired strings tuned in unison. Although this mandolin-guitar design did not find a market, it illustrates many of the design elements of Orville Gibson's highly successful mandolin models, including the star-and-crescent inlay, the lines of the lyre, and the flat center portion of the back. This instrument does not have a label, but a small pearl medallion engraved "1894." It is impossible to determine whether the medallion is original or was added at the time the instrument was refinished. Gibson USA/WC*

His contract was rewritten in 1915 so that he received a royalty, but he was never a partner. He left Kalamazoo to return to New York State in 1909 and died there in a sanitorium in Ogdensburg on August 19, 1918, of chronic endocarditis.

In light of Orville Gibson's profound influence on mandolin and guitar design, one might reasonably expect his instruments to be among the best of their kind ever made. One would probably be disappointed. Although a fair assessment of their quality is difficult, since genuine Orville-made instruments are rare and seldom found in good playing condition, these instruments typically are rather hard to play. Furthermore, to modern ears, the large bodies give them a deeper, deader tone that makes them sound decidedly inferior to the instruments the Gibson company was making by 1908.

The company quickly abandoned most of Orville Gibson's designs. By the end of the company's first five years, the heavy one-piece back with the flat middle section was replaced by a much thinner carved back of either one or two pieces. The one-piece carved neck and sides design was replaced by a separate neck and two side pieces that were bent into shape. The scale length was reduced to 13 7/8 inches (Gibson took a standard 13-inch violin scale and added 7/8 of an inch to account for the width of the frets). Guitars, too, decreased in size, to dimensions closer to those of other manufacturers.

Orville Gibson did, however, live to see his carved tops and his new body shapes not only survive but revolutionize the mandolin world and boost the Gibson company into a dominant position. When the guitar finally began its rise as a versatile orchestral instrument in the late 1920s and early 1930s, it would be another Orville Gibson concept—the large-body archtop (improved by the addition of *f*-holes)—that would take the guitar to the forefront of the fretted instrument world.

The Gibson company's first catalog, published in 1903, emphasized mandolins over guitars. It was one of the most important publications in the history of fretted instruments for it introduced not just one but two new mandolin body styles, both quite different from the standard bowlback models of the period and both hugely successful. Orville Gibson's symmetrical A-style and scroll-body F-style would be refined through the years, but they are in essence the two mandolin styles that remain the standard today. The switch to *f*-holes on both styles and a longer neck on high-end models would be the only major changes after 1910.

♦ Gibson A, circa 1907 (above). Even the plainest A-series mandolin of this period has a pickguard inlaid flush with the top. From 1908 until its discontinuation in 1933, the A is distinguishable from higher A models (A-1, A-2, etc.) by its lack of a peghead logo. Early Gibson models have a top finish of amber or, on the higher models, black. Gruhn Guitars/DL

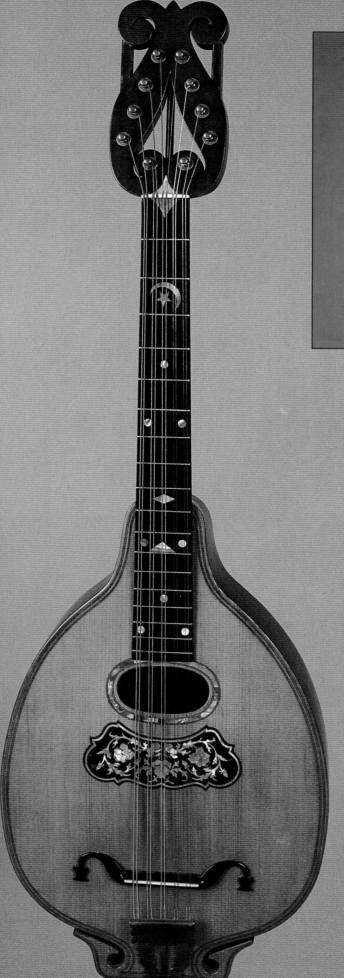

♦ Gibson A-3, late 1921 (above). The A-3, one of the models in the original Gibson line, was spruced up with an ivory top finish from 1918 until its discontinuation in 1922. The ivory top was also offered (but is extremely rare) as an optional finish on companion instruments from the mandolin family: the H-2 mandola, K-2 mandocello, and L-3 guitar. This example is one of the last A-3s made, and it is one of the first Gibson instruments to be fitted with an adjustable truss rod. The peghead ornament is obviously a pre–truss rod design, as the hole for the rod has been drilled through the inlay. This instrument also sports the first version of another important Gibson innovation, the height-adjustable bridge, which was introduced in early 1921. Gruhn Guitars/DL

♦ *Gibson catalog, 1903. After opening the catalog to a picture worthy of pin-up status, who could resist buying a Gibson instrument? Although instrument makers from the Vinaccias to the Martins would dispute the pronouncement on the title page—the first serious mandolins and guitars ever made—it set a standard of lofty catalog claims for many years to come. Gruhn Guitars/WC*

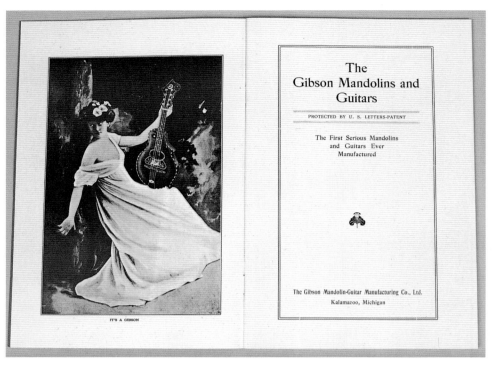

♦ *Gibson label, 1906. Orville Gibson's likeness and his lyre-mandolin were featured on his personal labels and on company labels up until about 1908. The lyre-mandolin was registered as a company trademark. This label is on a Style L guitar. Gruhn Guitars/WC*

♦ Orville Gibson A-style mandolin, 1901. The A-style, with a rounded symmetrical body and oval sound-hole, was the first mandolin style developed by Orville Gibson. Although a simpler design than the scroll-body F-style, the A is still radically different from the Neapolitan bowlback style that had been the standard of the nineteenth century. The large, plain "paddle" peghead is typical of the earliest Gibson company guitars as well. The symmetrical pickguard inlaid under the strings shows some of the ornamentation of Orville-made instruments (A-style mandolins pictured in the company's 1903 catalog have a smaller pickguard on the treble side of the strings or else no pickguard at all). This instrument was signed by Orville Gibson in 1901. A similar example, but with no pickguard, is the first instrument pictured in the 1903 catalog. This mandolin has the walnut back and sides typical of low-end and midline models prior to about 1907. The peghead is spliced on, and a splice mark on the neck just above the heel shows that Orville's concept of one-piece sides and neck was not economically practical (it required a very large piece of wood). Both splices are common on early Gibson company mandolins.
Jim Reynolds/DL

♦ Gibson A-4, 1923. The top model in the A line was given a dark mahogany sunburst finish in 1918. The tapered "snakehead" peghead appeared on A-style mandolins from 1923 through 1927. As a result of the growing acceptance of f-hole models and the general decline in the mandolin's popularity in the 1930s, the A-4 was discontinued in 1935. Gruhn Guitars/WC

♦ *Girls High Alumnae Association Mandolin Orchestra, Atlanta, 1917 (above). In the same way that turn of the century band instrument manufacturers promoted community bands as a way to sell instruments, Gibson promoted mandolin orchestras, featuring group pictures in ads and catalogs. Gibson captioned these pictures "Every One a Gibson-ite," so this picture was probably not used in Gibson literature, thanks to the non-Gibson bowlback mandolin in the back row. It did appear in the December 1917 issue of Cadenza magazine. Author Walter Carter's grandmother stands in the front row, third from left, playing a Gibson K-1 mandocello. In the process of promoting mandolin orchestras, Gibson became the prime force in standardizing the tunings of the mandola and mandocello to those of the viola and cello, respectively. The obstacle, as it had been in the era of the five-string banjo, was notation. In order to read a part for a "tenor" mandola, which was tuned a fifth below the mandolin, a player had to be able to read music written in the tenor clef. A mandocello tuned an octave below the tenor mandola presented a similar problem. Mandola players routinely tuned an octave below standard mandolin pitch so that the notation would be in the same key. Gibson's 1903 catalog stated that its mandolas were suitable for tenor or octave tuning, but by the 1908 catalog the company had changed its tune. In typical prosaic form, the catalog made a case for tenor tuning and then included a list of music publishers who offered treble-clef arrangements for tenor mandola and mandocello. Walter Carter/WC*

♦ *Gibson piccolo mandolin, circa 1915 (center). This rare instrument, possibly one of a kind, was no doubt inspired by the small banjos of an earlier time. Piccolo banjos of the classical five-string era are small, but they still have five strings. This piccolo mandolin has only three pairs of strings. Mark O'Connor/DL*

♦ *Gibson H-2 mandola, late 1915 (upper left). Gibson mandolas and mandocellos have equivalent mandolin models, but the model numbers do not necessarily correspond. The H-1 mandola and K-1 mandocello are similar in trim to either the A-1 mandolin, the A, or the A-2, depending on the period. The H-2 and K-2 are similar to the fancy A-4. The H-4 and K-4 are similar to the scroll-body F-4. Gibson's first deviation from a black or amber top finish is this slightly shaded mahogany finish, introduced in 1914. Gruhn Guitars/WC*

♦ *Gibson K-1 mandocello, 1928 (upper right). The K-1 started with an amber top finish, then went to a very plain-looking brown. In 1925 it was given a black top. In the late 1920s Gibson began placing the logo straight across the peghead rather than at an angle. Although listed until 1943, very few K-1s were made after 1930. John Hedgecoth/WC*

♦ *Kalamazoo KK-31 mandocello, 1939 (lower left and right). Gibson inaugurated the Kalamazoo brand on an in-house budget line of instruments in 1937. The KK-31 mandocello uses the body of a 16-inch–wide f-hole archtop guitar. Unlike most Kalamazoo models, the KK-31 has no equivalent Gibson model. The only mandocello with an archtop guitar body ever offered in the Gibson line is the high-end model, the K-5, with maple back and sides. The KK-31, however, is mahogany. Furthermore, the K-5 had been discontinued from Gibson catalogs for three years and had probably been out of production for closer to ten years by the time this instrument was made. Bernie Leadon/WC*

• *Gibson A-4 Special, 1929 (upper left). This instrument was custom-made for someone who wanted the trim of an F-5 (see page 83) on an A-style mandolin. The F-5 of that period had a longer neck than any other model, and this mandolin has a standard-length neck. Thus the label reads "A-4 Spec." Gruhn Guitars/WC*

• *Gibson Alrite or Style D, 1917 (upper right). Despite the dressy appearance of colored wood purfling, the Alrite or Style D, with its flat top and flat back, was offered as a budget model. Gibson literature called it "The most dangerous competitor the matchless 'Gibson' has." This seemingly self-contradictory statement was intended to separate the Alrite from a true Gibson, even though a special label made it clear that the Alrite was made by Gibson. It was only available for about a year but led the way for future budget models. Gruhn Guitars/WC*

• *Gibson Army and Navy (Style DY), circa 1918 (lower left and right). The Army and Navy has one of the simplest and cheapest mandolin designs conceivable. It replaced the Alrite in 1918, just after World War I. Designed for sale at military post exchanges, it lasted in the line about five years. The Flatiron company, founded in 1977 in Bozeman, Montana, revived the flat top concept. Gibson acquired Flatiron in 1987 and built a new plant in 1989 to handle all of Gibson's acoustic instrument manufacturing. One new Gibson model of 1990 was the AN Custom, a deluxe, longneck version of the old Army and Navy. Gruhn Guitars/DL*

♦ *Gibson A-5, 1963 (upper right). This 1960s A-style version of the Style 5 is a far cry from the F model (see page 83), in construction as well as reputation. Gibson introduced this model in 1957 but in 1971 switched the A-5 to a modified F-style body with a scroll-type extension but no actual cutout (referred to by collectors as "lump scroll" or "Gumby" model). It was discontinued in 1979. Gruhn Guitars/DL*

♦ *Gibson J mando-bass, circa 1920 (above). For the mandolin orchestra to be a true orchestra, it needed a bass instrument, and Gibson introduced one in 1912. Style J, Gibson's only mando-bass model, is 24 inches wide with the full 42-inch scale of a standard (three-quarter size) upright bass. Roy Acuff Museum, Opryland USA/WC*

♦ *Gibson A-50, late 1930s (center). The A-50 was introduced in 1933 with an oval soundhole. A year later the A-50, along with the fancier A-75 and the plainer A-1, became the first Gibson A models with f-holes. By 1937, in response to the success of their new large-body guitars, Gibson increased the body width of the A-1 and A-50 (the A-75 had been discontinued) from 10 to 11 1/4 inches and the scale length from 13 7/8 to 14 3/8 inches. While some of the wide-bodied examples are excellent instruments, either sales or quality of sound did not increase enough to justify the expense of the new design. Just before Gibson's wartime production hiatus in 1942, these models reverted to their former dimensions. Encore/BM*

♦ *Orville Gibson F model, signed June 10, 1900 (upper left and right). The scroll-body or F-style was the second new mandolin style designed by Orville Gibson. This example has an ornate butterfly inlaid under the strings and Orville's trademark star and crescent peghead inlay. According to Gibson historian Julius Bellson, the peghead inlay was done by a Turkish man in Kalamazoo. For such a fancy example, the lack of body binding is curious; even the plainest early Gibson company model had a bound top. As the neck splices indicate, Orville Gibson found it either impractical or uneconomical to follow his own patented design for integral sides and neck. Jim Reynolds/DL*

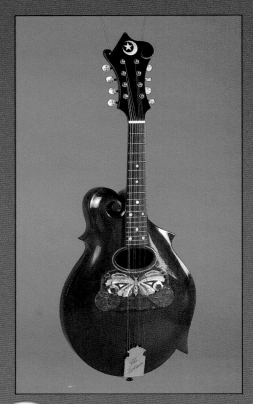

◆ *Gibson F-2, circa 1904. By 1904 the star and crescent inlay has disappeared from the peghead, but otherwise this example is identical to the catalog picture of the model in 1903. The edge trim is mother-of-pearl and ebony. At the time, there were two fancier F models, the F-3 and F-4, and two plainer models, the F and F-1. The back still has the contours of Orville's design but is of two pieces. Also, there are no neck splices. This instrument has metal tuners replacing the original friction pegs. Most of these replacements appear to have been factory jobs, performed shortly after geared pegs became available. Jim Reynolds/DL*

◆ *Gibson F-4, 1915. In 1910 Gibson replaced Orville Gibson's three-point body with a two-point body. This version of the double flowerpot adorned the F-4 peghead (opposite bottom) from 1911 until the truss rod appeared in late 1921. After a few examples were made with the truss rod slot drilled through the bottom part of the inlay, a single-flowerpot design was adopted to leave room for the truss rod cover. "The Gibson" is inlaid at a slant so that it becomes horizontal—for easy reading—when the instrument is held in normal playing position. The F-4 was the top model in the line when this example was made. Gruhn Guitars/DL*

♦ Gibson F-2, 1908 or 1909 (upper left). By 1908 the F-2 and F-4 were the only scroll-body models left in the line. This F-2 is rather plain compared to the pearl and ebony bordered example from 1904. It is one of the earliest to be fitted with Gibson's elevated pickguard. This one has the notice "PATAPPLIEDFOR" where later examples have the patent date of March 30, 1909. Gruhn Guitars/DL

♦ Gibson H-4 mandola, 1923 (upper right). The H-4 mandola has all the trimmings of the F-4 mandolin. Although Gibson took great pride in its elevated pickguard, many players found it to be in the way and removed it. Bill Camp/BM

♦ Gibson K-4 mandocello, 1924 (center). Unique among Gibson instruments, the mandocello was made in three distinctively different body styles. The lower models have an A-style body, the K-4 has the scroll-body of an F-style mandolin, and the K-5 has the same body as the L-5 guitar. The pickguard has been removed. Mark O'Connor/DL

Gibson F-5, signed by Lloyd Loar on July 9, 1923. (See page 85.)

MANDOLINS
◆ ◆ ◆

Lloyd Loar's Master Models

Lloyd Allayre Loar had a most appropriate surname, since he has inspired as much lore as any figure in the history of fretted instruments. Born in 1886 in Cropsey, Illinois, he already had an international reputation as both a mandolin and viola virtuoso and an expert on the science of acoustics when he joined the Gibson staff in 1919. According to legend, he designed Gibson's crowning achievements of the 1920s, the exalted Style 5 instruments: the F-5 mandolin, the H-5 mandola, the K-5 mandocello, the L-5 guitar, and the TB-5 banjo (forerunner of the Mastertone banjo line). From June 1, 1922, to December 1, 1924, he signed the labels of as many as 350 Gibson instruments,

(an estimated 250 of them mandolins), and his magic touch has elevated this group of instruments to Holy Grail status. He was a visionary as well as a genius, foreseeing the future of electric instruments more than a decade before the Gibson company did, and his belief was so fervent that he and Gibson parted ways over the issue. When he finally did bring his own electric designs to market, they were not just 10 but almost 50 years ahead of their time—harbingers of the piezo bridge pickups that brought electric-acoustic flat top guitars into popularity in the 1980s. So the legend goes.

This much is true: Loar-signed mandolins are indeed considered by most collectors and players to be the finest ever made. The most highly respected mandolin makers today, from individual luthiers to the Gibson company itself, have modeled their instruments on the Loar F-5. Loar mandolas, mandocellos, and guitars also inspire the highest regard.

The F-5, introduced in mid-1922, represented the pinnacle of mandolin design. The primary differences between the F-5 and the models that preceded it were the soundholes, the top bracing, the raised fingerboard, and the longer neck. A quarter century after Orville Gibson borrowed the carved-top concept from the violin, the Style 5 family took the next logical step—to violin-style *f*-holes. The top of a Style 5 instrument was braced with two tone bars, versus one on the violin (on the bass side only) or one small lateral brace on Gibson oval-hole mandolins. The fingerboard raised off the top—a violin design concept and also a feature of some European guitars—allowed the top to vibrate more freely. (The design had actually been perfected and patented at Gibson by George D. Laurian in 1917 but was not introduced on a production model until the F-5.) The neck on the F-5 was significantly longer, with three more frets clear of the body than earlier Gibson models. The height-adjustable bridge is also commonly accepted as an F-5 innovation, although it was actually introduced by Gibson in early 1921.

Loar's many responsibilities at Gibson included overseeing research and development as well as quality control. He certainly made sure that the instruments he signed were of the highest quality, but design credit may well go to Guy Hart, who would become secretary and general manager of the company shortly after Loar's departure. As Loar scholar Roger Siminoff wrote in the June 1975 issue of *Pickin'* magazine, "The 'Loar mandolin' should more properly be called the 'Loar-Hart mandolin.'" Siminoff's research led him to the conclusion that Hart was the man chiefly behind the development of the instrument line, while Loar was responsible for testing and approving. The innovations that almost surely should be attributed to Loar—and they are crucial to the success of the Style 5 line—are the *f*-hole design, a reflection of Loar's deep interest in the viola and violin, and the double–tone bar bracing system.

As with most innovators, Loar and Hart were not the first. The Shutt company of Topeka, Kansas, made a model A-7 possibly as early as 1913 with *f*-holes, a raised fingerboard, and a long neck (although not as long as the F-5's). The Gibson F-5 combined these innovations, of course, with Gibson's highly perfected scroll-body design and Gibson's high level of craftsmanship. The result was an instrument of monumental importance, whereas the Shutt A-7 remains a mere footnote.

Loar's legend and his reputation as a visionary are enhanced by his departure from Gibson in December 1924 in a dispute over electric instruments. While at Gibson he built a very minimalist, modernistic electric bass (much like the one Rickenbacker would market in the late 1930s), and he also built an electric viola that he used in performances. Gibson usually comes out as the villain in this story, as a stodgy, conservative company afraid to take a chance, but that judgment is unduly harsh considering Gibson's point of view. Total sales of 350 Style 5 mandolin-family instruments over a period of two years was not bad, but not all that good when the startup costs of four new models were factored in. Since none of these models was a new version of an existing model, all four required some degree of new tooling. Furthermore, the mandolin boom had ended several years earlier, as every instrument manufacturer knew. It was no coincidence that the company name changed from Gibson Mandolin-Guitar to Gibson, Inc. in 1924. To Gibson management, Loar must have seemed like the opposite of a visionary, focusing his efforts on not just one out-of-style instrument, but an entire family of out-of-style instruments. (In fairness to Loar, he is also credited with developing the spring-loaded, ball-bearing tone chamber for the tenor banjo, the dominant instrument at the time. Today, however, that design is the least desirable type of Mastertone tone ring, and it was not on a par with the contemporary designs of Vega, Bacon, Epiphone, or Paramount.) As if that were not enough, 1924 was hardly the time to embark on a wild new project. The economy had peaked in 1920 and then slowly but steadily fallen for three years. Coupled with declining mandolin sales, the economy had to be especially threatening to a company founded on the mandolin; it must have made Gibson executives wary of a man like Loar.

♦ *Gibson F-5, signed by Lloyd Loar on July 9, 1923 (pages 83 and 84, and above). The finish is Gibson's Cremona brown sunburst, named after the Italian city where Antonio Stradivari made his famous violins. Although associated with the Style 5 series, the finish first appeared in 1921 on the Style 4 mandolin line on a limited-edition basis. The metal plating is silver on these early F-5s. The tailpiece cover is the standard Gibson shape but the logo and ornamentation are hand-engraved rather than stamped. Most F-5s have a two-piece back but some, like this example, have a one-piece back. Anonymous collector/DL*

♦ *Gibson F-5, signed by Lloyd Loar on July 9, 1923. Although signed on the same day as the previous example, this F-5 has a two-piece back and "side binding," with the white-black-white of the binding on the side of the instrument rather than on top. Bluegrass patriarch Bill Monroe's F-5 was signed on the same day and also has the side-facing binding. In 1991 Gibson reissued this variation as the F-5L Bill Monroe model. Darryl Wolfe/DL*

One rumor floating around through the years should be put to rest, and that is the suggestion that Loar's departure was the result of a conflict of interest. Many of the Style 5 instruments he signed were fitted with a Virzi Tone Producer or, as Gibson called it, Tone Amplifier, an oval piece of wood suspended from the underside of the top that supposedly improved tone and balance. Loar was a consultant to the Virzi Brothers (who were based in New York with a factory in Palermo, Italy) prior to his employment by Gibson, and by early 1922 Gibson had gained exclusive rights to the Virzi device. However, in all the interviews Roger Siminoff conducted in researching Loar's life, including many conversations with Loar's widow, Loar was remembered without exception as a man of the highest honor and integrity. A kickback arrangement with Virzi would have been completely out of character. The disagreement over electric instruments was reason enough for Loar to leave Gibson. It was such a controversial issue that it became a divisive force throughout Gibson's upper management, and Loar was not the only one to leave, nor even the first.

Gibson may actually have given Loar's electric instruments a fair chance. "In 1924 Gibson electric instruments were shown to teacher agents, who, together with the public, were not yet ready to accept this great revolutionary discovery," wrote longtime Gibson employee Julius Bellson in his history of the company. In fact, it appears that the chief officers of the company actually sided with Loar on the electric issue. According to Bellson, "Differences of opinion in regard to marketing, and the type of instruments to make, resulted in a change of top management personnel in 1924." Secretary and general manager Lewis Williams, a founding partner and one of those involved in the development of the first pickguard clamp and the height-adjustable bridge, resigned in the fall of 1923, a year before Loar left. Sales and advertising manager C. V. Buttleman left in 1924. (If these three key men supported the development of electrics, one wonders who in a position of power was left to object.)

One can only speculate what Loar—and the entire Gibson company, for that matter—could have done had he stayed and enjoyed full company support for his electric vision. As it happened, he pursued the development of electric instruments, along with several other visions, independently. His patents included the electric viola that he often demonstrated and an electric keyboard instrument. His new guitar and mandolin designs were marketed in 1932 by the Vivi-Tone company, which he formed with former Gibson executives Williams and Buttleman.

Loar never achieved any degree of commercial success with his innovative instruments. He began teaching courses on the physics of music in 1930 at Northwestern University near Chicago, and he eventually married one of his students. In 1943 he traveled to Europe to perform for American servicemen, contracted an illness there, and died a short time after his return to the United States, on September 14, 1943.

The Loar-era F-5 mandolin remains the pinnacle of mandolin design, but ironically, by the time the pinnacle was reached, most manufacturers and players had forsaken the mandolin for the banjo. Gibson was no exception. Ads in late 1922 in *The Crescendo* touted an important new announcement, and the F-5 was indeed introduced in the next issue with a special full-page color picture, but Gibson's regular full-page ad, in that issue and in following issues, was for tenor banjos. The tenor banjo was booming and the Master Model name was revamped for the Mastertone banjo line, which eventually became the industry standard. In the ultimate irony, of all the Master Model and Mastertone instruments, the one that would have the greatest and most lasting mass-market impact was neither the mandolin nor the banjo but the archtop *f*-hole guitar—the L-5.

♦ *Gibson F-5, signed by Lloyd Loar on November 28, 1922. Instruments signed on this day have a lighter finish and a larger sunburst area than later Loar F-5s. The flowerpot peghead inlay was replaced on the F-5 and H-5 by a fern pattern in 1925 (a few 1924 examples have the fern). The flowerpot continued to appear on the L-5 and eventually returned to the F-5 in the late 1930s. Hank Risan/BM*

◆ *Gibson Style 5 mandolin family,
1924 (top), all signed by Lloyd Loar.
Gibson introduced the Style 5 line of
Master Model instruments in late
1922 with, from left, the L-5 guitar,
F-5 mandolin, H-5 mandola, and K-5
mandocello. This family portrait represents the ultimate dream of many
vintage instrument collectors. While
some individual models are more
prized than these, no set of instruments can compare in terms of rarity,
quality, and historical importance.
Joseph Nuyens/DL*

◆ *Second from top: The Master
Model label, visible through the bass
soundhole of the L-5, is one of two
labels affixed to all Loar-era Style 5
instruments.*

◆ *Third from top: Seen through the
treble soundhole, Lloyd Loar's signature verifies that he personally played
and approved this K-5 mandocello on
March 31, 1924. The H-5 mandola
was also signed the same day; the F-5
is dated February 18, 1924; the L-5
guitar (serial number 80263) is dated
Dec. 1, 1924. According to records
compiled by collector Darryl Wolfe,
this was the last day Loar signed instruments at Gibson, and this L-5 has
the highest known serial number of
any Loar-signed instrument.*

◆ *Bottom: The Virzi Tone Amplifier,
with which some Loar instruments
were fitted, also carries a label with a
serial number, visible through the
treble soundhole, but their numbers
do not necessarily match the chronol-
ogy of the instruments. This label for
Virzi number 10063 is on the H-5
with Gibson serial number 76487; a
supposedly later Virzi label, number
10172, is on the F-5, which has Gibson serial number 75692 and was
signed by Loar 42 days before he
signed the H-5.*

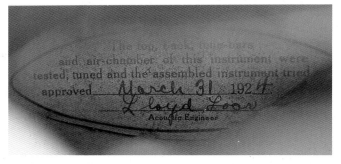

♦ Gibson F-5, 1925 (upper left and right). In the first part of 1925, shortly after Loar's departure from Gibson, fern peghead inlay and gold-plated metal parts became standard on the F-5. This unusual example has a brown-stained peghead overlay rather than the standard black, and the pearl inlay has taken on a golden color due to the aging of the varnish. The muted effect of the gold and brown is quite different from the gleaming black veneer and white pearl of the typical F-5 peghead. Gruhn Guitars/DL

♦ Gibson F-5, signed by Lloyd Loar on March 31, 1924 (above and left). Loar signed at least 50 instruments on this day, including the first examples with fern peghead inlay. Most of the instruments, like this one, have silver-plated hardware, but a few are gold-plated. Gary Burnett/DL

• *Gibson F-5, 1926. Ungrained white plastic binding was phased in to replace grained ivoroid on the F-5 beginning in late 1924. Otherwise, an F-5 from the years immediately following Loar looks almost the same as a Loar-era example. In sound, however, post-Loar F-5s have a different, slightly brighter voicing. That—and, of course, the Loar signature—make for a significant difference in value. Gary Brown/BM*

• *Gibson F-5, 1956. The F-5's original pearl dot fingerboard inlays gave way to pearl blocks in mid-1929. Other changes between the early 1930s and early 1950s include a return to the flowerpot peghead inlay (late 1930s), a stamped "clamshell" tailpiece cover (post–World War II), larger f-holes, and, of course, the postwar Gibson logo. The curl of the back wood is fairly nice, but the finish is a far cry from the rich Cremona brown sunburst of the 1920s F-5. The Kluson enclosed tuners definitely place this instrument in the electric guitar era rather than the classic mandolin era. The pickguard has been removed. By the late 1970s, the F-5 had gone through so many changes that it was hardly the same model as its original namesake. The F-5L was introduced in 1978 as a reissue of the Loar model, thus the L in the model name. However, with fern peghead inlay and gold-plated metal parts, the F-5L more accurately copies the F-5 of 1925, the year after Loar's departure. Blaine Hampton/DL*

♦ *Gibson F-5M, circa 1940 (above). Gibson had great success in the mid 1930s with large-bodied guitars and moderate success with several larger A-style mandolins, such as the A-1 and A-50. Perhaps someone reasoned that the F-style would also benefit from expansion. This fat custom-made example was the result. The meaning of the M in the model name is a mystery. Owner unknown/WC*

♦ *Gibson F-7, 1937 (center). In late 1933 Gibson phased out the F-2 (oval-hole model) and introduced three new F models with f-holes: the F-7, F-10, and F-12. Although the idea was apparently to create a line based on the F-5, none of the new models had the long neck of the F-5. Some F-7s have a fleur-de-lis peghead inlay; others have the curlicue design of the F-10 and F-12. The F-7 retailed for $125, which was $25 more than the oval-hole F-4. It was discontinued in 1940. Marketwright/BM*

♦ *Gibson F-10, late 1933 (above). For $25 more than the F-7, and for a limited time only, a mandolin buyer could get the F-10, with an extended fingerboard, fancier inlay, and black finish. For an additional $25, one could buy the F-12— essentially the same as the F-10 but with a sunburst finish, pearl tuner buttons, and gold-plated metal parts. The F-10 was only available from 1933 to 1935. Paul North/DL*

• *Gibson F-5L custom, 1988 (upper left and right). Gibson mandolin production moved to the Flatiron plant in Bozeman, Montana, in 1987, but this F-5L came from the Gibson Custom Shop in Nashville. Gibson's Jim Triggs built this instrument, and Greg Rich finished it out in a way that Lloyd Loar probably never imagined. They named it the Knucklehead Florentine model. Gibson USA/DL*

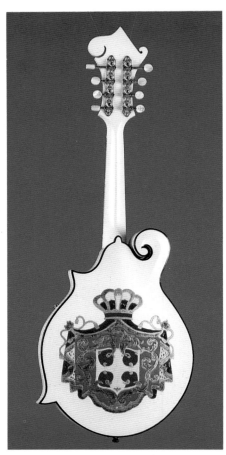

• *Gibson F-12, 1950 (lower left). Of all the F models, only the F-5 and the F-12 survived World War II. The postwar F-12 was fitted with the long neck of the F-5 but did not get the raised fingerboard until mid-1950, when the peghead was also enlarged. The F-12 was revamped in 1970 and lasted in the Gibson line until 1980. The pickguard on this example has been cut out to accommodate a pickup. Gruhn Guitars/DL*

• *Gibson TL, 1924 (lower right). The tenor lute bears a Master Model label, but aside from the f-holes and raised fingerboard, it has little in common with the Style 5 line. The neck and peghead design are from the Style 3 banjo, a midline model. The rest of its features are from low-end mandolins: natural top finish, brown stain finish on the back and sides, and birch (rather than maple) back and sides. Not surprisingly, it was never called a Style 5, and it never carried a Loar signature label. It was discontinued by 1926. Darryl Wolfe/DL*

MANDOLINS
◆ ◆ ◆

Martin Mandolins

Martin has always had the image of a small, family-owned company, insulated by the hills of Pennsylvania from fads and fashions, content for more than 150 years to make the finest flat top guitars in the world, giving only a nod to such important developments as the archtop and electric guitar. In the 1890s, however, the mandolin's growing popularity tempted Frank Henry Martin, president of the company since 1888 and grandson of the founder, to attempt a major expansion into mandolin production. Opposition came from the Zoebisch company of New York, the longtime exclusive distributor of Martin instruments, but F. H. Martin was so bullish on mandolins that he terminated his agreement with Zoebisch.

♦ *Martin Style 7. Martin's fanciest and rarest bowl-back model was made from 1899 to 1917. Its list price of $100 put it midway between Martin's top two pearly guitar models, Styles 42 and 45, although the mandolin's trim is more elaborate than that of any standard guitar style. Martin made a total of only 32 Style 7 mandolins. George Youngblood/GY*

As a mandolin maker, Martin would never be a serious threat to Gibson or Lyon and Healy, but the advent of mandolin production, nevertheless, turned out to be an important date in Martin history. It led to a change in the Martin brand, on guitars as well as mandolins. The brand had always said "New York," where the company had been founded in 1833 and where the distributor was located, even though Martin guitars had been made in Pennsylvania since 1839. With the dissolution of the Zoebisch agreement, Martin began distributing instruments directly from the factory, and consequently in 1898, the Martin brand was changed to read "Nazareth, Pa."

Like all mandolin makers in the late 1890s (except, of course, Orville Gibson), Martin made bowlback instruments, some of them highly ornate. After Gibson revolutionized the market with carved-top designs, Martin took off in an altogether different direction. The new mandolin models of 1914 looked like they were designed by guitar makers. The top was bent, as on a Neapolitan bowlback, but the back was flat like that of a guitar. The back and sides, like those of guitars, were of rosewood. Not surprisingly, in 1917, when Martin's Style 18 guitars changed from rosewood back and sides to mahogany, so did the low-end mandolin model in the new line. Other specs reflected the guitar line, too, with such Martin trademarks as herringbone purfling on one model, snowflake fingerboard inlay on others, and in the mid-1920s, koa wood bodies. By the end of the 1920s the mandolin boom was a distant echo, and Gibson had established a new standard with the *f*-hole F-5. Martin's response was to introduce a new series in 1929 with carved top and back—but with an oval hole. Not until 1936 did Martin finally introduce carved-top models with *f*-holes.

By the end of 1990, after 96 years of mandolin production, Martin had turned out only 26,316 mandolins, for an average yearly production of 274. The biggest production years were in the late 1910s and early 1920s when annual production averaged 600 to 800. The record year was 1920—the only year that production topped 1,000—when 1,524 mandolins were made. After a small surge in the late 1940s, when production hit around 500 per year, demand sagged. The low point was 1978, when Martin made no mandolins at all. Production has been sparse since then, with a total of 190 from 1979 through 1990, including eight for the year 1990.

♦ Martin A, 1937 (above). With bent top, flat back, and mahogany back and sides, the A model is Martin's cheapest and by far the most successful. Production averaged several hundred a year from 1914 into the mid-1970s, accounting for half of Martin's total mandolin output. The only other models to sell more than 200 in one year—and each for one year only— were the AK, B, and 2-15. The A is similar in wood and ornamentation to Martin's Style 18 guitar. The sunburst top finish is relatively rare but was offered as a standard optional finish. Bart Wittrock/BM

♦ Martin AK, 1925 (above). In Martin's model nomenclature system for guitars and mandolins, the K stands for koa wood body. The AK had its heyday in the 1920s, when acoustic Hawaiian guitars of koa wood were also popular. Blaine Hampton/DL

♦ Martin C, 1921 (center). Style C, available from 1914 to 1932, is more or less similar in wood and ornamentation to the Style 42 or Style 27 guitar, depending on the year. Examples made between 1917 and 1921 have this abalone pearl top border and soundhole ring. Those made before 1917 and from 1921 on (beginning sometime after this example was made) have a top border of wood purfling. Style C's highest production year was 1926, when Martin made a total of 50. Gruhn Guitars/DL

♦ *Martin E, 1920. The Style E has the same body trim as a Style 45 guitar, but the neck is fancier. With a total production of 62 instruments, Style E is rarer than any of the pre–World War II Style 45 guitar sizes, though not nearly as valued by collectors. Inlaid tuner buttons and engraved silver-plated tuner plates are standard on the Style E. Some, but not all, Style 45 guitars have these appointments. David Levin/JL*

♦ *Martin 2-20, 1938 (lower left). Martin finally responded to the success of Gibson's maple-body, carved-top, f-hole models with the Style 2 line of 1936. The 2-20 is the midline model in terms of ornamentation and success, with a total of 106 produced through 1941. The plainest, the 2-15, does not have the body points nor the ornamental peghead cutout of the 2-20, but it was fairly successful by Martin standards, lasting in the line until 1964. Gruhn Guitars/WC*

♦ *Martin 2-30, 1939 (lower right). Of the three models in the Style 2 family, the 2-30 is the fanciest, with more binding than the 2-20 and an extended fingerboard. It was the least successful commercially, with a total production of 64 from 1937 to 1942. Gruhn Guitars/DL*

MANDOLINS
◆ ◆ ◆

Other Mandolin Makers

Orville Gibson's influence on the mandolin world is without parallel in any other family of fretted instruments. No guitar maker or banjo maker has ever come up with even one new design—much less two—as radically different and, ultimately, as completely dominant as Gibson's carved-top A- and F-style mandolins. Almost all modern mandolin makers base their designs on the instruments conceived by Orville Gibson and perfected by the Gibson company in the years prior to World War II.

♦ *Washburn A, circa 1920. Lyon and Healy had been a successful manufacturer of bowlback mandolins for several decades before Gibson was founded, and the older company was understandably slow to respond to the success of Gibson's new styles. The 1912 Lyon and Healy catalog featured a full page of color illustrations of Washburn bowlback mandolins plus a new L. H. Leland line of bent-top, flat-back models. By 1917, however, the superiority of Gibson's carved styles was widely accepted, and Lyon and Healy introduced a model with carved top and back. The concept was Gibson's but the body shape differed from a Gibson. The earliest Washburn A, also marketed under the Lyon and Healy brand as the Deluxe, had a symmetrical body with two points. By 1920 this asymmetrical shape had been adopted. In quality, the A was the top of the line, although it was priced a bit lower than the most ornate bowlback Washburn. Gruhn Guitars/DL*

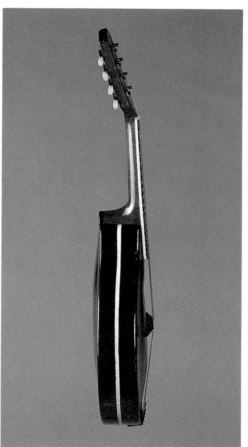

♦ *Lyon and Healy B, circa 1918 (upper left). Lyon and Healy's mandolin styles become plainer rather than fancier as the model names ascend. Style B's body is symmetrical and the peghead lacks the scroll of the Style A. Jacksonville Guitars/SE*

♦ *Lyon and Healy C, circa 1920 (upper right). Even plainer than Styles A and B, Style C has a shape similar to Gibson's A-style, with no body points. Ironically, it was called the Aristocrat model. Gruhn Guitars/DL*

♦ *Dayton, 1910s. The Dayton company patented this design in 1911. From the front it appears to be similar to Gibson's A models, but it actually has a double-stage construction. The binding material does not go around the middle of the sides. It goes around the back, or at least the piece of wood to which the inside label is affixed. A second stage or back is attached behind the first, giving this instrument a sort of double-boiler design. Jim Reynolds/DL*

♦ Stahl, circa 1925 (above and center). This odd-shaped model, made by the Larson brothers of Chicago for the Wm. Stahl Co. of Milwaukee, combines elements of various styles—the bent top of a Neapolitan bowlback and the three-point scroll body (albeit a weird suggestion of a scroll) from Gibson. Some manufacturers referred to flat-back models as "lute models," an ironic misnomer, since lutes have a rounded back. The flat back, rosewood back and sides, and ornamental backstripe are more closely associated with guitars than mandolins, and not surprisingly, the Larson brothers are better known for their guitars. This same body style was also offered on cheap models sold by the Regal company of Chicago. Gruhn Guitars/DL

♦ Lyon and Healy, circa 1920 (above). This instrument bears a Lyon and Healy label. The same model, but with a fancier fingerboard, appears in the catalog of distributor Carl Fischer. Again, the same model, but with an ornamental peghead cutout and a label from the Chicago-based Regal company, appears in the Tonk Bros. catalog in the late 1920s. Regardless of the brand, it was modeled on the flat-top, flat-back Gibson Army and Navy model, but with a symmetrical Florentine two-point body shape. With pearl borders and an ornamented pickguard, it was the top model of the budget line. Tonk Bros. listed it in 1928 for $54, which was almost nine times the price of the cheapest model in the catalog but still more than $130 less than a Washburn Style A. Gruhn Guitars/WC

♦ *Epiphone Strand, circa 1937. Epiphone entered the mandolin market by 1934 with a full array of styles. Scroll-body models appeared in catalogs, but it is questionable whether they ever went into production. Just below the scroll models is the Florentine-body Strand, which debuted with an oval hole but acquired f-holes by 1937. The Strand is the only high-quality Epiphone model to last until the company was sold to C. M. I. (Gibson's parent company) in 1957. This instrument still has its original case and guarantee card. The Masterbilt label, used on Epiphone's better models from 1931 to 1937, is visible through the f-hole. Gruhn Guitars/WC*

♦ *D'Angelico, late 1930s (lower left). John D'Angelico modeled his first guitars after a Gibson (the L-5 f-hole archtop), so it is not surprising that his mandolins would also have f-holes. In body shape and peghead style, however, this instrument resembles a Washburn Style A. Gruhn Guitars/DL*

♦ *D'Angelico, 1950s (lower right). About half of D'Angelico's mandolins have a two-point Florentine body; the others have a symmetrical A-style body that his ledger describes simply as "plain." This is D'Angelico's only known scroll-body mandolin. His version of Gibson's F-style has a neck-body joint at the 12th fret (giving it a shorter neck than the Gibson F-5), a "lump" scroll with binding material inlaid to suggest a scroll, and a peghead similar to that of his Excel guitar. Gruhn Guitars/DL*

101

♦ *Gilchrist mandolin family, 1981–1984. Australian Stephen Gilchrist began making mandolins in 1976 and spent a year in the United States perfecting his craft. Like most modern makers, he used Gibson's Loar-era F-5 as a starting point. The piccolo mandolin, modeled in size after Gibson's one-of-a-kind piccolo mandolin, has the flowerpot peghead inlay of most Gibson/Loar models; the standard mandolin has the fern pattern of the years immediately following Loar; the mandola, which is slightly larger than a Gibson mandola, borrows the inlaid tuner buttons from high-end Gibson mandolins of the pre-1918 period. Gilchrist also makes oval-hole mandocellos based on Gibson's K-4. Gruhn Guitars, Dan Mills/DL*

♦ Monteleone Grand Artist 10-string, 1980 (above). John Monteleone, now based in Islip, New York, started making guitars as a teenager. In 1974, he began building mandolins along the lines of the Gibson F-5 and eventually refined that design into his own Grand Artist model. This special 10-string Grand Artist shows Monteleone's open scroll design, which makes for a larger body cavity. Gruhn Guitars/DL

♦ D'Aquisto, 1972. James D'Aquisto, former apprentice to D'Angelico, is renowned for his archtop guitars. This 1972 mandolin was made, as the peghead engraving indicates, for Lydia Merriman and is one of only three mandolins built by D'Aquisto. Gruhn Guitars/DL

♦ Andersen F-5, 1992 (above). Steven Andersen of Seattle built his first guitar in 1973 and his first mandolin in 1978. Of his 150 instruments, about half are mandolin family (some A-style) and half are flat top or archtop guitars. In the 1990s, he began concentrating on archtop guitars. Gruhn Guitars/WC

◆ *Leedy Hollander tenor, late 1920s. (See page 119.)*

TENOR AND PLECTRUM BANJOS
◆ ◆ ◆

Tango to Jazz Age

By the early part of the twentieth century the mandolin overshadowed the five-string banjo, but by the end of World War I in 1918, the tables had turned, and the banjo was pushing the mandolin back into the shadows of popularity. For five-string banjo players, however, the victory was hollow because the new banjo—called by various names, including tango banjo, mandolin-banjo, or (the one that stuck) tenor banjo—was too much mandolin and not enough banjo. Rather than representing a triumph of banjo over mandolin, the tenor gave the mandolin a new voice, and those who profited most from the new banjo were not five-string banjoists but mandolin players.

The tenor banjo looked innocent enough—like a short-scale five-string banjo that was missing the fifth string. Its mandolin characteristics were subtle but significant: strung with metal strings, not the gut strings preferred by classical banjoists; tuned in fifths rather than to standard banjo tuning; and played with a plectrum instead of the fingers or "thimbles" (fingerpicks).

In 1907 the J. B. Schall company of Chicago advertised a four-string "banjorine" with mandolin tuning and later claimed it to be the first tenor banjo. The founder of the company was a noted five-string banjoist, and he died, appropriately enough that same year. Even if the claim were true, the tenor did not catch on for several years. Lyon and Healy, for example, still offered five-strings only in its 1913 catalog.

The rise of the four-string, mandolin-inspired banjo is often attributed to its association with the tango dance craze, which arrived in America from Argentina in 1910. The new banjo was indeed called the tango banjo, but the explanation seems too superficial. Granted, the sharp attack of the plectrum style was well suited to the start-and-stop tango rhythms, but the average five-string banjo player would have had no trouble adapting to a tango rhythm. With a set of steel strings and a pick, the banjo—any banjo—was well suited for tango music. The most likely reason that the four-string banjo supplanted the five-string was because of its mandolin tuning. Mandolin had become the dominant fretted instrument, and when mandolin players switched off to banjo, they no doubt took the easiest route—a mandolinlike banjo.

The tango banjo outlasted the dance fad that gave it its name, as pointed out by the editor of *The Crescendo*, Herbert Forrest Odell, in the May 1915 issue: "What is a tango banjo? In reading various magazines and advertisements we have seen the words 'tango-banjo' applied, as we suppose to the mandolin-banjo.... Is it a mandolin-banjo strung and tuned like a mandolin or is it a tenor mandolin-banjo strung and tuned like a tenor mandola or is it an octave mandolin-banjo, strung and tuned like an octave mandola?

"Why is the word 'tango' used anyway?...The tango is rather a back number now. One-steps, hesitations, fox-trots and canters are decidedly more popular than the tango.... If a uniform name is not applied to it, it is possible that we shall hear of hesitation mandolins, one-step mandolas or fox-trot mando-cellos, etc."

Odell suggested that the instrument, because of its mandolin characteristics, should properly be called the mandolin-banjo. A 1915 catalog from C. Bruno and Son, a New York distributor, illustrated Odell's complaint about confusing names with a "Tango Banjo-Mandolin." To add fuel to Odell's fire, Bruno referred to the tango not as a back number but as "America's foremost amusement." The catalog also listed two "club and quartette" banjos: a cello banjo with four strings tuned in fifths and a guitar banjo with a six-string guitar neck. Both were large, with a 14-inch head versus the 11-inch head of the standard tenor.

A little more than a year after Odell's article, the name tenor, as well as the instrument itself, had become entrenched in the music world. The title of the banjo column in the November 1916 issue of *The Crescendo* was "The Tenor-Banjo, a Fixture." The first sentence told the story: "Without doubt the tenor-banjo is now considered the best instrument of the banjo family for playing lead in dance orchestras…. So far as the regular [five-string] banjo is concerned, it has been found that its peculiar tuning renders it very difficult for the performance of melody parts in the orchestra."

Not long after the tenor banjo became popular, a new variation bridged the gap between the tenor and the five-string. The scale on the new model ranged from 25½ inches to full classical banjo scale of 27 inches, but the instrument was essentially a five-string without the short fifth string. The tuning was the "drop-string" of the classical five-string, with the interval of a fifth between the third and fourth strings (rather than the fourth of modern bluegrass tuning). This banjo was called a "plectrum" model—a curious name, since the tenor was played with a plectrum. Guitar players also doubled on plectrum banjo by tuning it to the highest four strings of the guitar.

Gibson company historian Julius Bellson attributed the death of the mandolin orchestra to "the swinging marching songs and the trend toward boisterous spontaneity after the war." The tenor banjo was an ideal instrument for that atmosphere, able to pick out a cutting melody line or to keep a percussive rhythm to the new sounds of the 1920s. The tenor banjo's featured role in modern Dixieland bands might seem to indicate that it was as closely identified with the "Dixieland" music of the 1920s as it had been with the tango a decade earlier. Several misconceptions cloud that assumption, however. The Original Dixieland Jass Band, a group of white New Orleans musicians whose recording of "Livery Stable Blues" sold a million copies in 1917, did not have a banjo player. Furthermore, according to jazz historian James Lincoln Collier, their music would more accurately be described as "some kind of advanced ragtime" than jazz. What came to be known as Dixieland jazz was defined on record in 1923 by Joe "King" Oliver's Creole Jazz Band, a group of black New Orleans musicians that included Louis Armstrong. Their records did include a banjo, but only by accident. On the primitive recording equip-

♦ *Vega Tu-ba-phone No. 9 tenor, 1926. Vega was founded in 1889 in Boston as a maker of brass instruments. It entered the banjo business with the acquisition of the Fairbanks company in 1904, and the Fairbanks brand name appeared on Vega models until 1922. Traditional Fairbanks models such as the Tu-ba-phone and Whyte Laydie continued as open-back Vega models. By the time this banjo was made, most players had switched to models with a longer scale, a 19-fret neck, and a resonator. Vega was sold to the C. F. Martin company in 1970, which in turn sold it in 1980 to a Korean company. The Deering banjo company of California acquired the Vega name in 1988 and offered the first new models for sale in 1992. Gruhn Guitars/DL* ment of the day, the group's standup bass caused the cutting stylus to jump out of the groove, so bassist Bill Johnson kept rhythm on a banjo—an open-back Vega Tu-ba-phone #9 tenor.

After the Oliver recordings, other important groups used a banjo. In 1924, Fletcher Henderson's dance band, which by that time featured Louis Armstrong, included a Paramount model with a resonator. Bix Beiderbecke's group of early 1925 recorded with a plectrum banjo. Louis Armstrong's famous recordings from late 1925 to 1928 with the Hot Five and Hot Seven included Johnny St. Cyr on banjo.

Aside from the name of the Original Dixieland Jass Band, "Dixieland" was not commonly used in the 1920s to refer to the music of the day. The music was "jazz," and tenor banjo aficionados refer to banjos of the era as jazz banjos. The Dixieland movement was an early 1940s revival of 1920s jazz. Dixieland bands on the West Coast strove to recreate the sounds of the early jazz bands, particularly Oliver's and Armstrong's, and the West Coast groups used a banjo and tuba for rhythm rather than the guitar and bass preferred by East Coast musicians. Not surprisingly, as "Dixieland" came into popular use, so did the term "Dixieland banjo." Had recording equipment been more advanced in 1923, the tenor banjo might have little or no association with Dixieland today.

Makers of five-string banjos had no trouble switching to tenor and plectrum production, and the high level of competition led to many improvements in design. Most of the resonator and tone ring designs that are industry standards today on five-strings first appeared during the tenor banjo era. The economic extravagance of the mid- to late-1920s resulted in some of the most highly ornamented and expensive fretted instruments ever made. Top-of-the-line models from most makers listed in the $400 to $600 range; Bacon's B&D Silver Bell No. 9 Ne Plus Ultra had a big name and a big list price to go with it—$900.

When the stock market crashed in 1929 and the Depression hit, the demand for fancy banjos crashed, too. At the same time, changing tastes—especially the decline of the Charleston and the rise of the fox-trot with its slower rhythms—called for an instrument with more sustaining power than the banjo. Enter the guitar. A Vega advertisement in the June 1929 issue of *The Crescendo* foretold the future. For the first time, a corner of Vega's standard full-page banjo ad was devoted to a guitar. The copy read: "Keep abreast of the times. The guitar is the newest attraction." The tenor banjo survives in Dixieland bands today, but it has never regained the glory it enjoyed in the 1920s.

♦ *Paramount Aristocrat Special tenor, circa 1929. William Lange introduced the Paramount brand in 1921 and with it the first modern flange and resonator design. The new models provided what catalogs and instrument labels described as "piano volume and harp quality tone." The original line included six models, with A the plainest and F the fanciest; the Aristocrat was added between Styles D and E in 1926. The fancier Aristocrat Special joined the Paramount line in 1929. Even with the Special's elaborate blossom design, it is still the third model from the top of the Paramount line. The tuners use a three-to-one gear ratio, a design patented in 1926 to compete with the Ludwig company's four-to-one Planet tuners. The knob extending from the flange near the neck controls a mute. Bill Camp/BM*

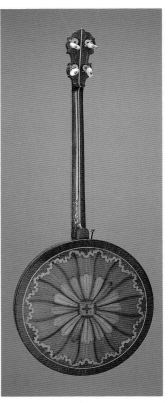

♦ *Super Paramount Artists Professional tenor, circa 1929. By 1929 virtually all banjo makers were using resonators and flanges derived from Lange's design, so he sought to improve it with a double-stage flange and resonator. Models with the new equipment carried the Super Paramount brand. Lange also marketed a double-stage guitar under the Paramount brand, although it was actually made by Martin. Bill Camp/BM.*

♦ B&D Silver Bell No.6 Ne Plus Ultra plectrum, circa 1927. Musician Frederick J. Bacon began marketing his own line of banjos in 1905. Initially, they were built by Fairbanks-Vega, then by William Lange. In 1912 he started making them himself, and in 1921 he incorporated as The Bacon Banjo Co., Inc., in Groton, Connecticut. In 1922 he hired former Fairbanks excecutive David L. Day as vice president and general manager and inaugurated the B&D (Bacon and Day) brand. Silver Bell was the company's high-end designation, and it included several endorsement lines, each with as many as nine different degrees of ornamentation. The Ne Plus Ultra (None Better) designation is found on Silver Bell models of No. 6 and higher. The heel of a No. 6 sports a carved lion's head. The f-hole flange, introduced in 1924, distinguishes B&D's Silver Bells from lower lines (earlier Silver Bell flanges have round holes). The knee pedal activates a mute against the back side of the head. Gruhn Guitars/BM

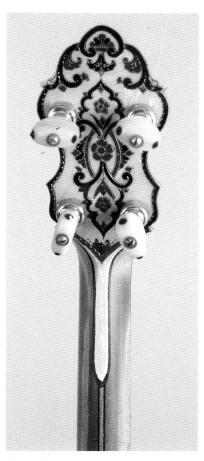

◆ B&D Montana Silver Bell No. 7 Ne Plus Ultra plectrum, late 1920s. Montana was the stage name of vaudeville star Ray Coleman. Billed as the Cowboy Banjoist or the Cowboy Beau Brummel, he would more accurately be described as a banjoist who dressed up in a white cowboy outfit. In 1926 Montana went on a promotional tour for B&D that included music store appearances, performances, and amateur banjo contests. The tour was so successful that in 1927 B&D gave Montana his own line of Silver Bells, with No. 7 at the top of the line. Ironically, one of the most famous banjo players of the tenor era played a five-string, but with a pick. Possibly to downplay his use of a five-string, his best-known publicity photo after the introduction of the Montana Silver Bell line shows him without a banjo, and the catalog illustration of the Montana No. 7 shows a plectrum model. Gruhn Guitars/WC

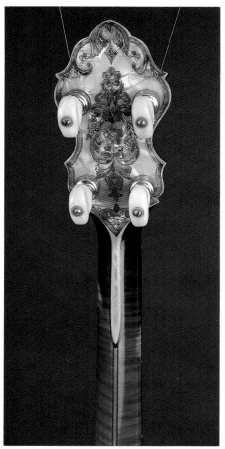

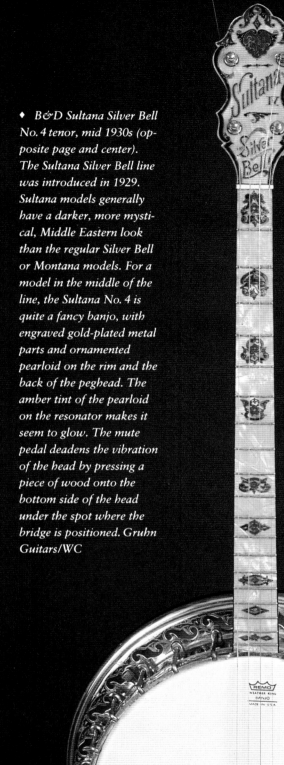

♦ B&D Sultana Silver Bell No. 4 tenor, mid 1930s (opposite page and center). The Sultana Silver Bell line was introduced in 1929. Sultana models generally have a darker, more mystical, Middle Eastern look than the regular Silver Bell or Montana models. For a model in the middle of the line, the Sultana No. 4 is quite a fancy banjo, with engraved gold-plated metal parts and ornamented pearloid on the rim and the back of the peghead. The amber tint of the pearloid on the resonator makes it seem to glow. The mute pedal deadens the vibration of the head by pressing a piece of wood onto the bottom side of the head under the spot where the bridge is positioned. Gruhn Guitars/WC

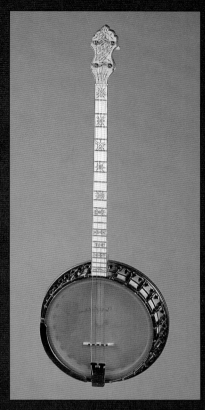

♦ B&D Radio Special plectrum, circa 1930 (above). The Radio Special is not a high-end model, as shown by the lack of a Silver Bell-type f-hole flange and by a cheaper tailpiece. It also lacks the Silver Bell tone ring. Nevertheless, its ivoroid fingerboard and radio wave ornamentation give it a striking look. Gruhn Guitars/DL

♦ *B&D Sultana Silver Bell No. 7 Ne Plus Ultra tenor, mid 1930s (this page and opposite left). The B&D catalog offered Sultana Silver Bells in Nos. 1, 3, 4, and 7. Like the other Silver Bell lines, No. 3 has gold-plated metal parts, No. 4 has engraved gold-plated parts, and No. 7 has engraved gold plus the lion's head heel carving. In contrast to the Silver Bell or Montana No. 7's resonator, the Sultana No. 7 has an intricate design and dark red coloring suggestive of a Persian rug. Gruhn Guitars/WC*

◆ *B&D Roy Smeck Silver Bell Stage Model No. 1 plectrum, circa 1930 (upper right). The gold-sparkle fingerboard and peghead overlay are befitting of the man known as the Wizard of the Strings. In 1926 multi-instrumentalist Roy Smeck made a short film for Vita-phone called* His Pastimes—*possibly the first music video—and immediately became a vaudeville star. He capitalized on his fame by endorsing the Harmony Vita-uke and Vita-guitar models, which have soundholes shaped like seals and a bridge like an airplane. He went on to become the most prolific model endorser in fretted instrument history. By 1930, Bacon offered three Roy Smeck B&D Silver Bell banjo models plus a line of Roy Smeck strings. He later put his name on acoustic Hawaiian guitars for Gibson, lap steels for Recording King (made by Gibson for Montgomery Ward), and an array of guitars, lap steels, and ukes for Harmony. His seemingly unquenchable taste for endorsements came back to haunt him, however. In a 1989 interview for* Guitar Player *magazine, he noted that his contract required him to play guitars that were inferior to a Gibson or a D'Angelico. Gruhn Guitars/WC*

♦ *Epiphone Recording Deluxe tenor, late 1920s. Epiphone was a brand name of the House of Stathopoulo, founded in 1873 by Greek violin and lute maker Anastasios Stathopoulo. The Epiphone Recording line of highly ornamented banjos was named after the founder's son Epaminondas. In 1928 the company name changed to the Epiphone Banjo Corporation. Of the nine Recording models, the Deluxe was two models away from the top of the line. Pearloid, a plastic material made to resemble mother-of-pearl, is sometimes referred to today as "mother-of-toilet-seat," but it was considered quite elegant in the 1920s. Hank Sable/DL*

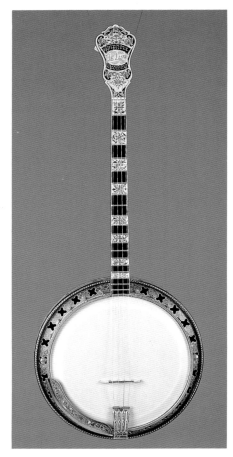
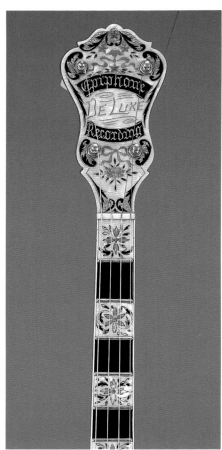
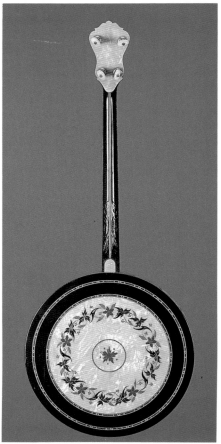

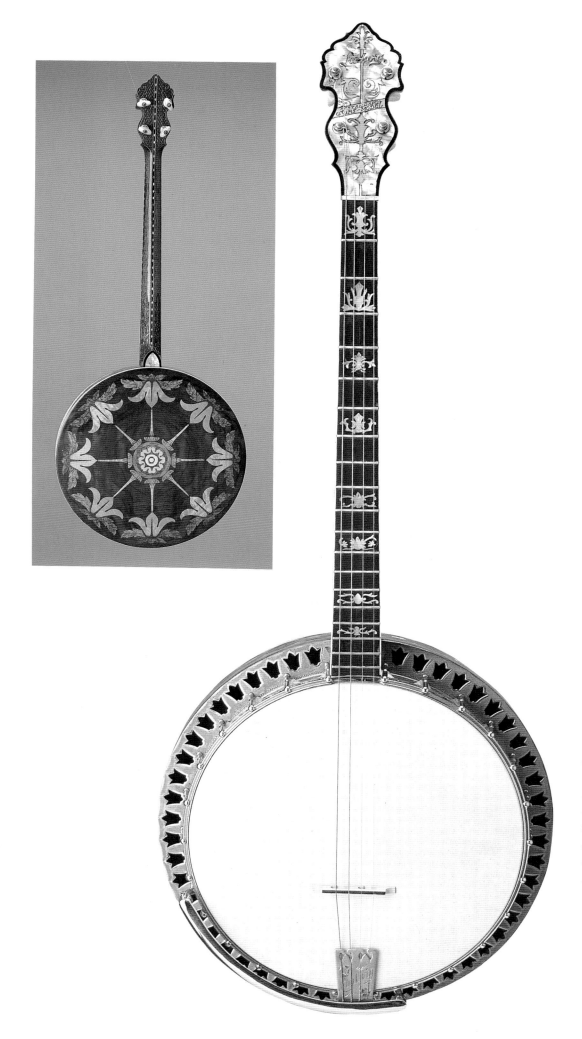

◆ *Ludwig Standard Art tenor, late 1920s. Like many banjo makers of the 1920s, Ludwig and Ludwig, Inc., started out as a drum company. Established in Chicago in 1907, Ludwig introduced a line of banjos in 1924. The company's patented Planet tuning peg, with a four-to-one gear ratio, was widely used during the tenor banjo era. Ludwig was sold to the C. G. Conn band instrument company in 1930 and merged with the Leedy banjo company, which Conn had also just bought. The Ludwig family later reacquired rights to the brand and continued to be a leading drum manufacturer. The Ludwig name is probably best known to the post-World War II generation as the logo above the Beatles' logo on Ringo Starr's bass drum. The Standard Art banjo is Ludwig's second from the top of the line, with fancy crown-shaped flange holes and pearl peghead ornamentation inlaid into a pearloid peghead veneer. The resonator inlay on the Standard Art is not the most artistic of patterns, but the model does have such high-end features as a carved heel and an unusual line of purfling running along the center of the neck. The rim engraving, according to the catalog, exhibits "exquisite tracery." Bill Camp/BM*

♦ *Ludwig The Ace plectrum, late 1920s. Ludwig was a leader in the development of "top tension" banjos, with tension hooks a player could adjust without taking the resonator off. Earlier models have a brass tension hoop, but top-tension Ludwigs have a pot metal hoop, which is much less desirable. The Ace is the middle model in the Ludwig line—fifth from the bottom and fifth from the top. With pearloid peghead veneer, it is not nearly so striking a model as the Standard Art, at least not from the front. Viewed from the back, The Ace is in a class of its own. The entire neck and resonator are covered in "Avalon pearl" (pearloid), a catalog option. Other available options included silver- or gold-plated metal parts. None of these features were offered as options on any other Ludwig model of the time. Music Makers of San Antonio/BM*

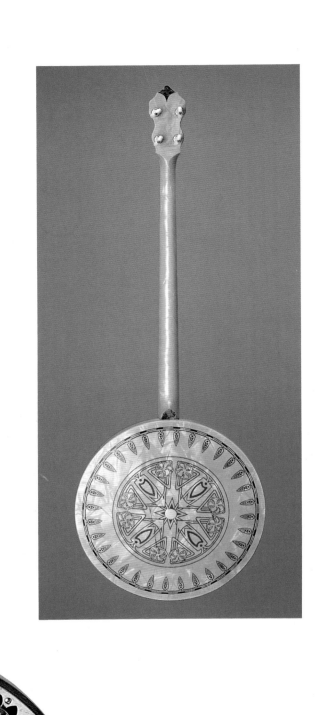

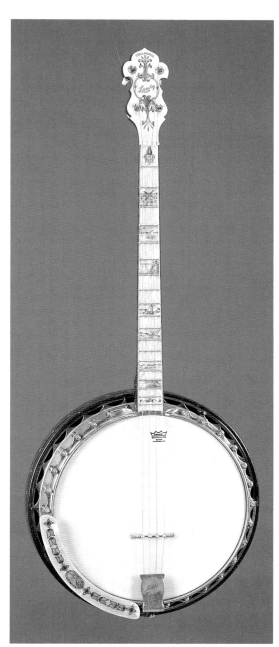

♦ *Leedy Hollander tenor, late 1920s. Professional drummer U.G. Leedy established the Leedy company in Indianapolis in 1898. In 1924, after hiring a former Ludwig employee, Leedy began making banjos. Like Ludwigs, Leedys employ top-tension adjustment, but with all brass parts rather than the pot metal hoop of Ludwig's late 1920s models. The brass parts make Leedy's tension adjustment superior to that of virtually all other makers, including Gibson's pot metal flanges of the late 1930s, but Leedy's metal rim produces a decidedly inferior sound. Intricate craftsmanship abounds on the Hollander—in the colored wood purfling, the carved and painted wood, and the engraved gold-plated metal parts. The resonator has been painted so painstakingly that the owner might hesitate to play this instrument for fear of damaging such a work of art. Leedy and Ludwig were bought by C.G. Conn in 1930 and combined into a single banjo division. Bill Camp/DL*

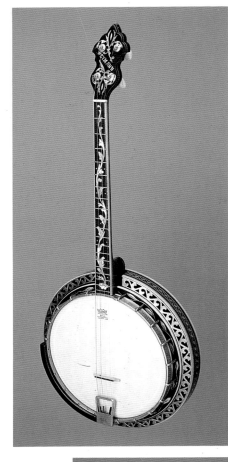

• *Weymann Orchestra No. 4 Deluxe tenor, late 1920s (upper right). Established in 1864 in Philadelphia, H. A. Weymann and Son, Inc., was a full-line instrument distributor. The company built its first banjos in 1900 and introduced a screw-on resonator (with no flange) by 1919. The Orchestra line was introduced in 1924 in five styles. Style 4 is nicely ornamented with floral designs on the rim and in the fingerboard inlay—even the flange holes incorporate a curled design. The "pop-on" resonator and rim are of rosewood, which is less common than maple or walnut on high-quality banjos of the period. Bill Camp/BM*

• *Weymann Orchestra No. 7 Deluxe tenor, late 1920s (center and lower right). In 1926, Weymann added a fancier model, No. 6, to its Orchestra line. The highly ornate No. 7 debuted in 1929 with walnut rim and resonator. The floral inlay runs up both edges of the fingerboard and practically covers the peghead. Bill Camp/BM*

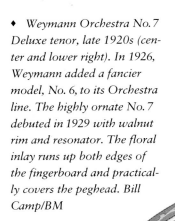

♦ *Slingerland Troubadour tenor, early 1930s. Slingerland was founded as a drum manufacturer in Chicago in 1916 and began making banjos in 1918. Though best known for its May Bell budget line of fretted instruments, the company produced five different resonator banjo models between 1925 and 1930, the most impressive being the Troubadour. The troubadour figure appears on a variety of instruments marketed by Lyon and Healy and by the Regal company of Chicago, indicating that the pearl figure may have been available to various manufacturers in precut form. The troubadour is walking, but the ships on the pearloid fingerboard markers and on the resonator markers imply that he is a seafaring performer. The hole in the resonator is for a mute pedal, which has been removed. Gruhn Guitars/WC*

♦ Vegaphone Artist tenor, 1928. Vega introduced resonators in the late 1910s. Flange-mounted resonators debuted in 1923, and Vega called the new models Vegaphones. The Artist is essentially a Tu-ba-phone #9 with a resonator. Like the Tu-ba-phone model, the Vegaphone Artist has a carved neck heel. The Vegaphone line lasted until 1940. Gruhn Guitars/DL

♦ *Gibson Florentine*
custom, 1927. (See page 129.)

TENOR AND PLECTRUM BANJOS
♦ ♦ ♦

Gibson Tenor Banjos

With revolutionary mandolin designs and aggressive marketing Gibson played a large role in creating the demand for mandolins and capitalized on the mandolin boom in the early twentieth century. Gibson no doubt expected continued success for the mandolin and consequently lagged far behind when it came to the tenor banjo. Despite its trail-blazing reputation, Gibson made a half-hearted entry into the banjo market in 1918. The line consisted of a single model, the TB (for Tenor Banjo), and it was a rather plain open-back instrument—hardly a challenge to established banjo companies, which had easily transformed full lines of five-strings into full lines of tenors. But as Gibson

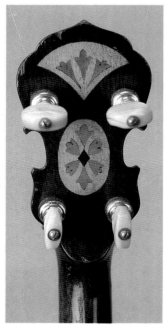

would do again and again when it got a late start on a new trend (such as electric guitars in the 1930s or electric solidbody guitars in the 1950s), once it entered a market, the company wasted no time in using a combination of aggressive marketing, innovation, and quality production to gain a competitive position.

Gibson's banjo line soon expanded to include the RB "regular" or five-string, CB cello banjo, MB mandolin-banjo, PB plectrum, UB banjo-uke, and eventually a giant bass banjo. In 1920 a plainer group of banjos was introduced and dubbed Style 2, even though the original line was never called Style 1.

Gibson threw its considerable marketing force behind the banjo. Even when the company introduced the F-5 mandolin and the Style 5 Master Model series in late 1922—one of the most important events in fretted instrument history—the focus of Gibson's ad campaign remained on the banjo line.

In the mid-1920s Gibson catalogs could hardly keep up with the banjo innovations. In the space of about four years, Gibson banjos went from an open-back design to a wooden, hinged, "trap-door" resonator to a "pyralin" plastic plate resonator and finally to the modern cupped wooden resonator. At the same time, the rim area underwent numerous innovations, including a hollow area between the head and the rim, then a hollow metal "tone ring," then a ball bearing and spring system to support the tone ring, then a cast tone chamber, and eventually a "flat-head" tone chamber. Two "coordinator" rods replaced the wooden dowel stick for neck attachment. Several innovations were implemented under the direction of Lloyd Loar, the man behind the Master Series mandolins and guitar, and a similar name—Mastertone—was appropriated for the top models of the banjo line.

Gibson never achieved the dominant position with tenor banjos that it enjoyed with mandolins. The company entered the competition late, and by the time it had perfected its designs, the tenor banjo was out of fashion. Consequently, tenor and plectrum players generally regard Gibson as only one of many good makers. Ironically, the most highly regarded banjo makers of the 1920s, such as B&D, Paramount, and Vega, have faded into relative obscurity, while Gibson is still going strong. The reason, of course, is the five-string banjo. Although the five-string's evolution in Gibson's line was merely coincidental with the tenor's, certain innovations designed for the tenor banjo are now considered by many bluegrass (five-string) players to be the ultimate in banjo design.

• *Gibson TB-5, 1925. In 1925 (center and opposite page), Gibson introduced a completely revamped model to compete directly with the modern flange and resonator of the Paramount models. Gibson's flange is different from Paramount's, but the tone ring is similar in appearance and function (though different in design), and the resonator is very similar. Collectors and players today call this new peghead the "fiddle" shape, but in the 1920s they would more likely have called it the Paramount peghead shape. This example was fitted with the new ball-bearing tone ring system developed by Lloyd Loar. The small round exterior holes appear only in 1925. By the time this instrument was made, most players preferred a banjo with a 23-inch scale and 19 frets. This example has a shorter neck, with a 20 ¾-inch scale and 18 frets, which was offered by Gibson as a catalog option but is relatively rare from this period onward. The tailpiece engraving refers back to a brief period when the TB was also called the Deluxe model and the TB-2 was called the Melody. Gruhn Guitars/DL*

• *Gibson TB, circa 1919 (above). Gibson entered the banjo market in 1918 with only one model, hence no number after TB. Although this is a fairly plain instrument, the fleur-de-lis peghead ornament puts it on a par with such high-end Gibson models as the A-4 mandolin or L-4 guitar, and when other banjo models were introduced, the TB was renamed the TB-4. The head on this example has a 12-inch diameter, versus the 11-inch head of later tenors. The peghead shape, which appears on the earliest Gibson banjos, was revived in the 1950s. The serial number of this instrument, 297, and the peghead suggest a very early example. There is no tone ring yet, but the rim is semi-hollow—made of two concentric rings separated by small spacer blocks. Brackets are anchored by a tube that circles the rim and is held in place by a "lip" milled into the rim. Gruhn Guitars/WC*

◆ *Gibson TB-3, circa 1923 (upper left and right). After the TB Gibson introduced two plainer models, the TB-2 in 1920 and TB-1 in 1922. The TB-3, introduced in 1923, is slightly less fancy than the TB-4 (formerly the TB). Although the modern flange and resonator design was introduced by other makers at about the same time this banjo was made, Gibson's first resonator, introduced in 1922, is a hinged wooden plate that can be opened for greater volume. Collectors call this resonator a "trap door" type; the official Gibson name is Tone Projector. Lloyd Chiate/BM*

◆ *Gibson GB, circa 1921 (center). This guitar banjo has the same rim construction and tube bracket system as the early TB, but the peghead is a later one, referred to by collectors as "moccasin" shape. The pickguard and extended fingerboard are catalog options, and some catalogs offered the option of one or the other but not both. The "trapeze" tailpiece with metal crossbar does not appear on Gibson guitars until 1923 (earlier guitars have a plastic crosspiece with pin string-anchors). Gruhn Guitars/WC*

126

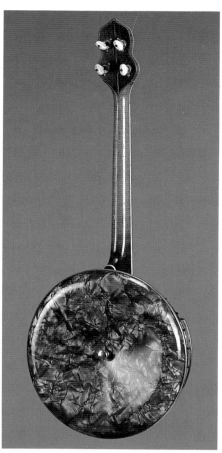

◆ Gibson TB-4, circa 1923. With bound fingerboard, bound peghead, and a fleur-de-lis peghead inlay, the TB-4 is a step up from the TB-3. The one-piece "pyralin" or pearloid resonator is simpler and flashier than the earlier trap door but a questionable improvement in terms of tone. It replaced the trap door as standard equipment on the Style 4 and the newly introduced Style 5 in 1923, but the trap door was still available as an option. Pyralin resonator models are much less common than trap door models, an indication that most players preferred the trap door. Gruhn Guitars/DL

◆ Gibson TB-5, circa 1924. Style 5 is essentially a gold-plated and more heavily ornamented version of the Style 4. The peghead inlay of a Style 5 banjo shows some of the fern pattern that was just beginning to appear in late 1924 on F-5 mandolins. This example, though later than the TB-4 with the pyralin resonator, has a trap door. Gruhn Guitars/WC

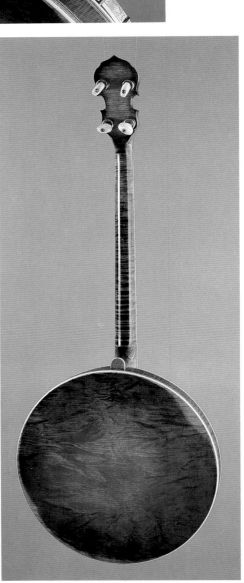

◆ *Gibson TB-6, early 1930s. Style 6 was introduced in late 1927. Examples from the late 1920s have eye-catching checkered binding. Gold sparkle binding (an option on the Florentine model) was featured in 1930 on a new model, the PT-6, which has a scale in between plectrum and tenor length, and the gold-sparkle was eventually adopted on all Style 6 models. Gibson called the dark, orangish sunburst finish "Argentine gray." Style 6 was discontinued in 1937. Gruhn Guitars/WC*

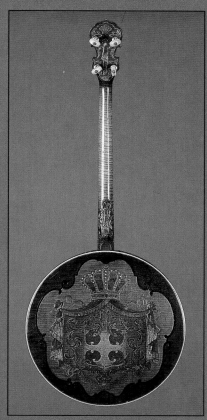

♦ *Gibson Florentine custom, 1927. A standard Florentine, the top of the line when it was introduced in 1927, did not suit the customer who ordered this banjo. The fingerboard and peghead ornamentation are unlike any in the Gibson line and are actually less fancy than the Florentine in the catalog. Apparently, that was the way Arthur W. Cook wanted it. Gruhn Guitars/DL*

♦ *Gibson Bella Voce, 1927. The Bella Voce and Florentine, both introduced in 1927, brought Gibson into competition with the fancy models of other manufacturers. "White holly" (actually white painted maple) sets off the elaborate carving and painting on the resonator, neck heel, and back of peghead. Both the Bella Voce and Florentine were offered in white holly, curly maple, rosewood, or burl walnut. The Bella Voce only lasted three years. Steve Soest/DL*

♦ *Gibson Florentine, circa 1934. The Florentine in white is a dazzling piece, especially with this transparent replacement head. The pearloid fingerboard is painted with Italian Renaissance scenes—interestingly, of Venice rather than Florence. The peghead is covered with pearloid and then garnished with a rhinestone border, rhinestone ornament, and even a rhinestone logo. This is an unusual late example of a Florentine, with a "double-cut" peghead shape (distinguishable by a point in the area on the sides between the pegs) and a one-piece flange. Gruhn Guitars/WC*

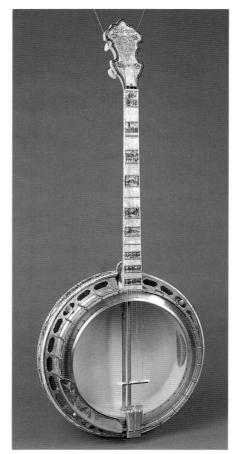
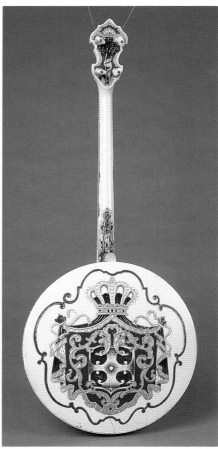

♦ *Bella Voce, circa 1928. This example sports standard Bella Voce appointments except for the 20¾-inch scale length and the 18-fret neck. The Bella Voce and Florentine were offered in woods described by the catalog as "the pick of American and foreign forests." Color schemes on the back carving differ from one wood to the next. The resonator and neck on this example are of maple. The peghead has the early floral-pattern inlay. Later Bella Voce models have the pearloid and rhinestone ornamentation of the Florentine model. The multicolored binding is one of six optional bindings offered on Bella Voce and Florentine models. The small metal accessory on the upper left part of the rim is a pick holder, and a mute has been added. Gruhn Guitars/WC*

♦ *Gibson MB-3, 1926 (above). Early tenor banjos were sometimes called "mandolin-banjos," but by the early 1920s, a more mandolinlike instrument, with double strings and mandolin scale, claimed the moniker. Gibson's MB-3 is a midline model, but it does not necessarily have the same fittings as a TB-3 of the same period. Gruhn Guitars/WC*

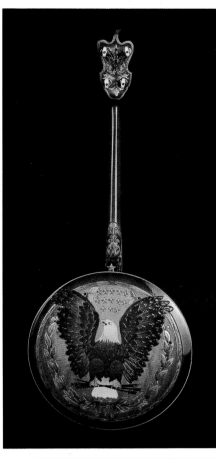

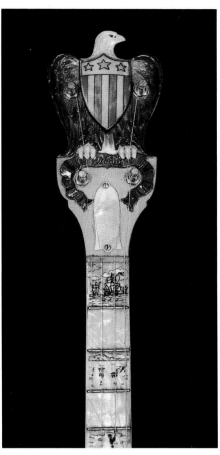

♦ *Gibson All American, 1932 (this page and opposite). The All American was introduced in 1930, the same year the Bella Voce was dropped, and was the most expensive banjo in the Gibson line. A bald eagle carved into the peghead presides over the history of America as told by the fingerboard scenes: the three ships of Columbus, the Statue of Liberty, the Washington Monument, a log cabin (the birthplace of Lincoln), and the White House. This example was refinished in the 1960s and replated. Len Jones/WC*

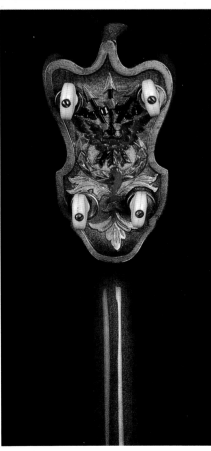

◆ *Gibson All American five-string, 1992 (this page and opposite). Most Gibson banjo experts believe that no five-string All Americans were ever made during the model's original run. This Custom Shop edition, made by Greg Rich, is a five-string, but the high degree of ornamentation carries on the tradition of tenor banjos of the Jazz Age. The peghead and fingerboard recreate the figures of the original models, but with more color. The signing of the Declaration of Independence is depicted on the resonator with inlays of pearl and several different types of wood. Gibson USA/WC*

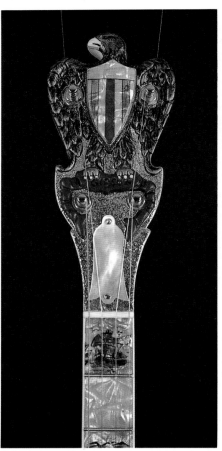

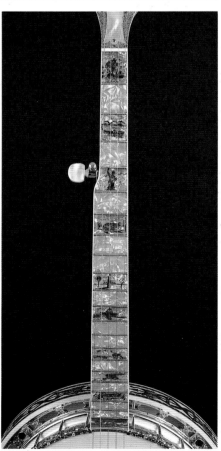

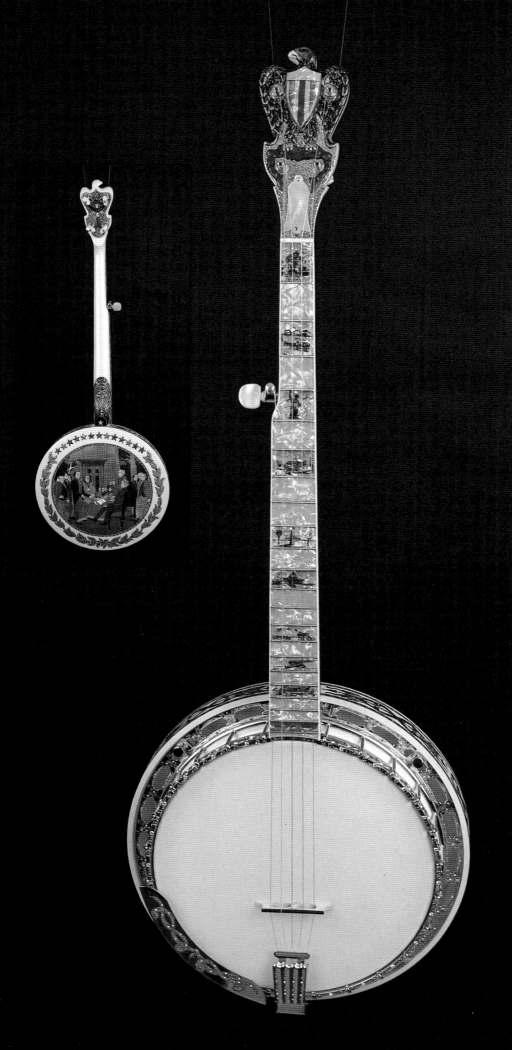

♦ Gibson UB-1, circa 1926 (above). The Gibson banjo family included ukulele-size instruments. Gibson's cheapest ukulele banjo or banjo-uke, the UB-1, debuted in 1926. Its 6-inch head diameter is 2 inches smaller than all other models except the original UB of 1924 and 1925, which also has a 6-inch head. The resonator is a flat wooden plate. The UB-1 was discontinued in 1939. Gruhn Guitars/WC

◆ *Gibson custom tenor, early 1930s. This unusual example combines features from three of Gibson's high-end models. All the body features of this banjo, including the checkered binding and the Argentine gray finish, are typical of a late-1920s TB-6. The fingerboard pattern belongs to the All American, the top of Gibson's banjo line from 1930 to 1934. The peghead of Gibson's Florentine model is ornamented with pearloid and rhinestones in this pattern. This example has the high-profile flat tone ring. Jim Bollman/WC*

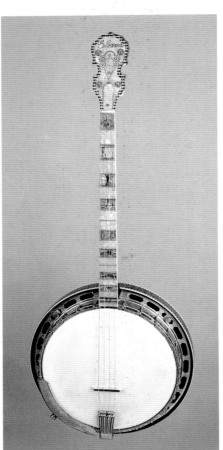

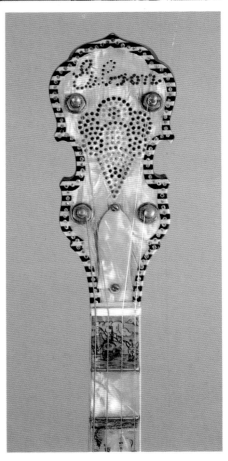

♦ *Gibson TB-11 and Kel Kroyden, early 1930s (above). From 1917 to the late 1920s, Gibson marketed various budget models—such as the Alrite and Army and Navy mandolins and a line of Junior models—that were Gibson-made but not of high enough quality to bear the Gibson brand. In 1930 the company introduced its first budget brand—Kel Kroyden. The line included two banjos, two mandolins, and two guitars. Kel Kroydens were dressed up with a stenciled pearloid fingerboard and peghead overlay to look more expensive than they really were. In 1931 Gibson apparently decided that the Kel Kroyden banjo was nothing to be ashamed of, and a nearly identical model was introduced as the Gibson TB-11. Aside from the logo, the only difference is the TB-11's adjustable truss rod; the Kel Kroyden has a nonadjustable rod or no rod at all. Both the TB-11 and the more expensive of the two Kel Kroyden models listed for $50. The tailpiece on this Kel Kroyden is not original. Gruhn Guitars/WC*

♦ *Gibson TB-18, 1940 (right). By 1937 banjos had fallen in popularity, and Gibson severely cut back its line, discontinuing Styles 2, 3, 4, 6, Granada, Florentine, and All American. Gibson probably should have retired from banjo making altogether, but instead introduced four new styles. In ascending order they were: 75 (a low-price Mastertone model), 7, 12, and 18. The top three models sported Gibson's version of top-tension head adjustment bolts, by which the head could be tightened without removing the resonator. Ludwig had introduced top-tension models by 1927, but the design was undermined by the use of a pot metal hoop and flange. Gibson's one-piece flange, introduced in late 1929 on Mastertone models, was also pot metal, which is prone to cracking and warping. (The two-piece flange, used on the models above the Granada, was brass.) The top-tension models were the first to be cataloged with the flat top or "flat-head" tone ring, which had been available as an option since the early 1930s. Gruhn Guitars/DL*

♦ Gibson UB-2, late
1920s. The UB-2 started
out as a big UB-1, with a
larger 8-inch head diame-
ter. In 1928, it was upgraded with fancier inlay and
fingerboard binding. The
UB-1 and UB-2 have a flat-
plate resonator. Higher
models have a flange and
resonator system. Gruhn
Guitars/WC

♦ *Orville Gibson guitar, circa 1900. (See page 140.)*

EARLY TWENTIETH CENTURY

♦ ♦ ♦

Early Gibson Archtops

Gibson's original company name identified it as a mandolin-guitar manufacturer, and indeed, the mandolin was Gibson's top priority. Well into the 1920s, Gibson treated guitars as members of the mandolin orchestra and built them accordingly, with carved top and back and oval or round soundhole.

In 1903 the first Gibson catalog assured customers that instruments would be made of woods with "the most durable, elastic and sonorous qualities," such as maple, mahogany, vermilion, and "other suitable woods." As Lyon and Healy had done in the 1890s, Gibson took issue with rosewood as a

♦ *Orville Gibson guitar, circa 1900. This instrument was made for Mrs. Donald O. Boudeman of Kalamazoo. It was acquired by the Gibson company and then restored and refinished. The body shape is the same as that of the Gibson company's O series. The butterfly is a common pickguard figure on Orville Gibson's fanciest instruments, but neither the butterfly nor the bridge ornamentation carries over into Gibson company production. Gibson USA/WC*

suitable material. "While rosewood is very beautiful," the catalog explained, "it is extremely treacherous and unreliable, because it checks [cracks] so easily. Even after years of preparation, it cannot be relied upon to retain the shape desired." Lyon and Healy had expressed a preference for mahogany; Gibson went for maple—at least in print. According to the catalog, "maple can be thoroughly dried, so that when made up into instruments it may be depended upon not to warp, bend or crack. It also takes a beautiful polish." However, despite the catalog's specifications for maple back and "rims" (sides) for all Gibson guitars and mandolins, in reality, only the high-end mandolins were made of maple. Guitars were made of walnut for several years. Birch then came into use for most guitars and mandolins until the mid- to late-1920s, when the instruments finally began to adhere to the catalog's maple specification.

Some of the earliest Gibson guitars differed considerably in size from Martins and Washburns of the day. Most models were offered in three sizes. The standard and concert were 12½ inches and 13½ inches wide, respectively—about the same dimensions as other makers' guitars. The next size up, grand concert, was 16 inches wide, a full inch wider than the widest Martin of 1903. In addition, some 18-inch guitars were made in Gibson's early years.

Another unique characteristic of early Gibson guitars was their steel-string design (gut strings were optional). Martin would not introduce its first steel-string models until the 1920s; Washburn guitars were guaranteed against practically everything except "the ravages of steel strings." At the time, the Larson brothers of Chicago were the only other makers of high-quality guitars whose instruments were built for steel strings. While Gibson may have seemed visionary in its steel-string design, more likely the steel strings were just another manifestation of the Gibson guitar's kinship to the mandolin.

The association with the mandolin finally paid off for the Gibson guitar, for it was a mandolin innovation—the violin-type *f*-holes that were incorporated into the L-5 guitar—that would set the industry standard for archtop guitars and eventually bring the guitar out of the mandolin's shadow.

♦ Gibson Style O, circa 1904. Style O is the plainest of the four O models in Gibson's first catalog. The 18-inch "special auditorium" size (this instrument actually measures 17 ½ inches) was discontinued in 1908, but it was revived in 1934 for the earliest version of the Super 400. Although this model appears without a peghead ornament in the 1903 catalog, the star and crescent are found on many early Gibson company instruments. Whereas the great majority of early Gibson mandolins have had the original friction pegs replaced by geared tuners, the original tuners are not unusual on an early guitar. There are at least two explanations: standard three-on-a-plate geared tuners of that time would not fit Gibson's "paddle" peghead, and these guitars were so cumbersome and hard to play that no one bothered to find replacement tuners. Style O is the only one of the original O-series models to survive more than a few years. Jim Reynolds/DL

♦ Gibson Style O, 1920. Gibson's perception of the guitar as a mandolin orchestra instrument is evident in the scroll and body point of the redesigned Style O, which debuted in 1908. Gibson sometimes called the scroll-body Style O the "Artist's Model," and collectors know it as the Style O Artist. Although it was Gibson's top of the line, it was not as successful as the slightly less expensive and more conventionally shaped L-4. The Style O was discontinued in 1923. Gruhn Guitars/DL

♦ Gibson L-2, 1924. An original but short-lived L-series model, the L-2 was reintroduced in 1924. It is the same size as the L-1 and L-3 and falls between the two in ornamentation. The thinner, tapered peghead shape—known among collectors as "snakehead"—is a feature of guitars and A-style mandolins made from 1923 to 1927. The metal trapeze tailpiece replaced the old trapeze-pin style in 1924. The gold-plated tailpiece on this example was lifted from a Gibson L-5 guitar. Hank Sable/DL

♦ Gibson Style L, 1906. Gibson's L-series models are much more common than O-series examples from the early 1900s, and they are closer in size to the parlor guitars of Gibson's contemporaries. Also like the typical guitar of the day, the smaller L models have a round soundhole rather than the oval hole of the O series. Style L is the plainest of the four original L models, all of which have an amber or, as the catalog calls it, "beautiful orange" top finish. The slotted peghead appears for only a few years and probably represents a transition between the problematic paddle peghead and the solid peghead design that would later accommodate three-on-a-plate tuners. Gruhn Guitars/DL

♦ *Gibson L-1, circa 1920 (upper right). By 1908 Style L had been discontinued and the L-1 had become Gibson's low-end guitar. That year the optional sizes of 1903 were standardized into one size— 13½ inches wide—for the L-1 and L-3 (the only two L models remaining in the line). In 1920, when most Gibson models had an amber top finish or a rich mahogany sunburst, the lowly L-1 came in a plain "Sheraton brown" wrapper. Gruhn Guitars/DL*

♦ *Gibson L-4, 1923 (upper left). The redesigned scroll-body Style O of 1908 left Gibson with no conventional 16-inch guitar. By the next catalog, in 1911, Gibson had filled the void with the L-4. Essentially the same guitar as the earlier Style O, it has an oval soundhole like virtually all 16-inch Gibsons of the period (whether O-series or grand concert–size L-series examples). Shortly after this example was made, the snakehead peghead was adopted. The L-4 was held in high regard by players into the early 1930s, even as the trend was shifting to f-hole models. In 1935 it was revitalized with f-holes. A later cutaway version lasted in the line until 1971. Blaine Hampton/DL*

♦ *Gibson L-3, 1918 (center). The fanciest of Gibson's 13½-inch archtops, the L-3 also lasted the longest, until 1933. Herringbone trim around the soundhole, a feature strongly associated with Martin guitars, is unusual on a Gibson guitar but was standard on this model from 1908 to 1927. Gruhn Guitars/DL*

♦ Gibson L-4, 1930 (above). Between the oval-hole and the f-hole versions of the L-4, a round-hole model appeared from 1928 to 1935. Strangely, in 1927 the L-3 went the other way—to an oval hole—and then returned to a round hole in 1929. Bill Camp/BM

♦ Gibson L-4 Custom, 1928 (center and above). Apparently not everyone in the late 1920s thought all the glory should go to the new f-hole guitars and mandolins. This custom-ordered L-4 has the scroll peghead shape of an F-style mandolin, the triple-bound body and pickguard of the top-of-the-line L-5 f-hole guitar, and the flowerpot inlay of the L-5 guitar and the F-4 mandolin. Most oddball or one-of-a-kind Gibsons are verified by the presence of a standard Gibson label and the appearance of factory-original work. This example has not only a standard label with "Spec." handwritten above the model name, but also has a second label that says it was "made special for" H. Schroeder of Lincoln, Nebraska. Jay Levin/WC

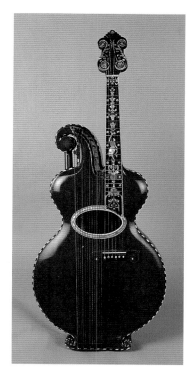

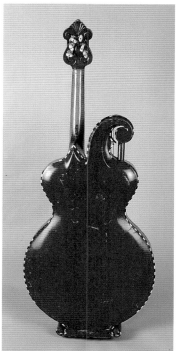

♦ Orville Gibson harp guitar, circa 1900. Forerunners of the harp guitar date back to the lute era. The ceterone of the 1500s, essentially a bass cittern, had a set of open strings that were much longer than the fretted strings. The harp guitar of the early 1900s represents one of the last waves of the experimentation and innovation that began around 1800, and this instrument certainly qualifies as an experimental model. It was designed so that the sub-bass string tuners as well as the string anchors are on the body of the instrument. Gibson USA/WC

♦ Gibson Style U harp guitar, 1919 (upper left). The harp guitar inspired some classic Gibson catalog text. "When gray hairs applaud, progress may well ask: What have I done amiss?" the catalog asked. Gray hairs, it seems, thought the standard six-string guitar was good enough, and they ignored the supposedly superior harp guitar. Under the innocent-sounding sub-head, "A Little Harp Guitar Talk," the company ranted about the superior concept of the instrument with an allegory comparing the guitar/harp guitar question to the harpsichord/piano question of a century earlier: "The mighty Bach and his contemporaries could not be persuaded to leave the harpsichord with its inferior capacity and power of expression for the piano…. Death alone saved Bach from the ridicule of the then rising generation." The discussion continued with the observation that "Bach's antiquated instrument is today but a museum curiosity…." Ironically, the Gibson harp guitar is today but a museum curiosity while the harpsichord enjoys a revival. The few musicians who play harp guitar today generally prefer a flat top instrument of the type made by the Larson brothers and marketed under the Dyer label. Gruhn Guitars/DL

♦ Gibson Style U harp guitar, circa 1906 (lower left). Gibson thought very highly of the harp guitar, and its image was double-trucked across the centerfold of company catalogs for 20 years. Gruhn Guitars/DL

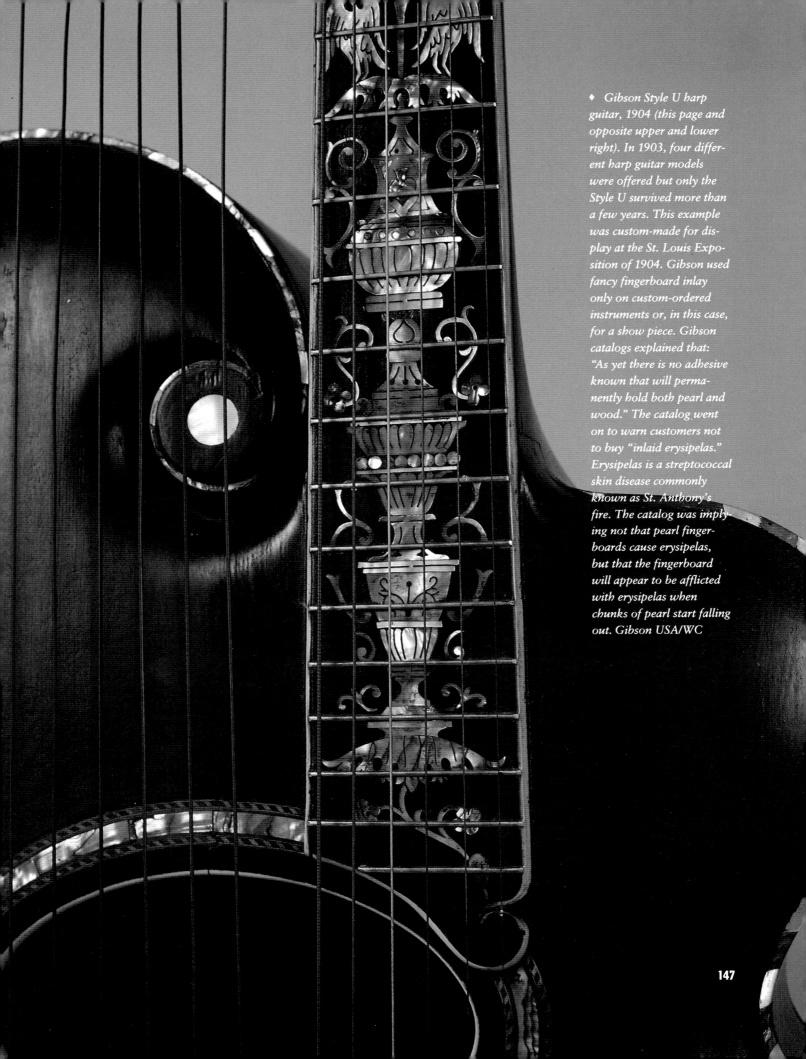

◆ Gibson Style U harp guitar, 1904 (this page and opposite upper and lower right). In 1903, four different harp guitar models were offered but only the Style U survived more than a few years. This example was custom-made for display at the St. Louis Exposition of 1904. Gibson used fancy fingerboard inlay only on custom-ordered instruments or, in this case, for a show piece. Gibson catalogs explained that: "As yet there is no adhesive known that will permanently hold both pearl and wood." The catalog went on to warn customers not to buy "inlaid erysipelas." Erysipelas is a streptococcal skin disease commonly known as St. Anthony's fire. The catalog was implying not that pearl fingerboards cause erysipelas, but that the fingerboard will appear to be afflicted with erysipelas when chunks of pearl start falling out. Gibson USA/WC

◆ *Hilo 670, mid-1920s. Model 670 is the fanciest of five Hilo models. Starting with the cheapest model, Hilos were available with all-cedar construction, spruce top and mahogany back and sides, all mahogany, spruce top and maple back and sides, and this all-koa model. The Hilo 670 is also the second fanciest of three koa models offered by the "First Hawaiian Conservatory of Music" in New York—actually the Oscar Schmidt company of Jersey City, New Jersey. Walter Carter/WC*

EARLY TWENTIETH CENTURY
◆ ◆ ◆

Hawaiian Guitars and Ukuleles

One of the most popular styles of music in America for most of the first half of this century was Hawaiian music. With the smooth, lyrical tones of a guitar played with a steel bar, the easy rhythm of a ukulele, and the romance of songs about an exotic land, Hawaiian music seemed immune to the faddish and fickle nature of pop culture. That immunity, strangely, worked both ways. Despite its unique popularity, Hawaiian music is essentially a sidebar to the history of American popular music. In the evolution from ragtime to early jazz to swing to rock and roll, little can be traced back to Hawaiian music. The only sounds of the last half of the twentieth century with Hawaiian roots are the pedal steel guitar in country music, the Dobro in bluegrass, and the slide or bottleneck style in blues.

In the history of instruments, however, Hawaiian music holds one of the most important places. As the first popular style based on guitar, it represents the guitar's first step on its way out of the parlor of the nineteenth century and into the spotlight of the 1930s.

In addition, the steel guitar, one of the signature instruments of the Hawaiian sound, evolved more quickly and more radically than any other instrument in American history—from a standard guitar laid flat in the lap to a hollow-neck koa wood guitar to a guitar with metal resonator cone (some with metal body as well); then to a 6-string solidbody electric (the "lap steel"); then to 7, 8, and 10 strings, then to double-, triple-, and even four-neck electrics, and finally to the modern pedal steel. At practically every step in its evolution, it led the way for important evolutionary change in the standard guitar—from the large-bodied acoustics and resonator instruments of the late 1920s to the first modern electric instruments of the early 1930s and the solidbody electrics of the early 1950s.

Traditional Hawaiian music derives from an odd union of influences. Musically, it is rooted structurally in classical European forms and tonally in the church music of American missionaries. As musician Bob Brozman observes, "There is a similarity between Hawaiian music and Mexican music or South African music or any primitive culture that had missionaries. It's all 'Bringing in the Sheaves,' all religious-based and all very beautiful." The Hawaiian repertoire in the early years of the twentieth century included marches and waltzes, reflecting the influence of a German bandmaster imported by the king and queen in the 1870s to organize and lead a brass band.

The instruments, however—the guitar and ukulele—were brought to the islands by Portuguese immigrants, and the playing style has Mexican roots. The guitar had arrived by the 1830s, but the instrument was probably closer to a Spanish classical guitar than to the Germanic guitar that evolved into C. F. Martin's American flat top. At about the same time, Spanish-speaking cowboys from southern California were brought to the islands. As in the continental United States, the cowboy became a legendary figure in Hawaii, complete with guitar. In the mid-1860s the Portuguese introduced metal strings. By the last

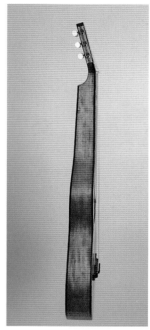

quarter of the nineteenth century native musicians had developed what became known as "slack key" tunings—tunings with a full or partial open chord that are the basis of the intricate but fluid style of modern Hawaiian music.

The earliest steel playing centered around chime tones—overtones actually—that were achieved by stopping the strings with the back of the hand. According to one story, James Hoa made chime tones by using a knife blade in 1876, thus inventing the steel guitar. Another account credits Gabriel Davion, a native of India who was kidnapped as a child by sailors, with appropriating the slide style from the *gootvadyam,* an Indian instrument played with an ebony rod or glass ball for a slide. The gootvadyam dates back at least to the eleventh century in India, the sliding technique as far back as the sixth century A.D. and possibly even to the second century B.C. Davion is said to have played melody on a single string that was not raised off the fingerboard. There is one and only one account of both Hoa and Davion playing with the slide technique at King Kalakaua's Jubilee Celebration in 1886.

The accepted father of the steel guitar is Hawaiian guitarist Joseph Kekuku. Even if he was not the first with the idea, he was the one who developed what had been an obscure novelty technique into a full-fledged playing style. According to Kekuku, the idea came to him in 1885, when he was 11 years old and walking along a railroad track playing his guitar. He picked up a railroad spike, and that became his first steel. Other versions of the story have him accidentally dropping a comb or knife on his guitar. He later experimented with various objects, finally settling on a steel cylinder that he made in machine shop class in high school. He also raised the strings so that they would not come into contact with the fretboard and used metal strings. By the mid-1890s Kekuku was a star in Hawaii. In 1904 he brought the Hawaiian style to the mainland and eventually to Europe.

Since a guitar does not project as much sound when laid in the lap as when held in standard playing position, special designs evolved for Hawaiian guitars. The earliest adaptations used a higher nut and a straight saddle. Gibson offered "Hawaiian equipment"—nut extension, steel bar, and finger picks—by 1917. At the same time, a distinct Hawaiian acoustic guitar appeared, with a shallow body, hollow square neck, and koa wood construction. These guitars were pretty, but they were not any louder than a standard guitar, and the major Hawaiian players stayed with a conventional-type guitar, such as a Martin. By the late 1920s Martin offered several standard models with

Hawaiian options, which included a flat fingerboard, flush frets, high nut, and heavier bracing for steel strings.

The next step manufacturers took was to increase the size of the guitar, which did result in greater volume. This development would have a profound effect on flat top and archtop guitar design, but by the time larger-bodied Spanish guitars had become standard, many Hawaiian players had already switched to the new resonator guitars made by National and Dobro. True to form, when yet another new design became available, most players forsook the resonator instruments for the revolutionary electric Hawaiian models. The evolution from flat top guitar to resonator to electric took place within a decade.

The forerunner of the ukulele, the *braguinha*, was a small four-string instrument tuned in fifths. Named after the town of Braga in Portugal, the braguinha arrived in Hawaii with the first group of Portuguese immigrants in 1878. The owner of the instrument did not know how to play it, however. A second boat, arriving in 1879, carried not only braguinhas but braguinha players and three braguinha makers—Augusto Dias, Jose do Espirito Santo, and Manuel Nunes. With a little adaptation—a more guitarlike body shape, native Hawaiian koa wood construction, and guitar-related tuning—the modern ukulele was born. King Kalakaua took up the uke and in 1886 featured it for the first time with hula dancers. It became the instrument of the islands.

On ocean liners and increasingly on the mainland, the sound of the steel guitar and ukulele grew in popularity through the first decade of the twentieth century. In the second decade Hawaiian music boomed. The boom can be pinpointed to the Panama-Pacific International Exposition of 1915 in San Francisco. The Hawaii Chamber of Commerce's Promotion Committee, forerunner of the Hawaii Visitors Bureau, had been sending musical groups to expositions and fairs to promote products of the territory. For the 1915 exposition, celebrating the completion of the Panama Canal, the Hawaiian legislature appropriated $100,000 for the Hawaii pavilion. Within a year, Hawaiian music was hugely popular. In 1916 the Victor company sold more Hawaiian records than any other style of music.

The ukulele was as big a hit as the music. Two of the best-known Hawaiian makers started their careers during this period. Jonah Kumalae, an ivory carver, switched to ukes in 1911. Samuel Kamaka of Honolulu began making koa ukuleles in 1916. Kamaka's company was incorporated in 1968 and is still in business. Mainland manufacturers quickly jumped on the uke

♦ *Weissenborn Style 1, mid-1920s. Herman W. Weissenborn of Los Angeles was the premier maker of koa wood guitars designed for Hawaiian playing, with a hollow square neck and fret markers flush with the fingerboard. Weissenborn began making guitars in 1916. Among his more noteworthy associates were Chris Knutsen, best known for early harp guitars marketed under the Dyer label, and Rudolph Dopyera of the family that founded the National and Dobro companies. Collector Mike Newton believes that Herman Weissenborn made Hilos, Konas, Shireson Lyric models, and virtually every other acoustic Hawaiian guitar that looks like a Weissenborn, regardless of label or advertising claims. Weissenborn died in 1936 and his factory ceased operation in 1937. Style 1 is the plainest of Weissenborn's four styles, which listed from $40 to $79. Real Guitars/BM* bandwagon. Ditson of Boston and Gretsch of Brooklyn advertised high-quality Hawaiian-made ukes as well as cheaper mainland-made models by 1917. Apparently not all ukes stamped "Made in Hawaii" really were, and in 1915 the Hawaii Chamber of Commerce took steps to protect Hawaiian makers by legislation. In addition, the Honolulu Ad Club tried to patent the ukulele.

Ukes remained popular through the 1930s, with styles ranging from colorfully ornamented novelty items to professional-quality instruments. Acoustic Hawaiian guitars fell out of favor when resonator guitars arrived in the late 1920s, but their unique look and their use in recent years by popular musicians have generated renewed interest from players as well as collectors.

♦ *Grossman catalog, 1935. The "steel" of the steel guitar refers to the implement by which it is played, not to a metal body or frame. Many makers tried to improve on Joseph Kekuku's cylindrical design, as shown by the variety of steels available in 1935. Earlier steels included a Rollers Royce, which utilized a roller bar to reduce string drag. In later years plastic-covered bars in a variety of colors were popular. The only one of these "improved" steels in wide use today is the Stevens, which is preferred by most bluegrass Dobro players. Most modern players of pedal steel, lap steel, and metal-body National resonator instruments use a chrome-plated cylinder (some of them much larger in diameter than those pictured here) with a rounded end, known as a "bullet" bar. Gruhn Guitars/WC*

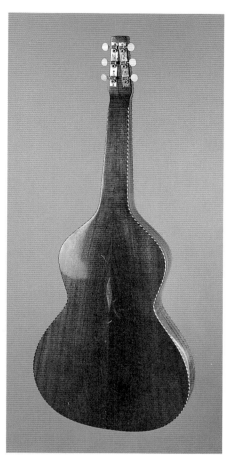

♦ *Weissenborn Style 4, mid-1920s. Weissenborn added rope-pattern binding in degrees to achieve four different styles. Style 2 has it around the soundhole only, with light wood binding on the fingerboard. Style 3 has rope around the soundhole, finger-board, and top edge. Style 4 features additional rope-pattern binding around the back and peg-head, plus a more ornamented fingerboard than the lower models. Although the Weissenborn-style Hawaiian guitar never surpassed the conventional guitar in popularity, it did experience a revival of interest among collectors in the 1980s, thanks to its use by recording artist David Lindley. Gruhn Guitars/WC*

♦ *Kona, mid-1920s (lower left). Kona guitars were marketed by C. S. Delano, a Los Angeles teacher, beginning by 1920. At first glance this guitar appears to be very similar to a Weissenborn Style 4, but the body is significantly deeper and the neck is round and solid. The neck may give this instrument different tonal qualities from a hollow-neck guitar, but with a neck-body joint at the seventh fret and flush frets, there can be little doubt that it was designed for Hawaiian playing. Ross Music/BM*

♦ *Washburn 5260, late 1920s (lower right). A rather large lap is required to play this bell-shaped Hawaiian guitar marketed by Tonk Bros. The top is spruce, and the back and sides are koa. The introduction of National and Dobro resonator guitars in the late 1920s put an end to this branch of innovation. Ross Music/BM*

◆ Groehsl, circa 1920. Groehsl (Groeschl, according to Chicago city directories; Groeshel, according to 1930s company literature) was founded in Chicago in 1890. It later became the Stromberg-Voisinet company and, in 1929, the Kay company. The body of this instrument shows the freedom of design allowed by a guitar played in the lap, Hawaiian style. Otherwise, it is more American than Hawaiian in design, with spruce top, pearl top trim, and rosewood back and sides. Gruhn Guitars/DL

◆ Martin 00-40H custom, 1932. C. F. Young was a teacher and musician who had Martin put his name instead of "C. F. Martin" on the peghead of this instrument. Although Martin made a few Style 40 guitars before the 00-40H was introduced, the 00 size with Hawaiian setup was by far the most successful. This example is not entirely true to Style 40 specifications. It has a solid, bound peghead rather than the slotted, unbound peghead of the standard Style 40, and the fingerboard inlay and binding are from the fancier Style 45. The shaded finish is rare, but it was an option offered by Martin. The slanted saddle shows that it has been converted to a standard setup. A total of 238 model 00-40Hs were produced from 1928 to 1939, plus five 00-40K koa wood Hawaiian models. Gruhn Guitars/DL

◆ *Martin 0-28K, 1927. In response to the rising popularity of Hawaiian music in the early 1900s, Martin introduced koa wood guitars, available with standard or Hawaiian setup. The 0-28K has herringbone purfling like any other Style 28 of the period. It is designed for Hawaiian playing, with a flat fingerboard, frets inlaid flush with the fingerboard, and the saddle mounted straight across the strings rather than at a slight slant. Dennis Watkins/BM*

◆ *Associated Teachers, 1930s (center). Like the Oahu guitars, this model was, no doubt, accompanied by an instructional course, in this case from Associated Teachers. It was not unusual for makers of cheap guitars to paint a wood grain on the body to make it look like a more expensive wood. Frogskin, of course, is not a wood. Walter Carter/WC*

◆ *Oahu, 1930s. Oahu, located in Cleveland, Ohio, was the dominant Hawaiian mail-order "school" in the 1930s. The company sold guitars made by Regal of Chicago, but the real money-making products were instructional courses —for teachers as well as students. "Oahu was the Amway of Hawaiian music," musician Bob Brozman says. "First you bought the student course, then they hooked you on the teacher's course." Gruhn Guitars/WC*

• *Gibson Roy Smeck Radio Grande, circa 1935. Gibson introduced a rather bizarre line of guitars in 1929 named "HG" (for Hawaiian guitar) models, but virtually all of the surviving examples appear to have been made for Spanish-style playing. Gibson's first truly Hawaiian models, with flush fret markers and straight saddle, were introduced in 1934 and endorsed by vaudeville star Roy Smeck. The Radio Grande was cataloged with rosewood back and sides and natural top, and the Stage Deluxe was described with mahogany back and sides and sunburst finish, but in reality the specs overlap. Because of their 16-inch dreadnought-size body and round neck, many Smeck models have been converted for standard play. They sound quite good, like most of Gibson's prewar dreadnoughts, but the extra-wide neck makes Spanish-style playing difficult. Gruhn Guitars/WC*

• *Gretsch Model 40 Hawaiian, circa 1939. Gretsch's effort in the Hawaiian market was nominal. Model 40 is the bigger of two Hawaiian models introduced in 1939 and is more noteworthy for being the company's first serious flat top model. The "smoked pearl" pyralin (pearloid) peghead overlay with real mother-of-pearl inlay gives this guitar a classy look (the tuners are not original). The big-bodied, big-sounding Model 40 listed for $40 and did not last through the 1940s. Gruhn Guitars/WC*

♦ *Gibson HG-2, 1950 (upper right). From 1937 to 1942 Gibson offered Hawaiian versions of several standard flat top models. These typically have a round neck and standard frets and are distinguishable from non-Hawaiian models by their 12-fret neck, straight-mounted bridge, and heavier top bracing. After World War II, Gibson made several HG-2 model guitars— essentially an LG guitar body (the LG, for "little guitar," series of 14¾-inch flat tops, was Gibson's most popular style) with a square, 12-fret neck. By the 1950s demand for this type of Hawaiian guitar was negligible, and the HG-2 appears neither in catalogs nor in shipping records. Rod Norwood/WC*

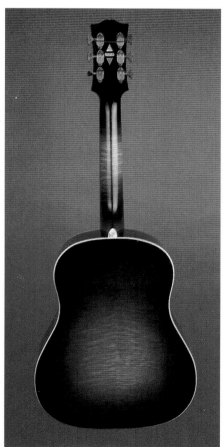

♦ *Gibson custom Hawaiian, 1935 (left and lower right). The body style is that of a Roy Smeck model, but otherwise this guitar matches Gibson's newly introduced top-of-the-line archtop model, the Super 400. Super 400 features include the fingerboard and peghead inlays, mosaic-pattern pickguard material, multiple body bindings, maple back and sides, three-piece maple neck, Grover Imperial tuners, and even a heelcap engraved with "Super." The original owner put his own label inside, which reads, "Howard Canford, Dec. 14, '35, Tulsa." Crawford White/WC*

• *Martin Style 2 uke (upper left). Style 2 is the middle model of three mahogany ukes introduced in 1918. The plainest, Style 1, has single-ply binding. Style 2 has triple binding. All three styles were also available as a taropatch, a slightly larger, double-strung ukulele. Gruhn Guitars/WC*

• *Martin Style 3 uke (upper right). The most elaborate of Martin's 1918 line of soprano ukes, Style 3 features a fancy inlay pattern. The earliest examples have this ornamental peghead inlay and the diamond inlays close together at the seventh fret. Style 3 and Style 0 (a model with no body binding, introduced in 1922) are still in production. Gruhn Guitars/WC*

• *Martin 3-K Taropatch, early 1920s. The taropatch is a double-strung ukulele, but the body of a Martin taropatch is the size of a concert uke (larger than a soprano). This example has the extra peghead ornament and the fingerboard inlay pattern of early Style 3 ukes. The earliest Martin ukes have wooden friction peg tuners. Metal "patent" pegs were phased in during the mid-1920s. Paul Gillette/WC*

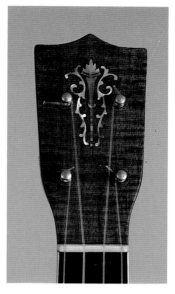

♦ *Martin 3-K concert uke, 5-K soprano uke, 5-K tenor uke, 1920s. Beginning in 1920 Martin offered koa wood versions of standard size ukes (6 3/8 inches wide), later known as sopranos, in Styles 1, 2, and 3. The koa taropatch and abalone-trimmed Style 5-K uke were introduced in 1922. (Style 5 was available in mahogany only in 1941 and 1942.) Just as earlier eras had a banjo family and a mandolin family, the rising popularity of Hawaiian music prompted Martin to expand the uke family to include the concert (7 5/8 inches wide) in 1925 and the tenor (8 15/16 inches wide) in 1928. Paul Gillette/WC*

♦ *Gibson Uke-1. Gibson entered the ukulele market in 1927 with three models, the plainest of which is Style 1. The tag was supplied by the Los Angeles Steamship Co. Gruhn Guitars/WC*

♦ *Regal Art Moderne ukulele, early 1930s (center). The typical mail-order house offered buyers a great variety of choices at low prices. This is the deluxe version of the Art Moderne, with pearloid fingerboard, and it listed for about $4, a dollar more than the wood-fingerboard version. Sam Calveard/WC*

♦ *Gibson Uke-3. Gibson's most expensive ukulele has fingerboard inlays patterned after those of Gibson's midline banjo, Style 3. Gruhn Guitars/WC*

♦ *Regal Harold Teen ukuleles, circa 1930. The ukulele was a serious instrument to makers like Martin and Gibson, but it also had a novelty image. Most mail-order houses in the 1930s carried a line of cheaply made but imaginatively decorated ukuleles. Harold Teen ukes feature scenes from a popular syndicated comic strip, drawn by Carl Ed, that ran from World War I into the 1950s. The model was also available in yellow. Walter Carter/WC*

PART TWO

◆ ◆ ◆

*The Guitar Steps Forward,
1930s to Current Times*

From the 1850s into the 1920s, a variety of new guitar designs surfaced. Some were outlandish, such as Lyon and Healy's giant 21-inch–wide Conservatory Monster. Some that seemed to be good ideas sank, like the harp guitar with its rack of sub-bass strings. Some were good ideas whose time would not arrive until decades later, like Gibson's carved top guitar and the Larson brothers' steel-stringed flat top—both turn-of-the-century innovations.

Essentially, the guitar rested on an evolutionary plateau from the 1850s into the 1920s, at least in part because of the perfection of C. F. Martin's design. A contributing factor was the playing public's preference for instruments other than the guitar. As a secondary instrument, the guitar was not subject to the same competition among manufacturers and the resulting race for innovation as the banjo and mandolin. The closest the guitar came to challenging the banjo or mandolin was through Hawaiian music from 1915 into the 1920s.

A significant factor in the evolution of the guitar in the late 1920s was a demand for louder instruments. The demand for greater volume first affected banjo evolution in the 1920s and continued to be the strongest force in new fretted instrument design through the next three decades.

At the same time, two technological advances in related fields were changing the musical instrument industry dramatically. The first advance, the phonograph, actually dates back to the late 1800s, but it did not muster full force in affecting popular culture until after World War I. Recordings made all kinds of music available to people who otherwise had access only to the music played by local performers or touring bands. The second advance was radio. The first commercial station signed on the air in 1919, and music quickly became even more readily available, and more cheaply than records. From 1920 to 1925 radio and record companies engaged in heated competition, with radio forbidding its artists from making records, and vice versa. With the resultant flood of accessible music, many different styles became popular. In addition to classical music and the "popular" music from Broadway and "Tin Pan Alley" in New York, such styles as "race" or blues, early jazz (later revived as "Dixieland"), and country music gained footholds in the music marketplace. In the late 1920s the guitar began to emerge as a sort of common denominator—the instrument most versatile and portable, best able to fill a role in an ensemble or accompany a solo performance.

Players with influential styles appeared in every genre, among them Eddie Lang in jazz, Lonnie Johnson in blues, and Jimmie Rodgers and Maybelle

Carter in country. In a replay of the European guitar scene of the late 1700s, as soon as the guitar became widely popular, it evolved like wildfire. The 1930s would be the most important decade in the history of the guitar, with more innovations—especially successful innovations—than any other period.

The guitar's impending rise was signaled by the appearance of the first tenor guitars. Just as the tenor banjo, or mandolin-banjo as it was called in its early years, owed part of its initial popularity to the ease with which a mandolin player could switch to it, the tenor guitar offered a shortcut for tenor banjo players to switch to the increasingly popular guitar. One of the earliest advertisements for a tenor guitar, placed by the Elias Howe Co. of Boston (the inventor of the sewing machine was also an instrument maker) in the July 1927 issue of *The Crescendo*, illustrated the change on the horizon in public taste: "Get the latest. An ideal instrument for those who cannot devote their full time to intensive study.... Can be tuned and played like the tenor banjo or ukulele."

Popular music in the late 1920s, was becoming louder and louder. The advent of electronic amplification raised the volume of radios and record players. The early five-piece jazz bands had given way to larger groups that would eventually swell to a dozen or more pieces. A guitarist no longer competed only with like instruments in a fretted instrument ensemble but vied with trumpets, trombones, and saxophones. The little parlor guitar from the previous century just could not cut it in the popular music of the day.

Even without the advent of records, radio, and big band music, the parlor guitar had no future after 1928. That was the year Andrés Segovia first performed in the United States, turning the world of classical and semi-classical music—the world of the parlor guitar—on its ear. The Spanish-born guitarist was more than a musician; he was practically an entire new style of music. He had revolutionized the guitar repertoire with transcriptions of lute music and other classical works, and his dedication had inspired some European symphonic composers to create works specifically for the guitar. He took this new classical guitar music around the world, touring South America in 1918, performing in Paris in 1924, and hitting New York in January 1928.

As with many later guitar stars, from jazzers to rockers, Segovia had a guitar as influential as the music he played on it. It was made in Spain, where in the early 1800s luthiers had branched off in a different evolutionary direction from the rest of Europe. Around 1850, when C. F. Martin was refining his X-bracing pattern and developing the American flat top guitar in Nazareth,

Pennsylvania, Antonio de Torres in Spain was perfecting fan-pattern bracing and other designs that would characterize the modern classical and flamenco guitars. After Torres, several Madrid makers came into prominence, among them Manuel Ramirez. Segovia's guitar was made in Ramirez's shop by his foreman Santos Hernandez, who would later gain fame in his own right.

The muted resonance of a typical American parlor guitar was no match for the hardy, robust sound of Segovia's guitar. In the hands of Segovia, the Spanish-made guitar captured the classical audience so completely that there was soon no one left to protect the tradition of the parlor guitar against the onslaught of new designs.

The importance of volume cannot be overstated. The quest for a louder guitar would be the driving force behind almost all the innovations of the 1920s and 1930s: the resonator guitars of National and Dobro, Martin's dreadnought-size flat tops, and Gibson's "advanced" (wider) archtops and large-bodied flat tops. When the limits of acoustic design were reached, the quest for volume would spark the invention and evolution of the electric guitar. Although experimentation continues on acoustic guitar design, the standard acoustic guitars of today were all well developed by the end of the 1930s.

◆ *Gibson L-5, signed December 1, 1924, by Lloyd Loar. (See page 169.)*

JAZZ AND ORCHESTRAL GUITARS
◆ ◆ ◆

Gibson f-Hole Archtops

The model that started the guitar on its rise to a position of dominance was an unlikely candidate for the leading role. It was conceived as a member of an improved mandolin family and introduced at a time when the mandolin was well on its way out of fashion, having been displaced by the tenor banjo. Its chances of survival were further lessened when the man who oversaw the moderately successful models left the company only two years after the line was introduced. The key man, of course, was Lloyd Loar, the company was Gibson, and the model was Gibson's first *f*-hole archtop guitar, the L-5.

Orville Gibson had implemented the concept of a carved top and back on the guitar and mandolin in the 1890s. By the 1920s several of the Gibson company's competitors had introduced carved-top mandolin models, but Gibson still owned the carved-top guitar market. In late 1922 the L-5 debuted as part of the new Style 5 Master Model line, which featured violin-type *f*-holes rather than the oval or round soundhole of earlier Gibson instruments.

Like the Style 5 mandolin, mandola, and mandocello, the L-5 guitar of the 1920s was the finest instrument of its kind from any maker, but then, other makers showed little interest in quality archtop guitars. They were busy making banjos or, in the case of Martin, content with their traditional flat top design guitars.

By the end of the 1920s, however, the guitar had begun to encroach on the banjo's popularity, and many musicians found that the L-5's archtop design, with maple back and sides, provided a desirable combination of banjo and flat top guitar characteristics. The L-5 was not quite as loud or percussive as the tenor banjo (which by that time had a modern tone ring, flange, and resonator), and it did not have the mellow tone or sustain of a rosewood-body flat top guitar, but for a combination of volume, attack, and sustain, the L-5 had no equal.

At the same time, individual guitarists began to gain some recognition. The first great jazz guitarist, Eddie Lang, began making records in 1926, and his instrument of preference was the L-5. In country music, Maybelle Carter had started out on a cheap Gibson flat top in 1927 but by 1929 was picking out her distinctive bass-string melody runs on an L-5.

By the late 1920s the archtop guitar had become the fretted instrument best suited for the horn-based bands of the day. Nevertheless, Gibson's *f*-hole archtop line of 1930 still consisted of one and only one model, the L-5, an indication that perhaps even Gibson was unaware of the superiority of its own creation. The wake-up call came in 1931 when Epiphone, one of the prominent banjo makers of the late 1920s, tried to swamp Gibson with a full line of nine "Masterbilt" *f*-hole archtops, plus related tenor models. Gibson responded immediately. From 1931 to 1933 Gibson introduced three new 16-inch models— some of them as ornate in appearance as the L-5, but none higher in quality— and two smaller, 14¾-inch models. In 1933 the competition heated up with the entry of Gretsch, which began marketing its own line in addition to distributing Harmony *f*-hole archtops and the odd-shaped Kay-Kraft roundhole archtops.

In late 1934 Gibson made a move to elevate its instruments a step above the competition. The four 16-inch *f*-hole models were "advanced" to a body width of 17 inches. Within a year, the smaller models were also advanced, to 16 inches, and two new 14¾-inch models joined the line. In addition, a new super wide, super deluxe model was introduced in late 1934. It was 18 inches wide and a great deal more expensive than any guitar Gibson or anyone else was making. With a leather-covered case it was priced at $400 and named accordingly—the Super 400.

The Super 400 was the pinnacle of archtop design—a standard for all who followed. And follow they did. Epiphone and Gretsch came with new models as large or larger than the Super 400. The two most respected individual archtop makers, John D'Angelico and Elmer Stromberg, had been making guitars modeled after the 16-inch L-5, though slightly wider. In 1936, D'Angelico began building 17- and 18-inch models; by 1940, Stromberg was building 17⅜- and 19-inch guitars.

By World War II the electric guitar was catching on and the archtop was on its way out as the dominant style of guitar. Gibson, the first major manufacturer of quality archtop guitars, became the last in the early 1980s, when it discontinued the L-5 and Super 400. The Heritage company, founded by former Gibson employees and located in Gibson's former plant in Kalamazoo, reintroduced acoustic archtops in 1985. By the beginning of the 1990s, demand was back on the rise, prompting Gibson and others to announce plans to reenter the market. In the meantime, a growing number of individual luthiers have begun making archtops, and some of their works bring the highest prices of any new fretted instruments.

♦ *Gibson L-5, signed December 1, 1924, by Lloyd Loar (pages 167, 168 and below). The L-5 is Gibson's first archtop with f-holes, a fingerboard raised off the top, and two parallel braces or "tone bars" (oval-hole models have H-pattern bracing, with two parallels plus a lateral brace). It may not be the first guitar ever made with these features (see page 216), but it is undoubtedly the first high-quality guitar of its type. The earliest L-5s—like all other Gibson guitars from about 1905 into the 1920s—have birch back and sides, even though catalogs specify maple. After Loar's departure in 1924, the L-5 and the K-5 mandocello (which has the same body as the L-5) were brought up to the standards of a Style 5 mandolin, with curly maple back and sides. Gibson's perception of the guitar as a mandolin family instrument is evident in the tuners and neck construction. Like a fancy mandolin, the L-5 has ornately engraved plates and mother-of-pearl buttons. The neck is maple with an ebony center laminate, like that of Gibson's high-end mandolins. The other guitars in the Gibson line at this time have a mahogany neck. L-5s from 1922 to 1934 (and a few later examples) are 16 inches wide and are not generally as highly sought by players as the later 17-inch examples, but collectors do value them as much as the larger version. A Loar-signed L-5 is quite rare—with an estimated production of 15 to 30 instruments—and highly sought by collectors. Joseph Nuyens/DL*

♦ Gibson L-5, 1929 (upper left). In a period when banjos are gaudy displays of rhinestone and pearloid, the L-5 has a conservative, stately aura like a piece of fine old furniture. The only concession to flashy fashion is the fingerboard, where in 1929 the pearl dot markers were replaced with large pearloid blocks. By the end of 1929 the end of the fingerboard would be squared off. Washington Street Music/BM

♦ Gibson L-5CP, 1949 (upper right). Cutaway body and natural finish were introduced as options in 1939. Cutaway models were originally called Premier, and a cutaway L-5 would be labeled L-5P. After World War II, the term Premier was dropped, but instrument labels carried the P designation until 1949, when cutaways were designated by a C after the model name. The label on this example has both designations: L-5CP. The pickguard-mounted pickup unit was introduced in 1948 and was available with single or double pickups. Gibson called it a "conversion" pickup; collectors refer to it as a "McCarty" pickup, after the man who developed it, Gibson vice president (later president) Ted McCarty. Gruhn Guitars/WC

♦ Gibson L-5, 1937. With the introduction of the 18-inch Super 400 in 1934, Gibson's 16-inch archtops moved up an inch in size. With the larger body, the L-5 was given more body binding, an inlay at the first fret, a wider peghead, a point at the end of the fingerboard, and an X-braced top. A more massive tailpiece, bound f-holes, and enclosed tuners were soon to follow. The top bracing returned to parallel bracing by 1939. Gruhn Guitars/DL

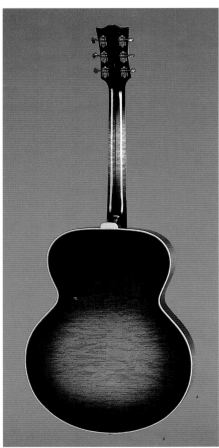

♦ *Gibson L-5CT, 1959. Gibson designated thinbody models by a T in the model name. The thinline electric guitars of the 1950s were quite successful, but an acoustic thinbody was a different matter altogether. The thin version of the L-5 is commonly called the George Gobel model because it was designed for and played by the comedian, but it would be an exaggeration to say he popularized it—during the L-5CT's three years of production, from 1959 to 1961, Gibson shipped a total of 43 of this model. The lack of volume inherent in the thinbody design prompted the original owner of this guitar to order a McCarty pickup unit. Tom Van Hoose/BM*

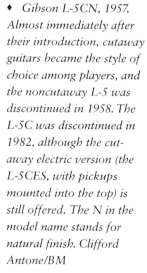

♦ *Gibson L-5CN, 1957. Almost immediately after their introduction, cutaway guitars became the style of choice among players, and the noncutaway L-5 was discontinued in 1958. The L-5C was discontinued in 1982, although the cutaway electric version (the L-5CES, with pickups mounted into the top) is still offered. The N in the model name stands for natural finish. Clifford Antone/BM*

♦ *L-10, 1936 (upper left). The L-10 was the second of Gibson's f-hole archtop models, introduced in 1931. Originally it was a rather plain guitar, with black finish and dot inlay. With the introduction of the L-12 in 1934, the L-10 adopted the fancy ornamentation of the L-12 but kept the black finish and nickel-plated metal parts. Later in 1934, with the increase in body sizes, the L-10 took on a dramatic new look, with bullet-shaped fingerboard inlays, a vase with curlicues on the peghead (replaced by the diamond a year later), checkered top binding, and a reddish sunburst top finish. While the models below and above it prospered, the L-10 did not. It was discontinued in 1939. Kinsey's Collectibles/BM*

♦ *Gibson L-7, 1933 (upper right). The L-7 was introduced in 1932. It occupied the lowest rung among Gibson's large f-hole archtops (then 16 inches wide, soon to be 17 inches), but it was the most successful. With the L-7 a player could buy a guitar that was almost as good as an L-5 but at no more than half the price. The earliest L-7s have fingerboard inlay appropriated from the Nick Lucas flat top, which, ironically, was the top model of the flat top line. Bill Camp/BM*

♦ *Gibson L-12, 1934 (lower left). The L-12 was introduced in 1933 and was the most expensive of Gibson's three midline 16-inch models: the L-7 at a list price of $125, the L-10 at $150, and the L-12 at $175. The L-12's fingerboard and peghead inlay patterns reflect some of the fancy ornamentation common on banjos of the period and its gold-plated metal parts make the L-12 appear even fancier than the L-5. The difference in quality, however, is evident in the difference in price—the 1934 L-5 listed at $250. W. T. Smith/BM*

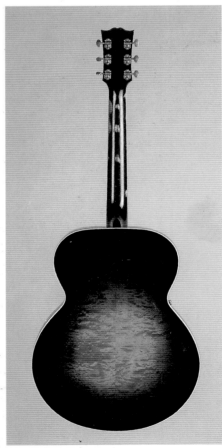

172

♦ *Gibson L-12, 1935 (center, above and opposite lower right). With the increased body size, the L-12 was given a new look. It was the first Gibson with the double-parallelogram fingerboard inlay that would later be featured on several of Gibson's most popular models, including the L-7, the ES-175 electric archtop, and the Southerner Jumbo (SJ) flat top. The new peghead inlay design was used for seven years on the L-12. In 1941 the L-12 became the first Gibson archtop to wear the "crown" peghead ornament that remains the standard today on many of Gibson's higher models. The playing wear on the neck reveals that the L-12, unlike the L-10 and lower models, has the three-piece neck of the high-end models. The L-12 was discontinued in 1955. Gruhn Guitars/DL*

♦ *Recording King M-5, 1939. By 1935 Gibson had begun making guitars under other brands for sale by various distributors. Recording King was a house brand of the Montgomery Ward company. The high-end, off-brand models are of a quality equal to the midline Gibson brand models, but no Recording King, Kalamazoo, Cromwell, Fascinator, or any Gibson budget-brand instrument has the adjustable truss rod of a Gibson. Gruhn Guitars/WC*

♦ *Gibson L-7, 1940 (upper left and right). The L-7 received this vase-and-curlicue peghead inlay shortly before going to the larger body. The fancy, rectangle-enclosed fingerboard inlay was introduced on the L-12 but was moved to the L-7 with the advance in body size of 1934. By the time this example was made, a three-piece maple neck had replaced the one-piece mahogany. The pickguard is not original. Blackwell Brothers/BM*

♦ *Gibson L-7C, 1963 (lower left). The L-7's ornamentation was revamped in 1942 with double-parallelogram fingerboard inlay and crown peghead ornament. The cutaway, first offered on the L-7 in 1948, quickly became the preferred version. The noncutaway model was discontinued in 1956, whereas the L-7C lasted through 1971. The DeArmond "floating" pickup, which is mounted on the fingerboard rather than on the top, was and still is a common accessory on acoustic archtops. Gruhn Guitars/DL*

♦ *Gibson L-50, circa 1944 (lower right). The L-50, introduced in 1932, began as a very small guitar —14¾ inches wide and 17½ inches long—with a round hole and flat back. The length was increased and f-holes were added in 1934. In 1935, following the lead of the higher models, the body width was increased to 16 inches, where it remained until the model's discontinuation in 1971. This example has the wartime peghead banner, which reads "Only a Gibson is good enough." The banner is common on several wartime flat top models but rarely seen on the L-50. Paul Carnes/WC*

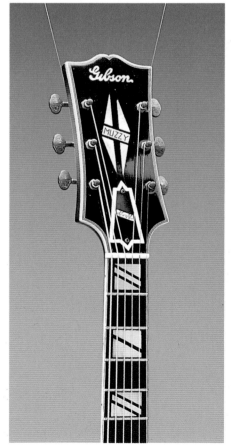

◆ *Gibson Super 400, 1934 (this and opposite page). Gibson's stand on archtop f-hole guitars could not have been made any clearer in 1934 had the company spelled it out in 10-foot-high letters. Gibson archtops were going to be the biggest thing the industry had ever seen—literally. As the four existing 16-inch models went to 17 inches, Gibson went the extra inch by introducing the first 18-inch f-hole model—the Super 400. Virtually nothing on the Super 400 is plain. The fancy engraved tailpiece is huge compared to the "trapeze" of the L-5 and other models. The seven-ply top binding is two layers better than that of the advanced L-5. Even the bridge base is ornamented with small triangular pearl inlays. The peghead, larger than that of other Gibson models, is inlaid with a slashed-diamond pattern, and the fingerboard is also inlaid with large slashed blocks. The inscribed "Muzzy" and "M. M." refer to the original owner, Muzzy Marcellino. The gold-plated tuners and the mounting plates are engraved. Though the body width across the upper bouts is relatively small compared to the lower bout, the body shape is identical to that of the 18-inch, Orville-style guitars that the company made only in its first few years. It produced the desired results: a big sound that could cut through in a big band, a big splash of visual features, and a big boost for Gibson's reputation. This example was one of the first, if not the first, Super 400. Hank Risan/BM*

♦ *Gibson Super 400PN, 1939.
In addition to the natural finish
and cutaway options of 1939, the
Super 400 (and all the 17-inch
archtops) underwent a change in
top bracing when the X-bracing
of the original Super 400 was replaced by two parallel tone bars.
The body was widened across the
upper bouts by 1⅜ inches in 1937.
In 1938 the open-back, engraved
tuners of the early Super 400s gave
way to sealed-back Grover Imperials with their identifiable stair-step
keys, which in turn yielded to these
sealed-back Klusons with buttons
of amber-colored Catalin in mid-
1939. This guitar is one of only 18
cutaway Super 400s with natural
finish shipped prior to World War
II. Tom Van Hoose/BM*

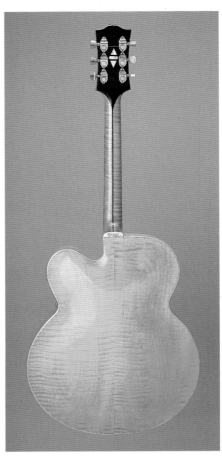

♦ *Gibson Super 400C, 1967. This
guitar has a nonstandard finish,
but despite the word "Custom" on
the truss rod cover, it may have
been experimental rather than custom-ordered. The uniform dark
back and sides finish with natural
top was never standard on any
Gibson f-hole archtop, but it is the
same finish that became standard
in 1968 on the Everly Brothers flat
top model. Whether the Everly's
finish was inspired by a custom-
ordered Super 400 or whether this
guitar served as a prototype for the
Everly's finish, this Super 400C is
unique. Lloyd Chiate/BM*

◆ *Gibson Super 300, 1953 (upper left). Before World War II, buyers of 17-inch archtops had several models to choose from, but the customer wanting an 18-inch Gibson had to buy the Super 400 or nothing. In 1948 the Super 300 was introduced to offer the same big sound at less than half the price—$200 for a Super 300 versus $425 (without case) for a sunburst Super 400. The 300, offered in sunburst finish only, is the same size and construction as the Super 400 but is trimmed more like an L-7. The Super 300 was last made in 1954, but a cutaway version, the Super 300C, was introduced that same year. It was discontinued in 1958. Tom Van Hoose/BM*

◆ *Gibson Johnny Smith, 1964 (center). All of Gibson's electric archtops—even the electric versions of the L-4, L-5, and Super 400, which have solid spruce carved tops—have pickups mounted directly on the top, thus destroying much of the instrument's acoustic capability. Jazz guitarist Johnny Smith played a D'Angelico archtop with a floating pickup, and when given the chance to endorse a Gibson model, he opted for the same concept. The body shape is that of a small D'Angelico, and the top is X-braced. Although the scale is a half inch shorter (25 inches), the neck ornamentation is that of a Super 400. The tailpiece is the same design as the L-5. The Johnny Smith model, also offered with two pickups beginning in 1963, stayed in the line until Smith's endorsement agreement ended in 1989. Clifford Antone/BM*

♦ *Gibson Kalamazoo Award, circa 1980. The Johnny Smith model was successful enough that Gibson made several very limited runs of a super-fancy archtop with floating pickup, the Citation, between 1969 and 1981. In addition, the Kalamazoo Award was introduced as a catalog model in 1978. Like the Johnny Smith and the Citation, it is 17 inches wide and a fully acoustic guitar, and it was always cataloged with a pickup. With an abundance of elaborate pearl inlay—in the peghead, wood pickguard, and tailpiece insert, as well as in the fingerboard—it was the most expensive model in the catalog. It was discontinued in 1984. Gruhn Guitars/WC*

♦ *Epiphone Recording D, late 1920s. (See page 182.)*

JAZZ AND ORCHESTRAL GUITARS

♦ ♦ ♦

Epiphone Archtops

Epiphone was one of the leading banjo companies of the 1920s, with some of the most ornate models of any maker. By the end of the decade, Epiphone saw the end of the banjo era coming and became one of the few banjo makers to switch successfully to guitars. In 1931 Epi beat Gibson to the gate by introducing a full line of *f*-hole archtops—nine archtop guitar models (plus an *f*-hole flat top) and five tenors—to compete with Gibson's lone model, the L-5.

◆ *Epiphone Recording C, late 1920s (upper left). Unlike practically all other manufacturers who tried to compete with Gibson, Epiphone was already familiar with the construction of archtop guitars. Granted, these small, ornate Recording Series models of the late 1920s are fundamentally different from the orchestra model f-hole guitars of the 1930s, but the higher-grade Recording models are indeed archtop guitars, and when the demand rose for archtops, Epiphone was ready and willing to give Gibson a run for the money. The pickguard has been removed. Dennis Watkins/DL*

◆ *Epiphone Recording D, late 1920s (lower left and previous page). Recording Series models are designated with letters, starting with A for the cheapest and going through E, the most expensive. Model A has a flat top and back, B has a flat top and arched back, C and higher have a carved spruce top and an arched back of laminated maple. The primary difference between a Recording C and D is in ornamentation. This example has been refinished. Gruhn Guitars/WC*

182

Taking a cue from Gibson's Master Model Series and Mastertone lines, Epiphone named its guitars the Masterbilt models.

Through the 1930s Epiphone provided fierce competition for Gibson. Epiphone catalogs, like Gibson's, were filled with photos of prominent musicians. Epi introduced the large-body Emperor shortly after Gibson's Super 400 and "advanced" its body sizes several years after Gibson did. Epi's natural finish option followed Gibson by only a year or so. It was no coincidence that Epiphone models were always a fraction of an inch larger than their counterparts in the Gibson line.

Gibson had the last word in the competition, however. In the years following World War II, Epiphone fell on hard times. The Stathopoulo family sold it in 1953 to the C. G. Conn company, which was and still is one of the most prominent makers of band instruments. The family regained ownership in 1955 but was unable to resume full-scale production. In 1957 the Chicago Musical Instrument Co., parent company of Gibson, bought Epiphone. C. M. I.'s purpose had been to acquire Epiphone's acoustic bass manufacturing equipment, but soon an entire new line of Epiphone guitars was being designed and manufactured by Gibson in its Kalamazoo plant. Although electric models have been the best selling of the postwar Epiphone models—both in the pre-Gibson and Gibson years—the company's reputation was built on banjos of the 1920s and acoustic archtops of the 1930s and early 1940s.

♦ *Epiphone De Luxe, 1933 (above, below and opposite). The De Luxe was the standard-bearer of Epiphone's 1931 Masterbilt line of f-hole archtops. It was designed to outshine Gibson's L-5, and to that end it is a little larger and noticeably fancier, with rope-pattern purfling around the top, fancy fingerboard inlays, and a very ornate peghead. The three-segment f-holes are characteristic of Epiphone archtops of the early 1930s. Lloyd Chiate/BM*

♦ *Epiphone De Luxe, 1947 (upper left and right). All Epiphones went through a number of design changes in the 1930s. In 1934 the floral motif of the De Luxe peghead inlay grew into the vine pattern of this example. In 1937 the body width increased to 17⅜ inches, standard one-piece cutouts replaced three-segment f-holes, the "cloud" fingerboard inlay appeared, and the peghead dip moved to the center. In 1939 high-end Epis were fitted with a Frequensator (for "frequency compensator") tailpiece, which allowed for a longer string length on the bass strings between the bridge and tailpiece. The gold-plated tuner enclosures are embossed with the stylized E—actually a lower-case epsilon, the Greek letter e—that would eventually become standard on all Epiphone peghead logos. Although the De Luxe, like the Gibson L-5, was no longer the top model in the line after the mid-1930s, it was still highly respected by musicians. Gruhn Guitars/DL.*

♦ *Epiphone Deluxe, 1962 (center). After its acquisition of Epiphone, Gibson continued to offer four of the acoustic archtop models upon which Epiphone had built its reputation: Emperor, Deluxe (the spelling changed in 1954), Triumph, and Zenith. As the added pickup on this example indicates, there was virtually no demand for purely acoustic archtops in the 1960s. In fact, beginning in 1965, all Epiphone acoustic archtops were available by special order only. From 1959 to 1970, Gibson made a total of 61 Deluxes—47 with sunburst finish and 14 natural. On this example the vine peghead inlay has been simplified, but the old Epiphone script logo remains. The effect of the Frequensator tailpiece design was apparently negligible; on this example, as on numerous other Epis, the Frequensator has been reversed in order to accommodate shorter string lengths. Lloyd Chiate/BM*

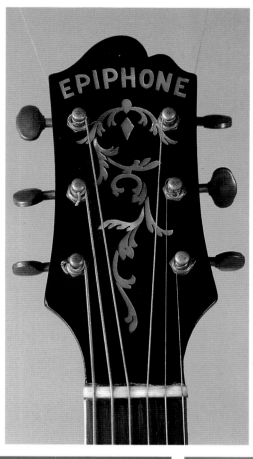

♦ Epiphone Tudor, 1934 (upper left and right). The Tudor held a place two models below the De Luxe in ornamentation, but it was still a professional-quality instrument, with a body width of 16 3/8 inches, maple back and sides, fancy fingerboard inlay, and gold-plated metal parts. The ornate banners of the earlier Masterbilt peghead had left the Tudor by 1934. The fancy appearance of the leafy vine is diminished somewhat by the lack of binding and the block letter logo. The model was discontinued by 1937. Gruhn Guitars/DL

♦ Epiphone Deluxe custom, 1967 (lower left). This is a standard Gibson-made Deluxe except for the oval hole and, of course, the pickup. Epiphone's Howard Roberts model is very similar in construction, with an oval soundhole and a floating pickup, but with a pointed cutaway shape. The customer who ordered this instrument apparently wanted the Roberts soundhole and pickup on a Deluxe. According to company shipping totals, this was one of the last two natural finish Deluxes ever made by Gibson. Lloyd Chiate/BM

♦ Epiphone Triumph, 1944 (lower right). One of the original Masterbilts, the Triumph was a step below the Tudor and was one of the more successful Epiphone archtop models. It lasted all the way to the end of Gibson's American production of Epiphones in 1970. Third Eye Music/BM

♦ Epiphone Emperor, circa 1941 (upper left and right, and lower right). The Emperor was introduced in 1936 to compete with Gibson's Super 400. At 18½ inches wide, it is a half inch larger than its competition. The Emperor body has rather small upper bouts, like the earliest version of the Super 400, but Epiphone did not follow Gibson in widening the upper bouts. The Emperor carries the vine peghead inlay of Epiphone's former top model, the De Luxe, but the "wedge" fingerboard inlay was no doubt inspired by the slashed blocks of the Super 400. On prewar Emperors, the inlays are three pieces of mother-of-pearl with wood spacing between them forming a V. With the exception of the Super 400, the Emperor is more highly regarded than any other large-body archtop by a major manufacturer. Gruhn Guitars/WC

♦ Epiphone Emperor Regent, 1951 (lower left). Although the Regent had been an early tenor model in the Masterbilt line, Epiphone began using the term in the late 1940s to denote a cutaway model. Epi uncharacteristically lagged 10 years behind Gibson when it came to cutaway guitars, offering the first ones in 1949. On postwar Emperors, the three-piece fingerboard inlays have no wood between pieces, but the wedge pattern is delineated by the use of a contrasting piece of abalone pearl for the center section. Ross Music/BM

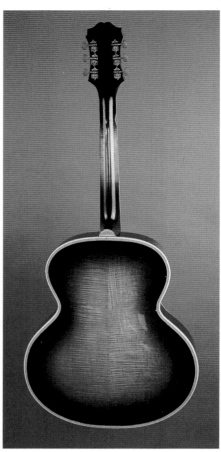

♦ Epiphone Emperor, 1962. Gibson never offered a noncutaway acoustic Emperor. This guitar was nevertheless made by Gibson from a neck and body left over from the period before Gibson's purchase of Epiphone in 1957. The lack of a truss rod cover suggests that the neck may have been made much earlier—before 1951, the year Epiphone introduced a truss rod that adjusts at the peghead. Gibson-made acoustic Emperors are quite rare, with a total of only 20 sunburst and 15 natural-finish guitars made from 1959 to 1970. Blackwell Brothers/BM

♦ Howard, early to mid-1930s (above). In contrast to Gibson and its many budget brands, Epiphone is not known to have made guitars for sale under other brands, but this instrument suggests that perhaps Epi did make some for a dealer or distributor named Howard. Except for the brand name and the fleur-de-lis on the peghead (an ornament associated with Gibson), this guitar is generally similar to Epi's Broadway model, which was one step below the De Luxe. Gruhn Guitars/DL

◆ *Gretsch Synchromatic 160, early 1940s. Model 160 is the lowest model of Gretsch's three 17-inch Synchromatics, but this example, with a natural finish and contrasting tortoise-grain plastic binding, has a most striking visual effect. Mike Larko/BM*

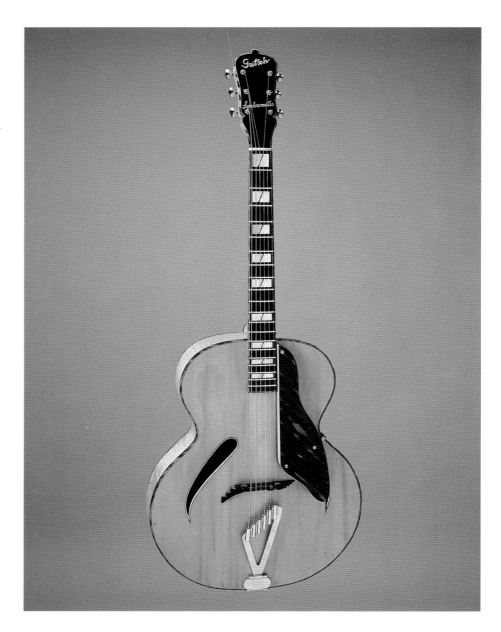

JAZZ AND ORCHESTRAL GUITARS
◆ ◆ ◆

Gretsch Archtops

Friedrich Gretsch, a German immigrant, formed a tambourine company in Brooklyn, New York, in 1883 that his son Fred Gretsch, Sr. took over after the founder's unexpected death in 1895. The similarity of tambourine rims to banjo rims led the company into banjo production by 1910 and into drum production by 1920. Today, the best-known Gretsch instruments from that period are the Broadkaster banjo and drum lines—known not for their quality but because in 1950 their makers forced the Fender company to change the name of its new solidbody electric guitar from Broadcaster to Telecaster. By the end of the 1920s Gretsch was a prominent distributor of band instruments as well as fretted instruments.

Gretsch offered a tenor guitar (although it may have been made by another company) as early as 1927. In 1933 Gretsch entered the archtop guitar market with a line of four Gretsch-American guitars, all 16 inches wide with maple back and sides. Model numbers corresponded to prices: $25, $35, $65, and $100. The 1933 catalog also included Harmony *f*-hole guitars and Kay-Kraft round-hole archtops.

The Gretsch line followed a different course from those of other banjo companies that ventured into the guitar market. Epiphone and Vega, for example, produced some of the most ornate banjos of any maker, but their guitars of the 1930s were plain by comparison. Gretsch, by contrast, had marketed a utilitarian line of banjos but was soon going to almost any length to create a visual sensation with its guitars. The Synchromatic models, introduced in 1939, sported a "synchronized" bridge with a stair-step bass-side footing and a "chromatic" tailpiece that also had a stair-step design. The 17- and 18-inch Synchromatics were easily distinguishable from their competitors by their teardrop-shaped or "cat's eye" soundholes.

Although the Gretsch models generally were not constructed as well as Gibsons or Epiphones during the 1930s and early 1940s (most that survive today need extensive repair and restoration), they were regarded as excellent instruments in their day. In the early 1950s Gretsch switched emphasis from fancy archtops to electric guitars and went on to create some of the most visually stunning models of the postwar period.

Fred Gretsch, Sr., retired in 1942, leaving management of the company to his sons. Fred Gretsch, Jr., managed the operation briefly before serving in the Navy. His brother, William Walter (Bill) Gretsch, took over from 1942 until his death in 1948. Fred Gretsch, Jr., then assumed the presidency until he sold Gretsch to the Baldwin company in 1967. Baldwin moved production to Booneville, Arkansas, in 1970 and sold Gretsch to Charlie Roy in 1978. The last American-made Gretsches were produced in 1981, but some were assembled in Mexico as late as 1984. In early 1985 Fred Gretsch, son of Bill Gretsch, acquired rights to the Gretsch name. In 1990 he introduced a new line, based on (but not replicating exactly) the company's classic models.

♦ *Gretsch No. 150, mid-1930s. Model 150 was only offered from 1935 through 1938, but it set the stage for the eye-catching Gretsch models of later years with its elaborate pearl peghead inlay and fancy engraving on the pickguard. Kinsey's Collectibles/BM*

◆ *Gretsch 6015, 1953 (upper left). Model 100 was the top model of the original Gretsch-American Orchestra models of 1933. It was also available with a round sound-hole until the late 1930s. In 1939, it was given Synchromatic status, but as the lowest model of the Synchromatic line. By the time this example was made, it was one of the cheapest of all Gretsch arch-tops. In 1949, it was known only by its catalog number, 6014. A natural-finish version, Model 6015, was available by 1951. The name was changed again to Corsair in 1955, and the model was finally discontinued in 1960. Irate Musician/BM*

◆ *Gretsch Synchromatic 400, early 1940s (upper right). Like Gibson's Super 400, Gretsch's 400 listed for $400. The fingerboard inlays are slashed "humptop" blocks rather than the slashed rectangular blocks of the Gibson model, and Gretsch's slashes go the opposite way from Gibson's. After 1951 the Synchromatic 400 was available by special order only. At that time it was given standard f-holes and named the Synchromatic 6040 (sunburst) or 6041 (natural). It was renamed the Eldorado in 1955 and continued in the line through the 1960s. The pickguard has been removed. John Brinkman/DL*

◆ *Gretsch Constellation, 1955 (center). The Constellation began as the Synchromatic 6030 (sunburst) and 6031 (natural), the cheaper of two 17-inch cutaway models introduced in 1951. By 1955, the model had lost the "Synchromatic" designation on the peghead, and the Synchromatic bridge and tailpiece had been replaced by a symmetrical bridge and a "G" tailpiece. The model was discontinued in 1960. Pittsburgh Guitars/BM*

◆ *Martin C-3, 1933. The fanciest of the C series has the fingerboard inlay of a Style 45 flat top, but no Martin archtop ever had the abalone pearl body trim of a Style 45. The C-3 was last made in 1934. Gruhn Guitars/DL*

JAZZ AND ORCHESTRAL GUITARS

◆   ◆   ◆

Martin Archtops

Throughout its history, Martin has consistently made one thing, and one thing only, better than any other company—flat top guitars. Aside from ukuleles (which are, after all, very similar to guitars in construction), practically every attempt by Martin to expand, from mandolins in the early part of the twentieth century to electrics in the later part, was ultimately unsuccessful.

♦ *Martin C-1, 1941. The C-1, the cheapest of Martin's three-model C-line, debuted in 1932. It is essentially the same guitar as a 000-18 flat top, but with an arched top and a bit more binding. The C-1 and C-2 were discontinued along with all Martin archtops in 1942. Thom Humphrey/BM*

Martin's archtops of the 1930s are a case in point—hardly worthy of a footnote except for the fact that they were made by Martin.

Martin archtops were archtops in top only. The top was carved or pressed, but the back and sides and neck were essentially those of a flat top. While every successful archtop maker used maple for the back and sides, Martin made archtops the same way it made flat tops—mahogany back and sides on the low-end and rosewood on the high-end models. The flat top characteristics even extended to a round soundhole on early examples.

The flat top design proved awkward, to say the least, when it came to setting the neck on a Martin archtop. The body, designed to accommodate the low bridge of a flat top, was not altered to compensate for the height of an arched top and the added height of a standard archtop bridge. Consequently, the neck has to be set at a radical angle. The angle is so great that when a Martin archtop is laid on a flat surface, the back of the guitar does not touch the surface. Only the end of the body and the end of the peghead make contact.

An additional problem was the size of the guitars. The first were 15 inches wide (Martin's largest flat top size at the time), followed by two smaller models at 14⅛ inches wide. Finally, in 1935 Martin came out with fancier, bigger F-size models. At 16 inches wide, they were the widest guitars Martin had ever made, but they were too little, too late to save Martin from archtop oblivion. By that time Gibson had advanced its best models to 17 inches wide and introduced the 18-inch Super 400. Martin mercifully laid all its archtops to rest in 1942.

If Martin archtops had had a superior sound, then what are now viewed as an awkward neckset angle and unsuitable woods would, no doubt, have been quickly adopted by other makers and made the standards for all archtops. Not surprisingly, however, the sound of a Martin archtop was closer to that of a Martin flat top—without the power—than it was to the Gibson or Epiphone archtops that set the standards in the 1930s. It is not unusual to find Martin archtops that have been converted to flat tops, and (again, not surprisingly) they typically have an excellent flat top sound.

♦ Martin C-2 12-string, 1932. Martin entered the archtop market with three C-series models. The first to appear was the middle model, the C-2, in 1931. The C-size bodies are those of the OM flat top models —15 inches wide with a 14-fret neck (Martin 000 models still had a 12-fret neck). The flat top styling extends to the round soundhole. The first f-hole C-series guitars appeared in 1932, but some round-hole examples were made into 1933. This custom-ordered 12-string is one of only six documented Martin 12-strings made prior to World War II, three of them archtops. One difference—and an important one in Martin history—between the C-series arch-tops and their flat top counterparts is the peghead logo. At the time, no Martin flat top guitars had a front peghead logo. The earliest C-2s have "Martin," without the initials, inlaid vertically on the peghead. The initials were soon added. In mid-1932 all sol-id-peghead models were given a decal logo on the peghead (except for those with pearl logo). In late 1933 the logo style, with initials, was appropriated for the Style 45. The pick-guard has been removed, and the tailpiece and bridge are not original. Mark O'Connor/DL

◆ *Martin F-9, 1935. Martin introduced 16-inch F-series archtops in 1935, the fanciest of which is the F-9, with rosewood back and sides. A total of 72 F-9s were made from 1935 to 1942, when all Martin archtops were discontinued. The body size and shape resurfaced with the introduction of the M-size flat top in 1980. Roy Acuff Museum, Opryland USA/WC*

♦ *D'Angelico Excel, 1937.*
(See page 201.)

JAZZ AND ORCHESTRAL GUITARS
♦ ♦ ♦

Stromberg, D'Angelico, and D'Aquisto

One of the more mystical skills of guitar making is the hand carving of an archtop guitar. Archtops require more time, more costly materials, and a higher degree of craftsmanship than any other style of guitar. Not surprisingly, a new acoustic archtop is one of the most expensive fretted instruments on the market, and the best examples from the premier independent archtop makers— Elmer Stromberg, John D'Angelico, and James D'Aquisto—are among the most revered of all fretted instruments. Although there have been highly respected independent makers of flat tops, resonator guitars, and solidbody electrics, none has achieved the respect among collectors as these three archtop makers. Their instruments have few peers on the vintage market, with many examples ranking in value with a Loar-signed F-5 mandolin or a Gibson Les Paul Standard solidbody electric from 1958 to 1960. Some of their large-body cutaways are rivaled only by such vintage market leaders as the prewar Martin D-45 flat top and Gibson's solidbody Explorer and Flying V models of 1958.

♦ *Stromberg G-1, circa 1940. Charles Stromberg began making banjos and drums in Boston around 1905. His son Elmer, born in 1895, joined him in the business in 1911. Most of the early banjos made by Chas. Stromberg and Son were rather plain and cheap, but later higher-grade models were of very fine quality. In the 1930s Elmer began concentrating on archtop guitars. The G-1 was the cheapest in the line. Early models, like Gibson's early L-5, were 16 inches wide, but by the time this instrument was made, Stromberg had followed Gibson's lead and increased the size of the G-1 to 17 3/8 inches. Gruhn Guitars/DL*

◆ *Stromberg Deluxe, mid-1930s. This Deluxe is very similar to the G-3 of the same period. In this early version, the body is 16 3/8 inches wide. After the mid-1930s, most Strombergs do not have a backstripe. This inlay is quite wide and ornate—an unusual feature on a guitar from any maker. Stromberg's pegheads, even on most of his fanciest models, are exceptions to the dressy mother-of-pearl inlay patterns and multiple bindings preferred by practically all major makers. He achieved the look of multiple binding with an overlay of alternating plastic layers whose edges are then beveled. The ornamental logo is not inlaid but engraved through the top layer of plastic. Gruhn Guitars/WC*

♦ *Stromberg G-3, mid 1930s (upper left). The G-3 is slightly fancier than the G-1, with some extra body binding and a gold-plated tailpiece. A Stromberg of the 1930s is not comparable in quality to the Gibson Super 400 or the Epiphone Emperor from the same period. Early Strombergs have a pressed plywood back, and the bracing system includes two parallel braces plus three lateral braces. Later 1930s models are braced like Gibsons of the same period, with two parallel braces. Music Ground/BM*

♦ *Stromberg Deluxe, early 1950s (lower left and right). Stromberg revamped his design in the 1940s. The f-holes went from three-piece to a single segment, and the bracing changed to a single diagonal. The laminated, beveled-edge pickguard gave way to a multiple-bound pickguard. Body size was increased on the Deluxe and the plainer G-1 and G-2 to 17 3/8 inches. These models and the larger Master 300 and Master 400 are the instruments upon which the Stromberg reputation rests. Hank Risan/BM*

♦ Stromberg Master 400, 1953 (above and opposite upper right). At 19 inches wide, the Master 400 is a huge instrument, and it produces a comparable sound—loud enough to be heard unamplified in a big band setting. This example's pickguard is unusual; most Master 400s have a stair-step pickguard shape. The engraved mother-of-pearl peghead ornamentation is unusual for a Stromberg and is somewhat suggestive of Stromberg's major competitor in the handmade archtop field, John D'Angelico. Hank Risan/BM

♦ Stromberg Master 400 cutaway, 1955 (center and below). Cutaway Stromberg guitars are very rare. This is one of the last of an estimated 640 guitars made by Elmer Stromberg. He died in 1955, only a few months after the death of his father. Hank Risan/BM

◆ *D'Angelico, 1933. John D'Angelico was born in New York in 1905. At the age of nine he was apprenticed to a granduncle whose shop produced violins, mandolins, and flat top guitars. D'Angelico established his own shop in 1932 to make violins, mandolins, and archtop guitars. His first guitars were modeled after Gibson's L-5 in body shape, fingerboard inlay, pickguard shape, triple-bound top, and even the unbound f-holes. The tapered point on the end of the fingerboard is like that of the pre-1929 L-5. D'Angelico's early creations are 16½ inches wide, a half inch wider than the L-5 of 1933. From the back, the triple binding, the pattern of sunburst on the sides and neck, and the gold-plated Grover tuners make this guitar look like a Gibson L-5. The only giveaways are the neck, which has three laminates in the center, compared to one on the L-5, and the smooth oval shape of the tuner buttons, which are different from those of the L-5. Lloyd Chiate/BM*

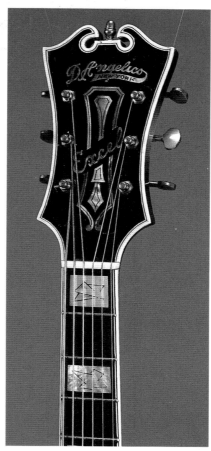

♦ D'Angelico Excel, 1937. By 1937, D'Angelico had standardized his models. Like all other makers, he had begun making larger guitars after 1934, when Gibson advanced its 16-inch models to 17 inches and introduced the 18-inch Super 400. D'Angelico offered models A, A-1, B, and Excel—all 17 inches wide—and the New Yorker at 18 inches. He modernized his f-holes with straight-line cuts in 1937 but returned to a more conventional shape in 1939. In addition, he developed many stylistic features that distinguish his work from that of any other maker. The Excel peghead is radically different in design and ornamentation from the snakehead type of D'Angelico's earliest guitars. The cutout and button—more formally, the broken-scroll pediment and cupola— became as well known as D'Angelico's signature, and the peghead design was eventually used on the New Yorker model as well. Michael King/DL

♦ *D'Angelico Excel, 1937 (upper right). The tailpiece on this guitar illustrates the transition from D'Angelico's early simple tailpieces to the large stair-step design that appears on some examples as early as 1937. This tailpiece has a slanted string-anchor angle but does not have the stair-step shape. The initials on the pickguard are those of Tom Johnston, for whom the guitar was made. Jay Levin/BM*

♦ *D'Angelico Excel, 1947 (center). Natural-finish guitars came into vogue in the years following World War II. Lloyd Chiate/BM*

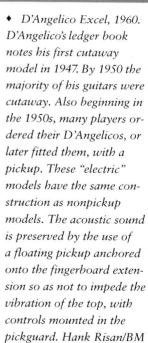

♦ D'Angelico Excel, 1960. D'Angelico's ledger book notes his first cutaway model in 1947. By 1950 the majority of his guitars were cutaway. Also beginning in the 1950s, many players ordered their D'Angelicos, or later fitted them, with a pickup. These "electric" models have the same construction as nonpickup models. The acoustic sound is preserved by the use of a floating pickup anchored onto the fingerboard extension so as not to impede the vibration of the top, with controls mounted in the pickguard. Hank Risan/BM

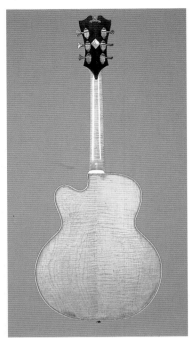

♦ *D'Angelico Excel Cut-away, 1954. D'Angelico had standard model specifications, but they were subject to change according to the whim of the maker or the customer. This Excel was a custom order from George Cabantino of New York City, whose name is engraved into the 12th-fret marker. "Top Steel" is engraved into the marker at the 15th fret. Gruhn Guitars/DL*

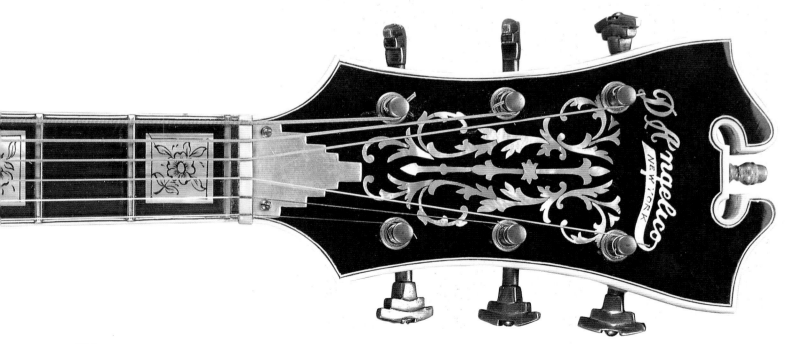

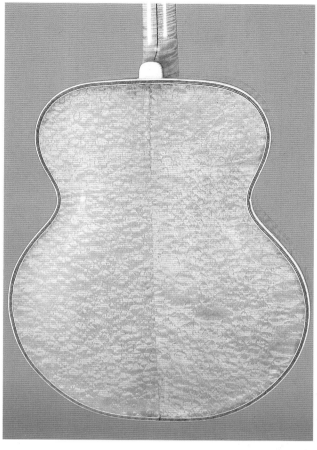

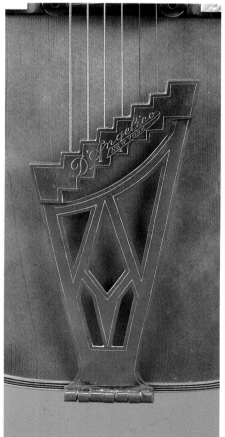

◆ D'Angelico New Yorker, 1946. John D'Angelico's ledger books note guitar models, serial numbers, and the dates they were finished, beginning in 1936. The first 36 instruments were mostly Excels, with a few Style B and "Special" models. In October 1936 the first New Yorker was notated. It is D'Angelico's only 18-inch standard model, although he made some plainer, custom-ordered 18-inch guitars and at least one 19-inch instrument. Like the top-line models of other makers, D'Angelico's New Yorker was not in such great demand as the models below it, particularly the Excel. D'Angelico's stair-step tailpiece was made by the Joseph Schaffner Company in Manhattan. The pearl signature piece was made and installed by the Louis Handel Company, which was located around the corner from D'Angelico's shop. The slashes on the fingerboard inlays of this example are engravings into a single piece of pearl rather than the result of separate pearl pieces. The neck construction, with one center laminate, represents a transition from earlier necks with three center laminates to later single-piece necks. Anonymous collector/DL

◆ *D'Angelico New Yorker, 1954 (above). This New Yorker varies from standard only by the pearl blocks on the fingerboard, which lack the usual slashes. The pickup is a DeArmond floating type. Hank Risan/BM*

◆ *D'Angelico New Yorker Cutaway, 1955 (center). The combination of natural finish, cutaway body, and New Yorker trim makes examples like this among the most valuable archtop guitars ever made. The slashes on the fingerboard inlay are formed by the use of two or three separate pieces of pearl. The f-holes on this guitar and later examples are slightly narrower than those of earlier years. Hank Risan/BM*

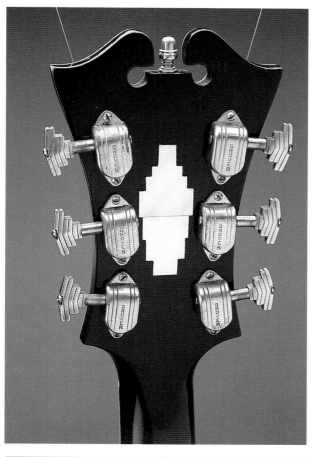

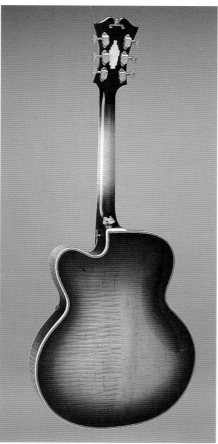

♦ D'Angelico Excel Cutaway 1000, 1954. This guitar combines features of the Excel and New Yorker. Many players ordered this style but D'Angelico never gave it its own model name. He listed it in his ledger under various terms, including Excel Special, Excel New Yorker, New Yorker Special (17 inch), and Excel Cutaway 1000. Excel features include the 17-inch body and the peghead shape; among the New Yorker features are the peghead inlay and extra layers of binding. The fingerboard inlays are New Yorker–style with an additional engraved border line, but other examples have the nonslashed blocks of the Excel. The floating pickup dates from a later era than the guitar and is the type used on Gibson's Johnny Smith model. As the engraving on the 15th-fret inlay shows, the addition of this pickup type was no coincidence—this guitar was made for Johnny Smith. Hank Risan/BM

♦ *D'Angelico Excel Cutaway, 1961. The New Yorker peghead ornament and extra binding identify this guitar as another Excel/ New Yorker combination. The DeArmond pickup was one of the most popular floating pickups among jazz players. The plastic pickguard has begun to deteriorate, a common condition. Gruhn Guitars/DL*

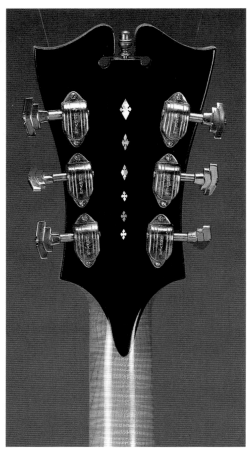

♦ *D'Angelico G-7, 1950s (above). The neck, pickguard, and tailpiece are authentic D'Angelico elements, but the plywood body was made by either Code or United, both New Jersey-based companies. These guitars may be D'Angelicos but they have neither the sound nor the value of a "real" D'Angelico. Gruhn Guitars/DL*

♦ *D'Angelico Excel Special, 1960 (left). The model name continues to change in D'Angelico's ledger, but this guitar is essentially a standard example of the Excel/New Yorker style. Joe Sanders/BM*

◆ *D'Angelico Excel Special, 1964. This guitar is undated in D'Angelico's ledger book and erroneously listed as being made for "Howard" rather than Harold Bradley, a top Nashville session guitarist. Its serial number, 2159, indicates it was the sixth from the last guitar made by John D'Angelico before his death in 1964. D'Angelico's model nomenclature can be confusing. The Special designation on this guitar may have been due to the three-ply peghead binding, which is different from the single-ply of the standard Excel, the five-ply of the Excel/New Yorker, or the nine-ply of the standard New Yorker. D'Angelico continued to refine his designs throughout his life. In 1963, and after 20 years or more of fitting his guitars with one-piece necks, he returned to a laminated construction, as illustrated by this unusual green-brown-green center laminate. Harold Bradley/WC*

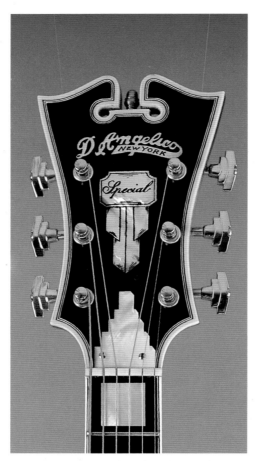

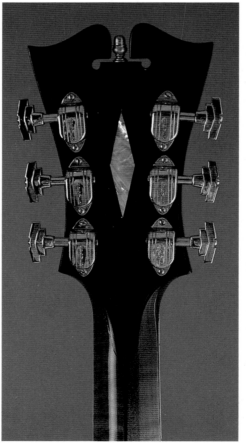
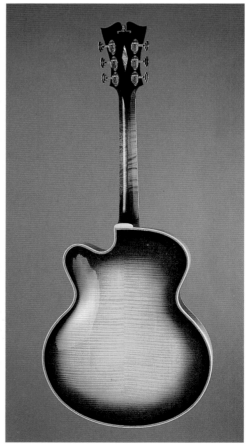

♦ D'Aquisto New Yorker Special, 1972. James L. D'Aquisto was born in 1935 in Brooklyn, New York. At the age of 17 he met John D'Angelico and began working in D'Angelico's shop. After D'Angelico died in 1964, D'Aquisto began making guitars under his own name, adopting the two basic D'Angelico models: the 17-inch Excel and 18-inch New Yorker. He began a series of design changes in 1967 that, by the time this guitar was made, had evolved into his own distinct style. In addition to his hand-made guitars, he designed models for Fender/Japan and Hagstrom. On this guitar, D'Angelico's broken-scroll pediment on the peghead has been smoothed to a circular shape. The soundholes have been widened and smoothed to an S shape. The pickguard and tailpiece are made of ebony in a simpler design than earlier examples. A scroll, with "New Yorker" engraved in script, has replaced the skyscraper peghead ornament. This example has no fingerboard inlay. Hank Risan/BM

◆ *D'Aquisto Excel, 1984 (upper left, right and opposite left). D'Aquisto's sunburst finish differs from that of most makers. The shading is more gradual and the outer edges are a lighter, more reddish brown. Anonymous collector/DL*

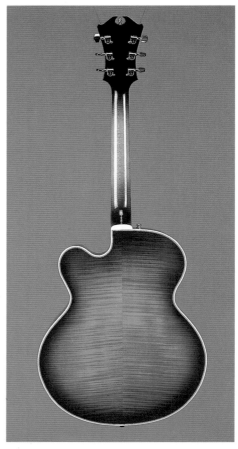

◆ *D'Aquisto New Yorker Delux, 1985. D'Aquisto's New Yorker Delux is a fancy model, 18 inches wide, with the slashed-block inlay of the traditional D'Angelico New Yorker. Jonathan Levin/JL*

◆ D'Aquisto New Yorker Classic, 1987. D'Aquisto introduced the New Yorker Classic in 1985 and offered it with a 17- or 18-inch body width. His goal was to make the entire guitar out of wood, and to that end, he used wood for the bindings, tuner buttons, tailpiece, and truss rod cover. The light body finish is a gleaming contrast to the dark shades of the ebony parts. David Levin/JL

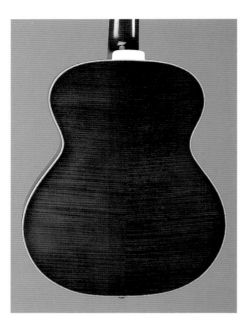

♦ *D'Aquisto 12-string, 1973. As is the case with most individual luthiers, D'Aquisto's guitars vary widely according to his customers' requests. This 12-string archtop, ordered by Sal DiTroia, is unusual in several ways, including the oval soundhole, the lack of ornamentation, the slotted peghead, the finish color, and the relatively small, 15-inch body width. Joseph Nuyens/DL*

♦ *Wilkanowski, late 1930s.*
(See page 217.)

JAZZ AND ORCHESTRAL GUITARS

♦ ♦ ♦

Other Archtop Makers

Many manufacturers and individual luthiers have experimented with archtop guitar designs since Orville Gibson's first efforts in the late 1800s. The most successful innovations, of course, were the Gibson company's in the 1920s and 1930s, and the most successful makers continue to use the classic designs of Gibson and the refinements of D'Angelico and D'Aquisto as a base.

◆ Shutt, circa 1915 (above). The Shutt company made some obscure but historically important mandolins and guitars that prompt a footnote every time Gibson's Style 5 series is mentioned. This unusual asymmetrical tulip-shaped guitar has f-holes and a fingerboard raised off the top. It also has a 1915 patent notice, which predates Gibson's introduction of these features. Shutt's ideas may have been on the right track, but the timing was bad. Mandolins were on the way out, and guitars would not come into vogue for another 10 or 15 years. Kevin Macy/BM

◆ Kay-Kraft, circa 1930 (left). The Kay company was still called Stromberg-Voisinet when these odd archtops appeared in about 1930. The body shape, the pearloid peghead overlay, and, on this example, the engraved pearloid fingerboard suggest that these guitars were designed to compete with Epiphone's Recording series. Three Kay-Kraft models were available: A, B, and C, with mahogany, maple, and rosewood back and sides, respectively. This example has a mahogany body, but the engraved pearloid fingerboard inlay is fancier than even that of a Style C. The gold stenciled design on the top is common but not pictured in catalogs. These small guitars were the archtop version of the parlor guitars, and like the small flat tops, they were no match for the powerful f-hole archtops that dominated the 1930s. They were offered through about 1935. Pearls Before Swine/BM

♦ Regal Prince, 1930s (above). Regal, a large mail-order house based in Chicago, made some of its own models, sold others under the Regal brand that were made by other makers, and also provided guitars to other distributors for sale under the distributors' brands. The Prince model illustrates some of the confusion as to who made what. The prince on the peghead inlay is merely a troubadour when the same figure appears on the Slingerland Troubadour banjo and some Washburn banjo models. Midwest Guitar Exchange/BM

♦ Wilkanowski, late 1930s (left). From the look of this guitar, one could guess that W. Wilkanowski was primarily a violin maker. He was born in Poland in 1886 and became a full-fledged violin maker at the age of 17. By 1920 he was living in the United States and working for the Oliver Ditson company. In 1938 he worked for Gretsch. The great majority of his output was violins—an estimated 5,000 instruments—but he made as many as 30 guitars. Dennis Watkins/BM

◆ *Vega Super Deluxe, circa 1940. Vega is best known as a prominent banjo maker, and the company's status as a major guitar maker in the 1930s and early 1940s is almost forgotten. Like some banjo makers—notably Epiphone and Gretsch— Vega foresaw the end of the banjo boom and made a successful transition to guitars. Not only did Vega offer a full line of acoustic and electric models, but the company was at the forefront of electric guitar innovation. Vega continued to offer guitars after World War II, but the company's highest-quality models were still banjos. The Super Deluxe was introduced around 1940. With a body width of 18 1/2 inches, it was obviously designed to compete with Gibson's Super 400 and Epiphone's Emperor. The vase-and-flower peghead inlay derives from that of two earlier Vega banjo models—the Tu-ba-phone #3 and the Whyte Laydie #7. The pearl block fingerboard inlays have almost imperceptible "slash" marks parallel to the strings. The heavy gold-plated tailpiece includes the company name and the model name, along with Vega's star logo. It is similar to a Stromberg tailpiece, and Elmer Stromberg may have been associated with Vega during this period. Gruhn Guitars/WC*

♦ National 1135, 1951. Even after National switched its emphasis to electric instruments in the mid-1930s, it never tooled up to make conventional wood-body guitars. National made its own necks and electronics but bought guitar bodies from other companies, primarily Gibson and Harmony. This model has the body of a Gibson L-7. The neck is National's "Stylist" heel-less design, introduced in 1949. Jim Reynolds/DL

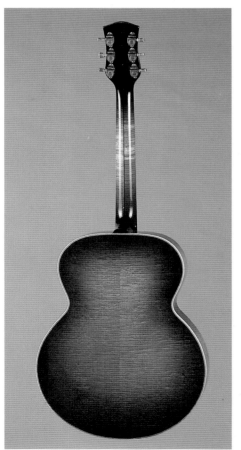

♦ National, 1950. The National-Gibson connection is obvious on this guitar. The fingerboard inlay is from Gibson's top-of-the-line flat top, the J-200. The body is that of a Gibson L-5, complete with a Gibson work-order number stamped inside. Unlike the great majority of Nationals with a Gibson body, this guitar also sports a neck made by Gibson. This is of the same construction as a J-200 or L-5 neck, although the heel is carved to a different shape. The tuners, too, are standard L-5 type. Jim Reynolds/DL

♦ *Harmony Mel Bay Model A, late 1940s. Mel Bay's name is well known to the thousands of self-taught guitarists who learned to play from a Mel Bay chord book. While Bay himself played a D'Angelico New Yorker, among other models, the guitars he endorsed cover a broader range of quality than those of any other endorser—from a D'Angelico to this cheap Harmony model. Dave's/WC*

♦ *Maccaferri, 1953. Mario Maccaferri came into prominence in Europe in the late 1920s as a guitarist. In the early 1930s, he designed guitars for the Selmer company in France with an internal sound reflector and a D-shaped soundhole. The most famous player of a Maccaferri was the legendary Belgian jazz guitarist Django Reinhardt. Maccaferri moved to the United States and in 1952 introduced several instruments made entirely of plastic. Both guitar models have f-holes, but the one on the right has a flat top. Although Maccaferri continued to believe in plastic—as late as 1990 he performed a recital on a plastic violin—the plastic guitars were not successful. His plastic ukuleles, however, were runaway best-sellers in the 1950s. Walter Carter/DL*

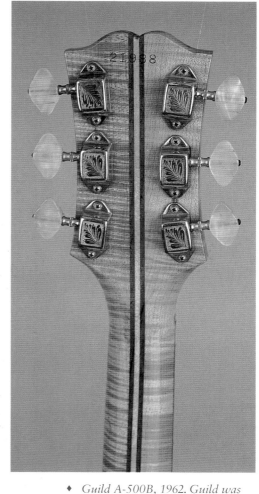

♦ *Guild A-500B, 1962. Guild was founded in New York in 1952 by Alfred Dronge. With a staff built around former employees of the Epiphone company, Guild quickly gained a reputation for acoustic and electric archtops. The company outgrew its New York facility in 1956 and moved to Hoboken, New Jersey. With the folk music boom of the 1960s, Guild successfully switched emphasis to its flat top line. The company relocated to Westerly, Rhode Island, in 1967. The A-500B (A for acoustic, B for blond) is the acoustic version of the Stuart 500 electric, although this example has been fitted with a floating pickup. Except for the Artist Award, which always came with a floating pickup, Guild discontinued its acoustic archtops in 1973. Jay Levin/WC*

♦ *Guild Artist Award, 1987. The Artist Award started out in the 1950s as the Johnny Smith model, which was similar to the A-500 but with a floating pickup. When Smith moved his endorsement to Gibson in 1961, Guild changed the model name and delineated the Artist Award from the Johnny Smith by this larger peghead shape and fancy inlay. The Epiphone influence is reflected in the fingerboard inlay, which is the same as that of Epi's post–World War II Emperor. Guild's tailpiece, similar in concept to that of Gretsch's Synchromatic models, is known as the "lyre" tailpiece. Harry Mulanax/DL*

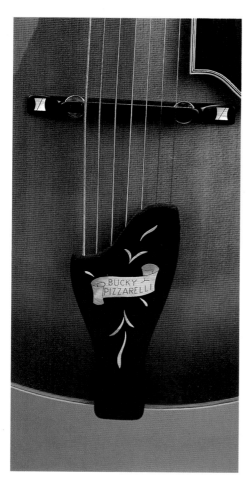

♦ Benedetto 7-string, 1981. Robert Benedetto finished his first guitar in 1969, using wood from his family's kitchen table for the back and sides. Based for many years in Clearwater, Florida, and since 1990 in Stroudsburg, Pennsylvania, he makes about 30 to 35 instruments per year. Benedetto fine-tuned his carving skills by concentrating almost exclusively on violins from 1983 to 1987. Seven-string models account for about 15 percent of his orders, and this early one was made for musician Bucky Pizzarelli. Robert Benedetto/BM

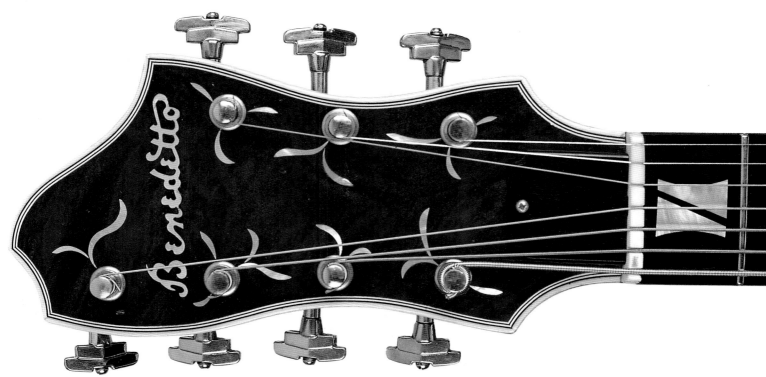

◆ *Benedetto Manhattan,*
1989 (upper left). Benedet-
to's Manhattan model is the
plainest of his five standard
models, but its lack of
heavy ornamentation lends
it a certain elegance. Like
D'Angelicos and advanced-
body Gibsons in the mid-
to late-1930s, Benedetto's
guitars have an X-braced
top. Gruhn Guitars/WC

◆ *Monteleone Eclipse,*
1984 (upper right). John
Monteleone has made few-
er guitars than mandolins,
but his guitars are respected
as highly. The Eclipse is
16 3/8 inches wide with
asymmetrical X-pattern top
bracing. Monteleone also
makes a Hot Club A model
f-hole archtop and a Hot
Club B model flat top with
D-shaped soundhole, plus
an 18-inch Radio City f-hole
archtop. Dixie Guitars/BM

◆ *Collings, 1992 (lower left*
and right). Bill Collings of
Austin, Texas, gained a
reputation in the 1980s as
one of the best makers of
steel-string flat top guitars.
By the 1990s, his reputa-
tion extended to archtops.
Collings guitars display a
great variety of styles and
appointments. This as-yet-
unnamed 17-inch model
has some D'Aquisto-like
features, such as ebony
pickguard, ebony tailpiece,
and S-shaped soundholes.
Bill Collings/Reagan
Bradshaw

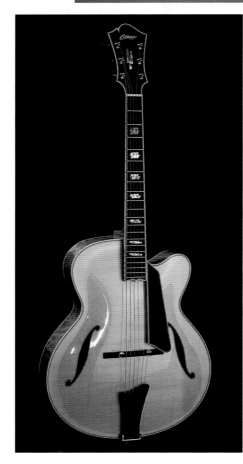
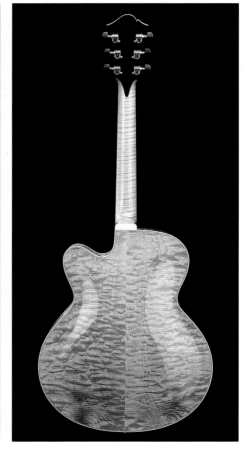

◆ *National Style 4, circa 1930. (See page 233.)*

RESONATOR GUITARS
◆ ◆ ◆

Nationals and Dobros

Up until the mid-1920s, every guitar or mandolin produced its sound by means of strings imparting vibrations to a piece of wood that formed the top of the instrument. The quest for greater volume pushed guitar makers to increase the size of guitars and refine their basic designs. In the 1920s the more imaginative designers saw that only a new concept of sound generation would achieve more volume. The most successful new concept, of course, would be the electric guitar, on which the strings do not move the top of the guitar at all but rather "move" a magnetic field to produce an electric signal.

Just before the development of the modern electric guitar, however, a new acoustic guitar appeared that was as different from the standard acoustic as the electric would be. The new design, like the electrics that followed, abandoned the idea that the top of the guitar must vibrate. Instead the bridge was mounted directly on a bowl-like aluminum cone, and when this "resonator" vibrated, it created a volume level that would overpower any standard guitar of the 1920s and rival the banjo. For a brief period, roughly from 1928 to 1933, these new resonator guitars were at the forefront of guitar evolution.

Resonator guitars were marketed primarily under the National, Dobro, and Regal brands. The early history of National and Dobro is a complex web of corporate and personal intrigue, and the controversy began even before National was formed. The National name first appeared on banjos made in Los Angeles by John Dopyera and his brothers. John, one of six children of a Czechoslovakian family living in Los Angeles, is generally credited with inventing the resonator guitar, but all the Dopyera brothers—John, Rudy, Emil (Ed), Louis, and Robert—were involved with National and Dobro in various financial and production roles. John was the constant experimenter (before resonator guitars he had taken out several patents unrelated to instruments), and both the National and Dobro companies were founded on his work.

Enter George Beauchamp, a vaudeville performer who played violin and steel guitar. Beauchamp's vision of additional amplification was a guitar with a phonograph horn coming out of the back, and he had the Dopyeras build him such an instrument. Then, depending on whose story is to be believed, either Beauchamp suggested building a guitar using a mica diaphragm like that used in phonographs, or John Dopyera built on his own experiments with various diaphragm materials, shapes, and configurations. In the end Dopyera came up with a system that rested the bridge on top of three aluminum cones. Dopyera's cones functioned as small megaphones opening toward the back of the instrument rather than projecting toward the front. It was a seemingly backward approach, but it worked, nevertheless.

John Dopyera applied for a patent on April 9, 1927, and the new guitars went into production. As if the tri-cone resonator system were not revolutionary enough, the new guitars were made of "German silver" or "nickel silver" (an alloy of copper, zinc, and nickel) and plated with nickel. The guitars bore the National brand, which the Dopyera brothers had registered in 1926 for their banjos. All of the 1927 models had a square, hollow, metal neck for Hawaiian

♦ *National Style 1 roundneck, 1929. National introduced squareneck tri-cone guitars in 1927 and roundnecks a year later. No doubt, the tri-cone's immediate association with Hawaiian music helped squareneck models outsell roundnecks by about three to one. Because of the relative rarity of roundnecks and the fall in popularity of Hawaiian music, roundneck tri-cones are much more valued by collectors today. Style 1 is the plainest of the four original models, with no engraving on the body. The posts on the tailpiece are to accommodate loop-end strings. Rick King/BM*

playing, which may have reflected Rudy Dopyera's former association with Herman Weissenborn, the best-known maker of hollow-neck, koa wood Hawaiian guitars. In 1928 roundneck models were added to the line. In the meantime, Beauchamp scored a publicity coup by putting a tri-cone prototype into the hands of Sol Hoopii, the most popular Hawaiian guitarist of the day.

The new National tri-cones had a high-tech look, with their gleaming nickel-silver bodies and varying degrees of ornamental engraving, but their high volume—seven times louder than a standard guitar, according to Dopyera—was their strongest selling point. The future looked so rosy that Dopyera and Beauchamp lined up investors and incorporated the National String Instrument Corporation on January 16, 1928. Beauchamp was appointed general manager, John Dopyera factory superintendent, and Paul Barth (Dopyera's nephew) assistant factory superintendent.

By the end of 1928 Dopyera had become dissatisfied with Beauchamp's management and formally resigned on February 19, 1929. He quickly developed a new, single-cone resonator design with the cone opening toward the top of the guitar and the bridge connecting to the cone by way of an eight-armed "spider" which rested on the edge of the cone or, in later versions, on indentations in the side of the cone. Dopyera telescoped the name Dopyera brothers to come up with the brand name Dobro and filed for a patent under Rudy Dopyera's name on June 29, 1929. The bodies of the new models were made of plywood and thus much cheaper to produce than the National tri-cone models. The immediate success of the Dobros forced National to develop a line of single-cone models to compete.

When John Dopyera left National, brothers Louis and Robert retained their financial interest in the company, and the infighting at National continued. Some stockholders pulled out, selling their shares to Louis Dopyera, and George Beauchamp was eventually ousted. Interestingly, Beauchamp's downfall, like Lloyd Loar's at Gibson a few years earlier, may have been a result of his determination to develop an electric guitar. Unlike Loar, however, Beauchamp was ultimately successful. Working with Paul Barth, he took a prototype to the man who handled National's metal stamping, Adolph Rickenbacker, and the company they formed made history with the first modern electric Hawaiian guitar.

National and Dobro existed separately for several years. Louis Dopyera eventually gained a controlling interest in National, and in or about 1932

♦ *National Style 1 roundneck, circa 1933. Although National listed only four engraving patterns on tricones, many variations exist. The most common is this wriggle pattern around the border of an otherwise plain Style 1. Collectors refer to it as "Style 1½." Gruhn Guitars/DL*

National and Dobro merged to become the National-Dobro company. Even though the two brands shared a factory and owned all the patents for resonator guitars, they behaved like separate companies, each with its own lines and its own distributors. In addition, Dobro—but not National—granted an exclusive license to the Regal company of Chicago in 1933 to make resonator guitars under the Dobro and Regal brands.

Resonator guitars were quite successful but only for a short time. As loud as they were, they were no match for an electric guitar. A viable electric guitar with a modern magnetic pickup was introduced by the forerunner of the Rickenbacker company in 1932. Again George Beauchamp, with Rickenbacker now, enlisted the aid of Sol Hoopii. By 1935 Hoopii had switched to an electric Hawaiian guitar, and he exerted the same influence on the electric market that he had earlier on the acoustic market. By the late 1930s, National turned its focus to electric instruments. Like most major manufacturers, the company diverted its production to support the war effort from 1942 to 1945. When World War II ended, National announced a line of resonator models but did not actually make any until a new, cheaper model appeared in the late 1950s.

The appeal and success of the various National and Dobro models is almost as complex and confusing as the company history. Despite their similarities in sound and concept, they are not interchangeable as far as players or collectors are concerned.

National's tri-cones were adopted by Hawaiian players, such as Hoopii, Benny Nawahi, and Jim and Bob, and are still identified with Hawaiian music. National's single-cone metalbody models caught on with blues players (who probably could not afford a tri-cone) and still retain that association in classic photos of such artists as Son House, Bukka White, and Blind Boy Fuller. Both single- and tri-cone models are highly regarded by today's blues players. The Regal-made metalbody Dobros, by contrast, may have been introduced too late, around 1935, to find acceptance among players of any style of music. To the ears of today's musicans, they do not sound as good as the National models, and that may have been true in the 1930s, too.

Judging by the number still around today, National woodbody models were moderately successful from a sales point of view but are generally viewed by players and collectors. alike as poor relations of the metalbody models. Dobro woodbody models did find a home in country music but probably would have been forgotten if not for Beecher (Pete) Kirby, better known as Bashful

Brother Oswald of Roy Acuff's band. Kirby joined Acuff's band in 1939, the year after Acuff joined the Grand Ole Opry, and almost singlehandedly kept up interest in the Dobro with, ironically, a heavily Hawaiian-influenced playing style. In the early 1950s the Dobro sound was carried into bluegrass music by Flatt and Scruggs bandmember Burkett (Uncle Josh) Graves, whose signature sounds were a blues lick and a banjo-type finger roll.

In 1942 National-Dobro was reincorporated as Valco, which combined the first initials of principals Victor Smith, Al Frost, and Louis Dopyera (although Valco was never used as a brand name). After World War II John, Ed, and Rudy Dopyera continued to make instruments under various brands. Family members reacquired rights to the Dobro brand in 1961 but sold them to Semie Mosely, maker of Mosrite electric guitars, in 1966. Dopyera family members formed the Original Musical Instrument company in 1967 to make resonator guitars under the Hound Dog brand, and they eventually regained the rights to the Dobro name in 1970. Today the company offers both wood-body models similar to the early 1930s Dobros and metalbody models, including some with the inverted National-type cone. In 1988 two former O. M. I. employees, Don Young and MacGregor Gaines, form-ed the National Resophonic company and began making instruments modeled after National's woodbody guitars, with single-cone metalbody models joining the line in 1992.

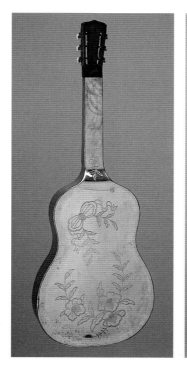 

◆ *National Style 2 square-neck, circa 1930 (this page and opposite). Style 2 is engraved with roses. A variation with the top engraving extending onto the cover-plate is known among collectors as "Style 2 ½." Except for a few models in the late 1930s, the entire neck on squareneck tricones is hollow and made of metal. Some players reverse the tuners so that the tuner buttons are on the top rather than the back of the peghead, which makes for easier tuning when the guitar is played in the lap. John Miller/BM*

♦ *National Style 2 ukulele, 1931. National offered single-cone ukulele versions of Styles 1, 2, and 3, but no Style 4. Several variations occur, including an earlier, larger version with screen holes in the coverplate. Bob Brozman/BM*

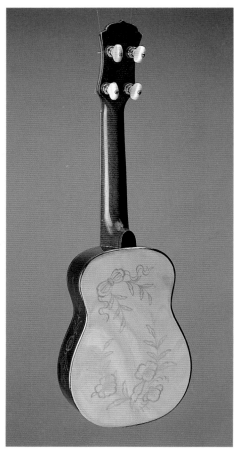

♦ *Styles 1, 2, and 3 plectrum, 1928 to early 1930s. National tenor and plectrum guitars in the Styles 1 through 3 went through several configurations. The Style 3 on the left is the earliest version, with three cones and a triangular body shape. The Style 1 on the right is the 1929 version, still with triangular body but with a single resonator cone. In 1930 the body shape changed to that of a conventional guitar, like the Style 2 in the center. Gruhn Guitars/WC*

♦ Style 4 roundneck, circa 1929 (upper left and right). The engraving becomes more elaborate as style numbers ascend. Style 4 features an intricate chrysanthemum pattern. Aside from slightly fancier ornamentation on the fingerboard and peghead, the only difference between tricone models is the degree of engraving. It made a considerable difference in price. The unengraved Style 1 listed originally for $125; Style 4 listed for $195. Jay Levin/BM

♦ Style 3 plectrum (center and above). Tenor and plectrum tri-cones were offered in Styles 1, 2, and 3 only. Style 3 tenor and plectrum models, with lily-of-the-valley engraving pattern, were the top of the tenor line, and they are not uncommon. Style 3 guitars, however, are quite rare. Once most guitar buyers chose to spend the money on a fancy tri-cone, they apparently went all the way to a Style 4. Gruhn Guitars/WC

◆ *National Style 4 square-neck, circa 1930. Style 4 remained at the top of National's tri-cone line until it was discontinued in 1940. Styles 1, 2, and 3 lasted until National's 1942 hiatus for World War II. Rick Schell/WC*

♦ *National tri-cone, 1928. This early roundneck has a nonstandard acanthus-leaf engraving pattern, possibly indicating that the company had not yet decided on a standard pattern for the Style 4 tri-cone model. The acanthus leaf is a common architectural ornamentation on columns. Mike Tepee/WC*

◆ National Style 97 square-
neck, 1936. Two new tri-
cone models were introduced in 1936, but with nickel-
plated brass bodies rather
than the German silver of
the original tri-cone series.
The brass-body tri-cones
were etched (sandblasted)
and then colored with en-
amel rather than engraved.
Style 97 has an ocean scene
on the back; Style 35 has a
lute player. Later Style 97s
have the same scene etched
but not colored. Unlike the
original tri-cone series or
the Style 35, squareneck
Style 97s have a solid wood
neck rather than hollow
metal. Dennis Watkins/WC

◆ National Triolian, 1929.
Tri-cones had been on the
market for a year or so
when Dobro's cheap single-
cone guitars forced National to come up with a less
expensive model. Cost-cut-
ting measures included a
wood body and a simple
round coverplate. The first
catalog depictions of the
Triolian show three cones
through the screen holes of
the coverplate—the source
of the "Tri" in the Triolian's
name—but a single-res-
onator design was quickly
adopted. The Triolian listed
at $45. Dennis Watkins/DL

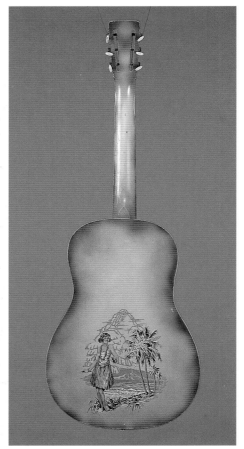

♦ *National Triolian, 1930. Throughout its 40-year history, National/Valco was always willing to try new materials. In 1930 the new material was Bakelite, and some Triolians from that year have a Bakelite neck. It proved unsuitable, however, as it is highly prone to warping. This body finish was called "polychrome," possibly in a reference to the multicolor scheme of earlier models. Polychrome Triolians have a uniform finish color, although they vary from one instrument to another, ranging from bright yellow to a bluish green. The Triolian was also available during this period with a yellow-to-brown sunburst finish, with no palm scene on the back. In 1937 the Triolian was given a simulated rosewood finish, with the wood grain painted on. Gruhn Guitars/DL*

♦ *National Triolian, late 1929. Perhaps the sound of the woodbody Triolian was too different from that of a metalbody tri-cone, or perhaps the National shop was not set up to work effectively with wood. For whatever reason, the wood body of the Triolian quickly gave way to a steel body. With the changeover, a silk-screened Hawaiian scene replaced the decal on the back. Like the woodbody models, this early metalbody has a painted fingerboard. Gruhn Guitars/WC*

♦ *National Triolian ukule-le, circa 1930 (above). National's early ukuleles are larger than the standard soprano uke. This example has the optional yellow-to-brown sunburst finish. Dennis Watkins/DL*

♦ *National Duolian, 1933 (center and upper right). By 1929 John Dopyera had introduced three woodbody Dobro models, the most expensive of which listed for $45—the same price as the cheapest National. In 1930 in an attempt to capture more of the budget market held by Dobro and, no doubt, in response to the onset of the Depression, National introduced the Duolian, with a list price of $32.50. The differences between the Duolian and Triolian are minor. The Triolian has a bound fingerboard, a neck of light-colored wood (probably basswood), and a polychrome or sunburst finish. The Duolian has no fingerboard binding, a mahogany neck, and a dusky greenish-gray "frosted duco" finish. Gruhn Guitars/WC*

♦ *National Style O, 1933. Style O was introduced in 1930. At $62.50, it filled the rather large gap between the Triolian and the tri-cones. Although the nickel plating gives the Style O an expensive look, the body is brass (or steel on the earliest examples). Hawaiian scenes are sandblasted into the body. Entertainer Bob Brozman, author of a book on National's resonator models, has recorded a dozen pattern variations on the Style O alone. A plain version was offered in 1930 and 1931 as the Style N. Walter Carter/WC*

♦ *National Style O square-neck, early 1937. In late 1934 National followed the lead of Gibson and Martin and switched to 14-fret necks on single-cone models. The changeover required a new body shape for the Style O, Triolian, and Duolian. A new etching pattern put palm trees on both sides of the resonator. Squareneck versions of the three single-cone models were available beginning in 1933. The diamond-hole coverplate appeared in 1935. The pickguard came in about 1936, but it is rarely seen because it tends to deteriorate with age, producing fumes that corrode the plating off the body. Gruhn Guitars/WC*

◆ *National Style O, 1939 (upper left and right). In 1937 the Style O was revamped a bit with parallelogram-shaped fingerboard inlays and an "ebonoid" (polished black plastic or Bakelite) peghead overlay. Square-necks from this period have an ebonoid fingerboard as well. Palm trees decorate the sides of the late 1930s Style O. Earlier models have sides roughed up by sandblasting but with no decorative pattern. Strings West/BM*

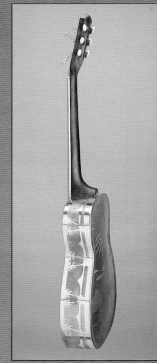

◆ *National El Trovador, 1933 (center). National began competing head-on with Dobro's woodbody guitars in 1933 with the El Trovador at $55 and the Rosita at $30. The El Trovador body, made by the Kay company, is of laminated mahogany while the Rosita has a maple veneer. The El Trovador was made for only about eight months in 1933. It was replaced in 1934 by the Estralita, which has fancier fingerboard inlay but is otherwise similar. Gruhn Guitars/DL*

♦ Airline Extra Volume Folk Guitar, circa 1963. In 1957, Valco made a half-hearted attempt to revive the single-cone resonator guitar with the short-scale, solidbody, pearloid-covered National Resophonic models. A full-scale, ultra-modern model debuted in 1963 with a hollow body made of "Res-o-glas" or fiberglass. The same guitar, with differences in trim, was marketed as the National Bluegrass 35 with white body, the Supro (Valco's budget brand) Folk Star with red body, and this black model under Montgomery Ward's house brand, Airline. Although these instruments are quite different from the engraved metalbody models of the 1930s, one characteristic of the originals remains, as expressed in Montgomery Ward's official model name: Extra Volume. Gruhn Guitars/WC

♦ National Trojan, circa 1937 (above). The Trojan was introduced in 1934 as a slightly upscale version of the low-end Rosita. This example shows some typical features of late-1930s Nationals, including a solid peghead and striped pickguard. Clifford Antone/BM

♦ National Aragon de Luxe, 1938 (center). This unique guitar is one of the last resonator models introduced by National before World War II. It has maple back and sides and an arched spruce top. The resonator coverplate is spruce. Its resemblance to a Kay archtop is no coincidence; Kay supplied the bodies and necks for the Aragon de Luxe. Roy Acuff Museum, Opryland USA/WC

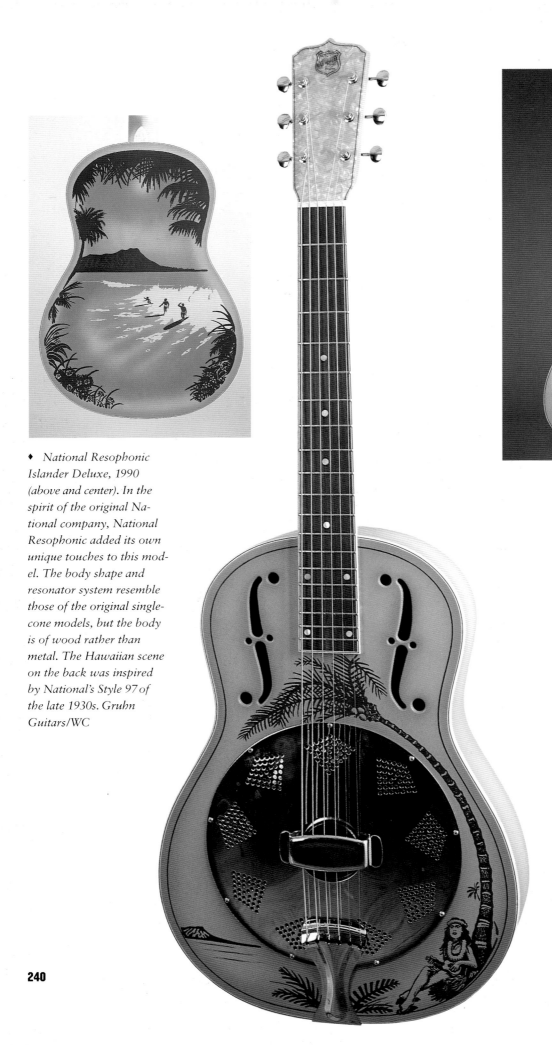

♦ National Resophonic Islander Deluxe, 1990 (above and center). In the spirit of the original National company, National Resophonic added its own unique touches to this model. The body shape and resonator system resemble those of the original single-cone models, but the body is of wood rather than metal. The Hawaiian scene on the back was inspired by National's Style 97 of the late 1930s. Gruhn Guitars/WC

♦ Dobro No. 45 square-neck, Regal-made, 1937. Dobro debuted in 1928 with three guitar models (available with round or square neck) plus three tenors, two mandolins, and one uke. Model No. 27 was priced at $27.50, No. 37 at $37.50, and No. 45 at $45. No. 27 is made of an unspecified type of laminated wood (typically birch), No. 37 is laminated mahogany and has more binding, and No. 45 has a laminated spruce top. The spruce top not only distinguishes No. 45 from the two cheaper models, but it also distinguishes the ultimate model, No. 206, from the walnut-top models below it. Mike Cass/DL

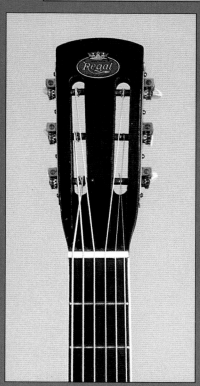

◆ Regal No. 45 round-neck, mid-1930s (upper and lower left) Dobro granted a license in 1932 to the Regal company of Chicago to make and market Dobros. The first Regal models, introduced in June 1933, are the same as the first three Dobro models. Within a few years, the Regal line expanded to include wood-body models with f-holes rather than screen holes, plus an array of metalbody models. The spruce top of this No. 45 has an unusual shaded finish. Some Regal-made Dobros have a Regal peghead decal, and some have the Dobro decal. Among the identifying marks of a Regal-made Dobro are routed peghead slots that have rounded ends. Dobros made by the Dobro company in California have sawn slots with square ends (except for those made in 1937, just before National-Dobro moved to Chicago). Gruhn Guitars/WC

◆ Dobro ukulele, late 1920s (right). From the beginning, the Dobro line included only one ukulele: this mahogany model. Regal later made a ukulele with screen holes sold under the Regal brand and a model with upper f-holes for sale by other companies. Dennis Watkins/BM

241

♦ Dobro No. 37 "double-cyclops" squareneck, 1932 (upper left). In 1931 some Dobros were made with a single screen hole; these are referred to as "cyclops" models. In 1932 some "double-cyclops" models were made with joined screen holes. Aside from the joined holes, this is a typical No. 37, with mahogany body, bound top and back, and bound fingerboard. Mike Cass/WC

♦ Magn-o-tone roundneck, 1932 (upper right). In addition to the Regal brand, both Dobro and Regal made instruments under various brands for other distributors. Magn-o-tones were made for Montgomery Ward. The square-end peghead slots reveal that this example was made in California. This guitar also illustrates the variation in trim common on Dobros. It is in most respects a No. 27, but the fingerboard is bound. Mike Cass/WC

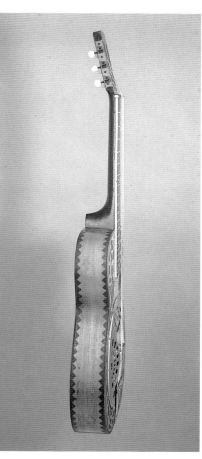

♦ Dobro No. 65 prototype, 1928 (lower left and right and opposite page). Unlike National, which started with fancy models and then expanded the line downward to reach the budget market, Dobro started with cheap models and quickly introduced fancier ones. The basic design stayed constant; only the wood and ornamentation changed. The body is of magnolia wood and the "French scroll" pattern is "carved" by sandblasting. A foreboding skull figure dominates the back pattern. The sawtooth pattern on the sides of the prototype did not continue on a production version of this or any other Dobro model. Walter Carter/WC

♦ Dobro No. 65 square-neck, circa 1936 (above). By the mid-1930s, Dobro seems to have chosen self-promotion over art and replaced the skull figure with a stylized letter D. Gruhn Guitars/WC

♦ Dobro No. 65 roundneck, 1928 (upper and lower right and center). The production model has the same pattern as the prototype, but the finish is reversed. On this one, the carved-out areas are lighter; on the prototype the carved areas have the dark finish. On the back, the reverse finish creates an entirely different effect. The dark hollow eyes of the prototype now appear to be greenish globes. The scroll carving on the sides appears to have been done by hand rather than sandblasted. Dennis Watkins/WC

♦ Dobro custom round-neck, Regal-made, circa 1935. Regal made several Dobros that were inspired by Martin's Style 28 guitars, with spruce top, rosewood back and sides, and herringbone trim. Gruhn Guitars/WC

♦ Dobro No. 125 round-neck, 1928. The most expensive Dobros were made of walnut. Model No. 125, also advertised as the De Lux, has an engraved, nickel-plated coverplate. Presumably, most customers elected to pay the extra $25 or so for gold-plated metal parts, because No. 125 is much rarer than the more expensive No. 156. The back of a No. 125, like all the higher models, is made of four book-matched pieces of walnut. The model immediately below it, No. 100 or 106, has a two-piece back. Mike Cass/WC

♦ *Dobro No. 156 round-neck, 1928. Model No. 156 is quite an eye-catcher with an engraved gold-plated coverplate. It listed for about $150. Jay Levin/WC*

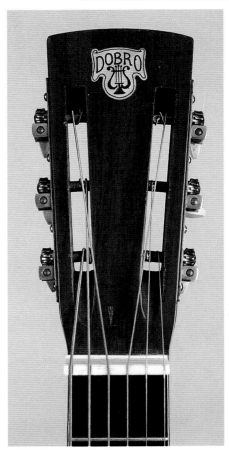

♦ Dobro No. 175 square-neck, circa 1929. The Dobro version of a presentation model, this instrument was made for Rudy Dopyera's niece Violette. A standard No. 175 has more engraving on the coverplate than a standard No. 156. Even the soundhole rings are engraved. Gruhn Guitars/WC

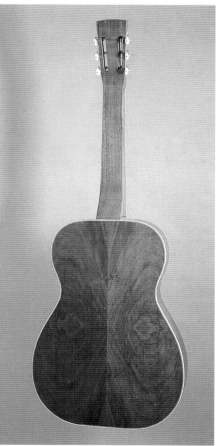

♦ *Dobro No. 175 square-neck, circa 1930. Model No. 175 is rare—both in literature and in reality. The only fancier Dobro model is No. 206, which has a spruce top. The coverplate identifies the No. 175 by its more descriptive model name: De Lux Special. Mike Cass/WC*

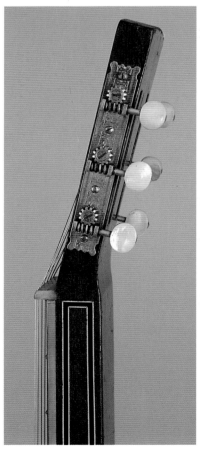

♦ Hollywood, mid- to late-1930s. N. W. Shireson of Los Angeles was granted a patent in late 1932 on a resonator system similar to John Dopyera's (which had been patented earlier in 1932 under Rudy Dopyera's name)—so similar, in fact, that Dobro sued for infringement and won. This model is nice-looking, but none of the Shiresons produced a sound competitive with a Dobro. Except for the absence of gold-plated metal parts, this guitar is as fancy as any high-end Dobro model, with spruce top, metal-clad soundholes, fancy fingerboard inlay, and an abalone pearl top border. The back is four-way matched walnut. John Bernunzio/BM

◆ *Dobro Professional No. 15H squareneck, Regal-made, late 1930s. In the early 1930s National introduced woodbody models to compete with Dobro. In the mid-1930s Regal (Dobro's exclusive licensee) countered with several lines of metal guitars, the fanciest of which were the Regal-Dobro Silver Guitars. This example has the fancy engraving of a No. 15, but it has "window" soundholes and a pearl-inlaid peghead instead of the segmented f-holes and pearloid peghead overlay of the standard No. 15. The back engraving has a floral motif quite different from those of National's tri-cones. Unlike the sides of National metalbody guitars, which are soldered to the top and back, the sides of Regal-Dobro models are rolled into the top and back to create what is commonly referred to as a "fiddle edge." Becky Dowling/DL*

♦ Slingerland Cathedra-
nola, late 1930s (above).
Some manufacturers, like
Slingerland, avoided in-
fringing on Dobro's patent
by avoiding a resonator altogether. The bridge of this
model sits on a spruce disk
recessed slightly into the
top. Except for the lack of a
resonator—which, of course,
is a monumental exception
in terms of sound quality—
this instrument has a look
of quality, with "ribbon"-
grained mahogany body,
checkered binding (including a backstripe), and
uniquely shaped screen
holes. The tailpiece is not
original. Dave's/WC

♦ Dobro No. 62, mid-1930s
(above and center). While
Regal's Silver Guitars competed with National's tri-
cones, the Regal-Dobro
No. 62 was designed to take
on National's Style O, with
an etched, nickel-plated
brass body. W. T. Smith/DL

♦ *Ward metalbody round-neck, Regal-made, late 1930s (upper left). Montgomery Ward referred to this model as "our finest professional guitar." It was not the Regal-Dobro Professional No. 15M, however, but the model just below it, the Leader No. 14M (M denoted a roundneck, H a square-neck). Becky Dowling/DL*

♦ *Alhambra, Regal-made, mid-1930s (upper right). This Alhambra-brand guitar is another version of the Leader No. 14M. Strings West/BM*

♦ *O. M. I. No. 75, 1980. Unlike the original Dobro company with its Regal-made metalbody guitars, the Original Musical Instrument company has been as successful with metalbody guitars as with woodbodies. This model has a Dobro-style cover-plate but a National-type resonator system. The engraving and etching patterns on the majority of O. M. I. metalbody models are inspired by original National models rather than Dobros. This pattern is modeled on the lily of the valley of National's Style 3 tri-cone. Gruhn Guitars/WC*

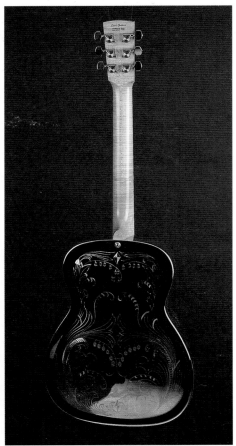

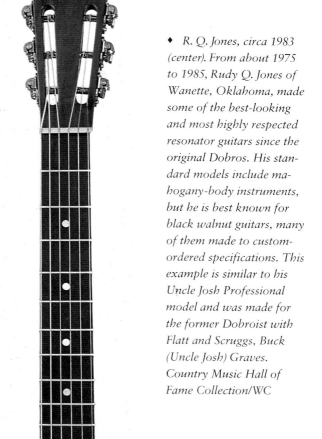

◆ R. Q. Jones, circa 1983 (center). From about 1975 to 1985, Rudy Q. Jones of Wanette, Oklahoma, made some of the best-looking and most highly respected resonator guitars since the original Dobros. His standard models include mahogany-body instruments, but he is best known for black walnut guitars, many of them made to custom-ordered specifications. This example is similar to his Uncle Josh Professional model and was made for the former Dobroist with Flatt and Scruggs, Buck (Uncle Josh) Graves. Country Music Hall of Fame Collection/WC

◆ Dobro No. 32, Regal-made, mid- to late 1930s (above). The sunburst finish of the No. 32 puts it in the same league as a National Triolian, but the gold-sparkle peghead overlay of this example upstages the competition. Dennis Watkins/DL

♦ *Martin D-45, 1939.*
(See page 265.)

FLAT TOP GUITARS

♦ ♦ ♦

Martin OMs and Dreadnoughts

Martin was especially vulnerable to changing tastes in the 1920s. Most companies had a healthy banjo line or a diversified line with banjos and mandolins as well as guitars, but while Martin did offer mandolins, the success or failure of the company depended on flat top guitars and ukuleles.

Even though Martin's sales rose steadily in the early 1920s, changes in the Martin line indicate that the company must have been aware of the changing marketplace. In 1922 Martin put a mahogany top on the low-end 2-17 and put heavier bracing under the top so it could be fitted with steel strings—the first steel strings offered on a Martin model. The mahogany top was probably an economizing move and the steel strings a response to the popularity of Hawaiian music and the consequent demand for guitars of greater volume.

By the end of the 1920s, however, steel-string design alone could not compete in any segment of the market. Dance band guitarists were moving toward the louder, more percussive *f*-hole archtop guitar. Hawaiian musicians were moving to National and Dobro resonator guitars. Classical and semiclassical guitarists were abandoning the parlor guitar, which had been the mainstay of Martin's success, for the more robust Spanish-style classicals.

The flat top guitar was not dead by any means. The biggest star of country music, Jimmie Rodgers, was identified with Martin and Weymann flat tops, and most of the singing cowboy movie stars of the 1930s would play flat tops. Nevertheless, any astute observer of industry trends in the late 1920s could have predicted that the flat top was in jeopardy. Martin's move to steel-string guitars was the first of several changes it made in an attempt to keep its primary product—flat top guitars—competitive with other new guitar styles. The second major move came in 1929 with the introduction of a 14-fret neck on a new model, the OM (for Orchestra Model). The 14-fret neck was a success and was adopted on the majority of Martins by 1934. The crowning innovation, the one that would reestablish both Martin and the flat top guitar as the standard bearers for the general guitar-playing public, was the introduction of a larger, more powerful guitar—the 15 5/8-inch–wide dreadnought or D size.

Like many successful innovations, Martin's dreadnought guitar of 1931 was not a new idea, not even to Martin. A full 15 years earlier, Martin had made dreadnought models for Chas. Ditson, a branch of the Boston-based Oliver Ditson Co. Although "dreadnought" usually connotes a 15 5/8-inch–wide guitar (or, in the case of Gibson, 16 inches wide) with a relatively thick waist, the dreadnought shape was actually used for three different Ditson sizes, only the largest of which was 15 5/8 inches wide. Gibson, too, used the dreadnought shape on several smaller bodies. Estimated production of Martin-Ditson D-size guitars from 1916 to 1921 is 14 with a total of 19 more made between 1921 and 1930.

The large, thick-waisted body style differed enough from the standard Martin bodies to deserve a new designation, one that broke from the numbered

♦ *Paramount Model L, 1930. Martin's period of inspired innovation in the late 1920s and early 1930s spawned one clunker that never made it into the Martin line. This double-stage guitar—the second stage, with the round holes, is meant to act as a resonator—was made for Paramount. Martin historian Mike Longworth estimates that about 36 of these were made, some with four strings and some with six. Most examples have no soundhole in the top, and that appears to have been the original design. Martin records do not specify a soundhole. The lack of any ornamentation whatsoever around the soundhole is highly unusual, and it makes the originality of the soundhole suspect. Roy Acuff Museum, Opryland USA/WC*

tradition. In World War I the largest class of battleship had been the dreadnought, after the HMS Dreadnought, a British ship built in 1906. Martin appropriated the name for its largest body size and used the letter D in model names.

Unlike the early Ditson models, which had fan-pattern bracing, the 1931 Martin D models were X-braced in traditional Martin fashion. The combination of X-bracing, steel strings, and large body gave the dreadnoughts a power greater than that of any previous Martins. The X-bracing is usually thought to have enhanced Martin guitars all the way back to the 1850s, but as the fan-braced, Spanish-made classicals showed, the X pattern was not the best for classical models. With the steel-string models, however, the X found its voice. Telling evidence for the superiority of the X pattern comes from the Gibson line. Gibson's first flat tops, in the mid- to late-1920s, were small-bodied models first with H-pattern bracing (like that of Gibson's round-hole archtops) and then ladder bracing. When Gibson increased body sizes in the early 1930s, the company adopted the X pattern not only on flat tops but for a few years on archtops, too. In the 1970s Gibson tried to "out-X" Martin with a double-X pattern but returned to the standard X in the 1980s.

As C. F. Martin had done in the 1850s, the Martin company in the early 1930s produced an instrument that would represent the height of flat top guitar design for many years to come. The mahogany D-18 and rosewood D-28 would become the favorites of an overwhelming majority of bluegrass guitarists from the 1940s on. The folk music boom of the late 1950s and 1960s inaugurated a production boom for Martin. In 1971, Martin's record production year, over 80 percent of Martin's 22,637 guitars were dreadnoughts. The D-18 and D-28 together accounted for almost half the total production that year.

While the D-18 and D-28 became the workhorse models of the guitar industry, the D-45, the top of the dreadnought line, also helped secure Martin's place in guitar history. On the vintage market today, the D-45 from the pre–World War II period has few rivals from any American maker of any time period.

◆ *Martin OM-28, 1931. The OM models with 14 frets clear of the body kicked off the era that would be dominated by the dreadnought. The OM-28 was introduced in 1929; the OM-18, OM-42, OM-45, and OM-45 Deluxe followed in 1930. The body is 000 width, 15 inches wide, but is shorter than the body of a 12-fret 000 model. The pickguard was also introduced with the OMs, and it is slightly smaller than those that would become standard on the rest of the Martin line in 1932. In the late 1800s and early 1900s, the occasional Martin had a solid peghead with friction peg tuners. The OMs are the first Martins with a solid peghead as a standard feature, and the tuners on early examples are banjo-style. Hank Risan/BM*

◆ *OM-45 Deluxe, 1930. In a departure from its traditional model numbering system, Martin offered an OM model fancier than the OM-45, but rather than giving it a higher number, called it the OM-45 Deluxe. In addition to standard Style 45 appointments, it has pearl inlay on the pickguard, snowflake inlays at the ends of the bridge, and mother-of-pearl tuner buttons. It is Martin's fanciest catalog model of the twentieth century. Only 14 OM-45 Deluxes were made, all of them in 1930. Martin reintroduced the OM-45 in 1978, and musician/collector Eric Schoenberg, working with Martin, revived the OM-45 Deluxe in a limited run in 1992. Eric Schoenberg/John Peden*

♦ *Martin D-28, 1932 (upper left). Like early D-18s, early D-28s have a 12-fret neck and a slotted peghead. In keeping with Martin's standard model nomenclature, a D-28 has the same materials and trim as any other Style 28. Anonymous collector/DL*

♦ *Martin D-2, 1931 (center and upper right), owned by Arkie, the Arkansas Woodchopper. The first Martin-brand dreadnought models were designated D-1, for the model with mahogany back and sides, and D-2, for rosewood. Luther Ossinbrink, better known to audiences of radio WLS in Chicago as Arkie, the Arkansas Woodchopper, had his name inlaid on the fingerboard. In every respect, including the zigzag backstripe, this D-2 is a Style 28 guitar. After two D-1s and seven D-2s were made, the model names were changed to D-18 and D-28, respectively. Country Music Hall of Fame Collection/WC*

♦ Martin D-18, 1947 (upper right). The D-18 has changed little in outward appearance through the years. The outer binding layer was changed from black plastic to tortoise-grain plastic by 1936, then back to black plastic in 1966. The rosewood finger-board replaced ebony at the beginning of 1947. The fin-gerboard dots were en-larged to this graduated-size configuration in 1946; in 1947, sometime after this guitar was made, the dots became uniform size. The shaded finish is fairly rare, but it was a catalog option. Steve Shaw/DL

♦ Martin D-18, 1933 (left). Martin's first dreadnoughts, like earlier Martins, have 12 frets clear of the body and a slotted peghead. The 12-fret neck with the long body style reappears in the postwar period first on 12-string models in 1964, then on special model dreadnoughts, denoted by the letter S after the model name. In Martin's postwar nomenclature, S stands for a 12-fret neck. Before World War II, S stood for Special, and was used on any guitar with a nonstan-dard feature. Tommy Gold-smith/DL

♦ *Martin D-28, 1956 (upper left and right). The most obvious change in the D-28 from the 1940s to the 1950s is the loss of the herringbone top trim. The changeover occurred in early 1947. The top wood changed, too, from Adirondack spruce to Sitka spruce in late 1945. Also, in late 1944 scalloped bracing was dropped, and the inlay began a series of changes, from slotted diamonds to small dots, then to larger uniform-size dots in 1946, and finally to these large graduated-size dots in 1947. In 1976 herringbone purfling and scalloped bracing were revived with great success on the HD-28 model (H for herringbone). The backstripe of the D-28 changed in early 1947 from the zigzag or "zipper" pattern to a narrow checkered pattern. A year later the wider pattern of this example was instituted. Scotty Jackson/WC*

♦ *Martin D-28, 1938 (center). In terms of value versus rarity, a Martin D-28 from the period prior to late 1944 is one of the strongest performers of any vintage guitar model. From 1931 through late 1944 Martin made 1,450 D-28s. By vintage standards this is not a rare model, but guitarists and collectors regard it so highly that it brings more on the vintage market than any other prewar production model except Martin's D-45 (91 made) or Gibson's SJ-200 (96 made). Danny Jones/BM*

♦ *Martin 0-42, 1927, owned by Gene Autry. This is obviously not a large-bodied guitar, but its ownership by Gene Autry helped to keep Martin flat tops in the spotlight at a time when archtops and resonator guitars were poised to take over the guitar market. It is unlikely that Autry bought it new—he was still a telegraph operator in Oklahoma when this guitar was made. He probably sent it back to the factory to have the script signature inlaid. The peghead decal, peghead binding, pearl tuner buttons, bridge, and pickguard were probably added at the same time. Autry also had a 1926 00-42 customized in the same manner but with his name in block letters on the fingerboard; that instrument is displayed at the Country Music Hall of Fame and Museum in Nashville. The back of this O-42 is of attractive Brazilian rosewood with the Martin stamp faintly visible on the back of the peghead. The decal on the front of the peghead was first used in mid 1932, but the stamp on the back continued until 1935. A third Autry guitar with his name on the fingerboard—a D-45—is one of the most famous guitars ever made. Gene Autry Western Heritage Museum*

♦ *Martin D-45, 1933, custom-made for Gene Autry. Gene Autry was a star on Chicago's WLS "Barn Dance" radio show when he ordered this guitar. Billed as "Oklahoma's Singing Cowboy," he had not yet appeared in a movie but had had a hit record in late 1931 with "Silver Haired Daddy of Mine." In anticipation of greater fame, he contacted the Chicago Musical Instrument Company (which, ironically, would later own Gibson) and ordered the biggest and best guitar Martin could make. The new dreadnoughts had been in production little more than a year and were available only in Styles 18 and 28. Autry special-ordered one with Style 45 trim and his name inlaid in script on the fingerboard. In 1934 he landed his first movie role as a singing cowboy in* Tumbling Tumbleweeds *and went on to become one of the most successful singers and movie stars in the business. Many collectors regard the prewar D-45 as the ultimate flat top guitar—in construction, aesthetics, and sound. The belt-buckle wear on the back and the capo marks on the neck show that Autry played it as well as displayed it. The decal on the back of the peghead probably indicates that the guitar went back to the factory at some point for restoration. Even without the celebrity connection, this instrument's status as the first D-45 makes it the most valuable American guitar ever made. Gene Autry Western Heritage Museum*

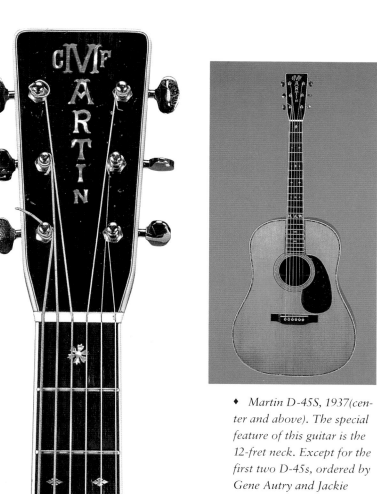

♦ Martin D-45S, 1936 (above), with D-28. The S in the model name of this guitar refers to an oversized body, 16¼ inches wide. The guitar on the left is a standard D-28, 15⅝ inches wide. Of the 91 prewar D-45s, only two were made with this large body, both of them ordered in 1936 through a Wurlitzer store in St. Louis. They are the widest guitars ever made by the Martin company. Steve Shaw/DL

♦ Martin D-45S, 1937 (center and above). The special feature of this guitar is the 12-fret neck. Except for the first two D-45s, ordered by Gene Autry and Jackie "Kid" Moore, this is the only other prewar D-45 with a 12-fret neck. Until 1939 the D-45 had snowflake and slotted-diamond fingerboard inlay. The "HAW" inlay is the monogram of the original owner, Harold Wagler. According to Martin records, this guitar was ordered through the Floyd L. Matthews company of Peoria, Illinois, for a wholesale price of $108.50; its value on the vintage market in 1993 is more than a thousand times greater. Charles Rosser/DL

♦ *Martin D-45, 1939 (this page and opposite left). The large hexagonal inlay pattern was adopted in 1939. In the traditional Martin scheme (before the introduction of the J-40), pearl top borders indicate models in the Style 40 series: Styles 40, 42, or 45. Only Style 45 has abalone pearl borders around the sides and back. Prior to 1934 Style 45 guitars have a torch-pattern inlay and no logo on the front of the peghead. The last original-series D-45s were made in 1942. In response to players' requests, Martin finally reintroduced the D-45 in 1968. Gruhn Guitars/DL*

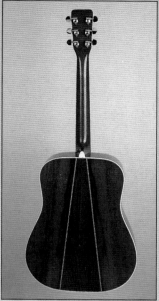

◆ *Martin D-35, 1968. In 1965 Martin found a way to use pieces of rosewood that were too small for a standard two-piece guitar back. The result was a three-piece back, and the model was dubbed the D-35. It became one of Martin's most successful models. This D-35 has a back of Brazilian rosewood. An embargo was placed on Brazilian rosewood in the late 1960s, and in late 1969 Martin switched to Indian rosewood on all rosewood models. Some D-35s from the transitional period have mixed Indian and Brazilian back pieces. The tortoise-grain pickguard is not original; it last appeared on Martin models in 1966. Gruhn Guitars/WC*

♦ *Martin J-40, 1991. In 1980 Martin introduced a new body size which it designated M. In the context of Martin bodies, it is the equivalent of a 0000 size—the same size and shape as the F-series models of 1935–1942. Although the M, at 16 inches wide, is 3/8-inch wider than a dreadnought, it is not as deep. In 1985 an M body with a dreadnought depth was introduced as the J (for Jumbo) size, and its model names included both letters. For example, this model was originally called the J-40M. Like many new Martin styles beginning in the 1980s, the J-40 does not conform to the traditional Martin scheme. It bears little resemblance to the Style 40 of 1874 to 1941. There is none of the pearl border that once distinguished all models in the Style 40 series. It does not even have the pearl soundhole ring and fancy purfling that distinguished the Style 30-series models prior to the introduction of the D-35 in 1965. The binding, rosette, and backstripe are similar to those of a Style 28. The only fancy features are the bound fingerboard, hexagonal inlays, and gold-plated tuners. In another break with tradition, Style 40 and various other new styles are not offered on all Martin body styles. A 000-40 or D-40, for example, is not a catalog model. From the back (upper right), the difference in body shapes is evident between the J-40 on the right and a D-28. Also evident is the difference between Brazilian rosewood on the pre-1970 D-28 and the Indian rosewood. Despite the wide difference in style numbers between these two models, the backstripes are identical. Gruhn Guitars/WC*

◆ *Maurer, circa 1915.*
(See page 269.)

FLAT TOP GUITARS
◆ ◆ ◆

The Larson Brothers

From 1900 to 1944 Carl and August Larson of Chicago made an estimated 11,000 to 12,000 guitars, harp guitars, and mandolins. They were the
first to build high-quality flat top guitars designed specifically for steel strings,
beating Martin by at least 20 years or more. Yet the Larson brothers remain

the most obscure of major American guitar makers of the twentieth century, primarily because they made few if any instruments bearing their name. Much of their production was sold under the distributor's brands of Stahl and Dyer. Unlike Martin, Gibson, Gretsch, Washburn, or even Epiphone, the Larsons' three in-house brands gave no clue to the name of the individuals behind the instruments. Euphonon suggested a guitar with an agreeable sound and Prairie State an instrument made in the Midwest (although Prairie State is a nickname for Illinois). Maurer was, in fact, someone's name—the surname of a maker who had previously employed the Larsons. Furthermore, the brands, whether their own or a distributor's, almost never appeared on the peghead but rather on a paper label or a small brand on the inside back center seam.

Many of the country stars on the WLS "Barn Dance" in Chicago, including Patsy Montana, Arkie the Arkansas Woodchopper, and Gene Autry, played guitars made by the Larsons, but if these had any logo at all on the peghead, it was the radio station's call letters, and consequently these guitars were commonly known as "WLS" rather than Larsons. Probably the most familiar, but typically anonymous, example of the Larson brothers' work in recent years is the fingerboard on "The Log," Les Paul's famous experimental solidbody electric guitar, a fingerboard usually attributed to Epiphone or Gibson—even by Les Paul himself.

The Larsons were born in Sweden and immigrated to Chicago in the 1880s. By the late 1890s they were building instruments under the Champion brand, among others, for Robert Maurer, a music teacher and instrument retailer. In 1900 Maurer sold his factory to Carl Larson and two other partners who were later replaced by August Larson.

The Larsons ran essentially a two-man shop. In their 44 years in business they never had a full-time employee, although they did rely on family members for part-time help. August worked the front of the shop while Carl did most of the instrument construction. Despite the smallness of the "factory," the Larsons produced a great variety as well as a great quantity of instruments. They made instruments in all different sizes, from mandolins, mandolas, and parlor guitars to large-bodied guitars and harp guitars. Styles ranged from oak body with plain trim to rosewood body with tree-of-life fingerboard inlays and presentation-grade ornamentation. The craftsmanship of their instruments also varied greatly, from some of the finest examples of American luthiery to guitars with unintentionally asymmetrical bodies.

From the beginning the Larsons built steel-string flat tops. Steel strings were standard on mandolins and had been available for guitars in the late 1800s, as shown by cautions against using them in the catalogs of S. S. Stewart and Washburn, but no major makers before the Larsons built guitars designed for steel strings.

In addition to steel strings, high-end Larson guitars typically featured several design characteristics that have never received any significant acceptance among guitar makers. The earliest Larson innovation, patented in 1904, was laminated top bracing. Because of the extra tension of steel strings, heavier braces were designed, with a rosewood or ebony center between two pieces of spruce. In Robert Hartman's book on the Larsons, Les Paul recalls that the string sets sold by the Larsons were of an extremely heavy gauge, with a wound second string, so that the added tension on a guitar strung with Larson strings would be tremendous.

The top of a Larson guitar is unique in that it is arched. Martin flat tops have a slight transverse arch, and Gibson's first flat tops were described as having an arched top, but neither company's "arch" is apparent to the casual observer. A Larson top has a noticeable arch from being bent and then braced while bent—"built under tension," as their literature described it.

A third Larson characteristic, patented in 1930 and 1931, was a double-rod body support and neck adjustment system. This innovation was advertised as a feature of Prairie State models but it appeared in some other Larson guitars as well.

The Larsons used the Maurer brand from the time they acquired it in 1900 to the mid-1930s, when they replaced it with the Euphonon brand. They made some instruments for Stahl and Dyer possibly as early as 1904. The first Prairie State models were probably made around 1927, the year August Larson applied for the patent on the double-rod system. The guitars made for Wack of Milwaukee, from 1930 to 1944, were Maurer, Prairie State, or brandless custom-ordered models. Some guitars with Euphonon characteristics but without the Euphonon brand were sold through Wack.

August Larson died in 1944, and Carl died two years later. No one continued with the Larson brands.

♦ *Maurer, circa 1915 (above and opposite page). This guitar is typical of the top of the Maurer line. The auditorium size is 15 inches wide and the largest body size in the catalog, but by no means the largest made by the Larsons. The Maurer brand is accompanied by a 1904 patent date; the patent was for laminated top braces. The fancy fingerboard may be the work of the Handel Company of New York City, which did pearl work for various makers, including Martin, Gibson, and D'Angelico. Gruhn Guitars/WC*

♦ *Stahl, circa 1916 (above). This guitar has the Stahl brand on the inside center backstripe, but it is typical of Maurer models of the period. It is 12 ½ inches wide, which is Maurer's "standard" size. J. Gravity Strings/BM*

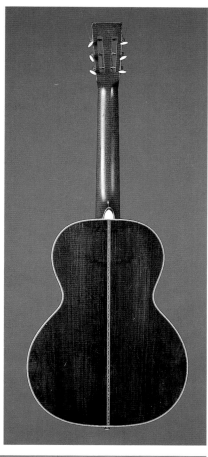

♦ *Stahl, early 1930s (opposite and upper left and right). The attractive pickguard with pearl inlay is a standard feature on bowl-back mandolins and appears on some Larson guitars. It is inlaid flush with the top of the instrument rather than glued onto the top in the manner of most makers. Aside from the pickguard, this guitar is essentially a Prairie State model. The label claim of Wm. C. Stahl of Milwaukee as manufacturer is obscured, appropriately, by the patented rod system found only on a guitar made by the Larson brothers. This model has the cheapest of the three ornamentation styles cataloged in the 1930s. Gruhn Guitars/DL*

♦ *Euphonon, circa 1938 (lower left). The Euphonon brand replaced Maurer in the mid-1930s. This model has a body shape similar to Martin's 000 size, with wider upper bouts than earlier Larson body lines. The dark-stained top is unusual on a Larson brothers guitar. Strings West/BM*

♦ *Euphonon, late 1930s (lower right). The thick waist and large body of this Euphonon show the influence of Martin's dreadnoughts. Its rosewood back and sides produce a classic dreadnought sound. Its classical features—the 12-fret neck; the flat, wide, unmarked fingerboard; and the classical bridge—are highly unusual, custom-ordered features. Gruhn Guitars/DL*

◆ *Prairie State, circa 1935. This huge guitar, 21 inches wide and 6⅛ inches deep, is the largest known guitar ever made by the Larsons. If the player's arm is long enough to reach the strings, the instrument will produce a huge sound. Martin's dreadnought was named after the largest battleship class of the early 1900s, but in terms of body width, the Martin D-18 is a ¾-size guitar relative to the Larson. The larger inner rod acts as a spacer to support the body, while the smaller one adjusts the neck angle. Dennis Watkins/DL*

♦ *Prairie State Style 450, mid-1930s. This instrument illustrates the inconsistency of the Larsons' brands. The large screw through the fingerboard and the single rod inside the body are, according to the Maurer & Co. catalog, characteristics of Maurer guitars, although most Maurer guitars do not have this feature. Prairie State guitars in the same catalog have a double-rod system. Although this guitar is branded with the Prairie State logo, it would more accurately be described as a Maurer Style 593. So that the neckset angle can be adjusted, the neck is not glued into the body but rather attached and adjusted by means of three bolts (the third bolt goes through the neck heel and is not visible). Gruhn Guitars/WC*

◆ *Dyer harp guitar, circa 1920. A harp guitar with a similar design was patented by Chris Knutsen in 1898. W. H. Dyer & Bro. of St. Paul, Minnesota, began marketing a Symphony line of harp guitars and mandolins made by Knutsen by 1912. August Larson also had an interest in harp guitars, and in 1912, the year Knutsen's patent expired, Larson was granted a patent for a harp guitar with a double-body design (the bass side of a standard guitar body is present but hidden under the top). By 1917 the Larsons were making all the instruments for the Dyer harp line, which by then included mandolas and mandocellos. Interestingly, the harp mandolin family models have the body extension of the harp guitar but not the extra strings. Although Gibson's carved-top harp guitars were more highly promoted and are more commonly seen today, most players of harp guitars prefer the Knutsen-Larson flat top design. Gruhn Guitars/WC*

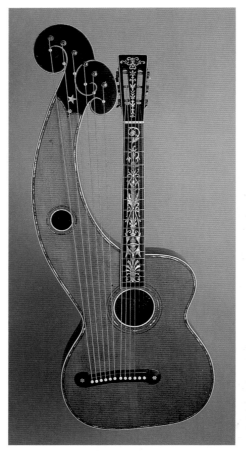

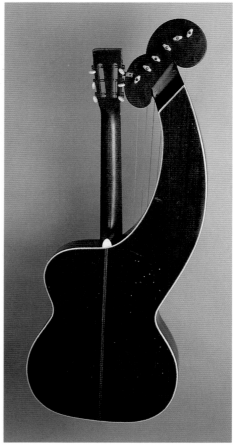

♦ *Gibson SJ-200, 1937.*
(See page 286.)

FLAT TOP GUITARS
♦ ♦ ♦

Gibson Flat Tops

It is not surprising that Gibson, as the inventor and standard-bearer of archtop instruments, would hold the flat top guitar in low esteem through the company's first quarter century. The earliest flat top made by Gibson, the GY, was a companion to the Army and Navy mandolin of 1918 and, like that mandolin, was advertised as being of decent quality but "not a Gibson." In 1926, 24 years after the company was founded, Gibson finally put the company name on two flat top models, but the model names revealed the company's ongoing low opinion of the flat top. Instead of creating a fanfare over a new line, Gibson simply discontinued its cheapest archtops, the L-1 and L-Jr., and put the L-1 name on the more expensive of the two flat top models. The less expensive model was given an even lower name, L-0. (In the 1930s there would be an even cheaper flat top, the L-00.) Two years later Gibson finally began to recognize the growing market for flat tops, or perhaps for guitars in general, and introduced a quality model endorsed by recording artist Nick Lucas.

In 1929, Gibson introduced one of the most important models in guitar history and, ironically, one of the most obscure. It was a 16-inch dreadnought with a 14-fret neck—the first by any maker. (Martin had made earlier dreadnoughts for the Ditson company, but no 14-fret dreadnoughts until 1934.) Unfortunately, Gibson's innovations did not stop with the large body and long neck. A second wall was added within the guitar body, and four *f*-holes in addition to the standard round soundhole were cut into the top. Gibson called the bizarre guitar the HG-24. "HG" stood for Hawaiian Guitar, although the few surviving examples appear to have been set up originally for standard playing, with raised frets and slanted bridge saddle. All of Gibson's later Hawaiian models had a 12-fret neck and a straight-mounted saddle. Two smaller models, the HG-22 and HG-20 were introduced with the HG-24, and they, too, had the dreadnought body shape, a 14-fret neck, raised frets, and slant-mounted saddle. The combination of radical design (double-wall body with four *f*-holes) and confusing marketing (a supposedly Hawaiian guitar set up for standard play) doomed the HG-series guitars.

After the HGs, Gibson adopted a more cautious approach to innovation on the flat top line, increasing ornamentation more than body sizes. Despite the failure of the HG-24, Gibson's reluctance to try a large-bodied flat top is curious, considering that the early Gibson line included 17- and 18-inch archtops and that the company had always offered at least one, and at times as many as three, 16-inch archtops. Finally, a rather plain 16-inch dreadnought, simply named the Jumbo, was introduced in 1934. It lasted only two years but set the stage for what would become a highly respected dreadnought history.

As usual, Gibson made up for a late entry into a market with a frenzy of innovation and marketing. By the end of the 1930s the company had established not just one but two new large-bodied flat top designs that would elevate it into a competitive position with Martin.

♦ *Gibson L-1, circa 1929 (opposite). The first models worthy of "The Gibson" on the peghead appeared in 1926. They are the same size and shape as the discontinued L-1 archtop— 13 ½ inches wide, with the same circular lower bout. The back and sides are of mahogany. Although the L-1 is not noteworthy for quality, it has gained a great deal of notoriety as the model in one of two known photographs of blues legend Robert Johnson (Johnson's guitar is a circa 1928 version, with unbound fingerboard). The L-1 did not come with a pickguard as standard equipment, but the archtop-style elevated pickguard is seen on many flat tops from the late 1920s and early 1930s. The bridge on this example is not original. Pearls Before Swine/BM*

After World War II Gibson made a full array of flat top models. Unlike Martin, which had smaller models but essentially only one style that might be considered a budget guitar (Style 17 or the nearly identical Style 15), Gibson had a strong low-end line with the LG series. Their prewar predecessors, the L-1, L-0, and L-00, accounted for over half of Gibson's flat top sales in the 1930s and early 1940s, and the postwar models were no less successful. The folk music boom of the 1960s prompted a further expansion of the flat top line.

Gibson was sold to the Norlin company in 1969. By the early 1970s the quality of Gibson products had become inconsistent, and sales of American-made instruments had fallen to about half the number of instruments sold in the peak years of the 1960s. A second plant was opened in Nashville in 1976, and production was split between Nashville and Kalamazoo until 1984, when the original Kalamazoo plant was closed. The company changed hands again in 1985, being acquired by Henry Juszkiewicz, David Berryman, and Gary Zebrowski; Zebrowski left the partnership in 1991. With the new ownership came renewed attention to quality. Gibson bought the Flatiron mandolin company of Bozeman, Montana, in 1987 and built a new plant in Bozeman in 1989 to handle all acoustic instrument production. By the 1990s Gibson had regained much of its former reputation.

Most players perceive the sound and feel of a Gibson to be quite different from that of a Martin. Both makers have a loyal following. Like Martin, Gibson has revived some of its more highly respected models to remain among the leading makers of high-quality flat top guitars.

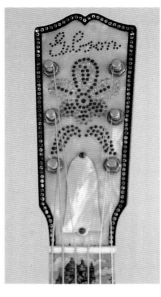

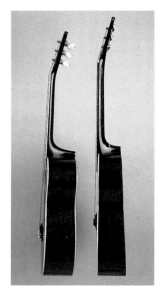

◆ *Gibson Nick Lucas custom, 1928. In 1928 Gibson introduced a quality flat top endorsed by Nick Lucas, who had just had a hit record with "Tiptoe Through the Tulips." The primary difference between the Lucas and the two earlier models is its deeper body and higher degree of ornamentation, though not as high as this instrument. The custom-ordered peghead and fingerboard were inspired by the Florentine model banjo, which had been introduced in 1927. All three flat top models of 1928 were small—only $13\frac{1}{2}$" wide—but the Lucas did attempt to meet the growing quest for volume with a deeper body. It is $4\frac{1}{4}$ inches deep at the neck and $4\frac{5}{8}$ inches at the endpin, deeper than Gibson's Jumbo dreadnought model of 1934. The mid-1930s L-00 next to it is $3\frac{1}{2}$ inches deep at the neck and $4\frac{3}{8}$ inches at the endpin. Gruhn Guitars/WC*

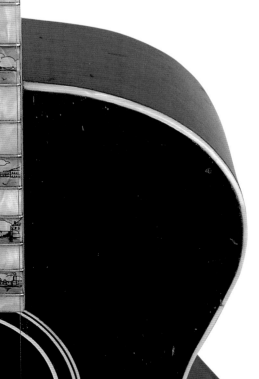

♦ Gibson Nick Lucas custom, 1928 (upper left). A customer apparently reasoned that if f-holes worked wonders on an archtop guitar, then the principle should hold true on a flat top. Dennis Watkins/WC

♦ Gibson Nick Lucas, 1936 (upper right). In 1929 Gibson increased the body widths of its flat top line to 14¾ inches. The Lucas model, listed in the catalog as the Gibson Special, of 1928 had mahogany back and sides. It switched to rosewood in 1929, then to maple (with some mahogany) from 1934 until the model's discontinuation in 1938. It was reintroduced, with optional rosewood or maple back and sides, in 1991. Gary Burnett/DL

♦ Recording King Lucas-style, mid-1930s. Recording King was the house brand of the Montgomery Ward company, and the better Recording King models were made by Gibson. Except for the lack of truss rod, this example is essentially a Nick Lucas model, with the extra-deep mahogany body. Gruhn Guitars/WC

♦ *Gibson custom-painted flat top, circa 1928. This guitar extends the Venetian motif (found ironically, on the fingerboards of Gibson Florentine banjos) over the entire guitar. It is one of the most unusual pieces ever produced by Gibson. Gruhn Guitars/DD*

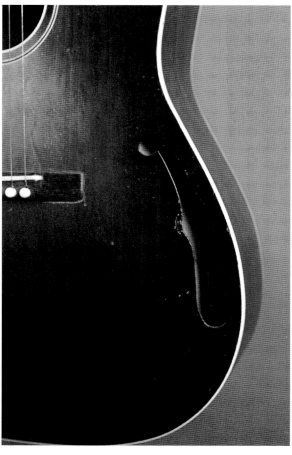

♦ *Gibson L-2, 1931 (upper left). With the introduction of the L-2 in 1929 all flat tops moved up to 14¾ inches. The original version had a rosewood back and sides and a 13-fret neck. With the move to this "Argentine gray" top finish (the standard finish on Gibson's Style 6 banjo), the body went to mahogany and the neck to 12 frets. Gruhn Guitars/WC*

♦ *Gibson L-2, 1932 (upper right). In 1932 the L-2 was given a new identity with a bright natural top finish. Other changes included a 13-fret neck and a new pickguard. By this time, a glued-down pickguard was standard on Martin guitars, but Gibson stayed with the elevated style for a brief period on the L-2 and the Nick Lucas. The L-2 was discontinued in 1934. Jim Reynolds/BM*

♦ *Gibson HG-24, 1929. Though designated a Hawaiian guitar, the HG-24 was set up for standard Spanish-style playing. It is the first 14-fret dreadnought by any maker, predating Gibson's Jumbo model and Martin's first 14-fret D-18 and D-28 by a full five years. The need for louder Hawaiian guitars may have inspired the inner wall and extra f-holes, although there is no known example of this model with original Hawaiian setup. The back and sides are of rosewood. Gruhn Guitars/WC*

◆ *Gibson HG-22 custom, circa 1929. The HG-22 and HG-20 are smaller than the HG-24, but they retain the dreadnought body shape. This example was custom-made for entertainer Jimmie Rodgers. The inlay designer apparently ran out of ideas after "Jimmie Rodgers" and "America's Blue Yodeler." Perhaps he thought Rodgers might forget how to tune his guitar so he engraved the notes of standard tuning, "EADGBE," at the ninth fret—yet another indication that these HG models were not Hawaiian guitars at all. The back speaks for itself. Rodgers also owned a Martin 000-45 with "Thanks" on the back. Roy Acuff Museum, Opryland USA/WC*

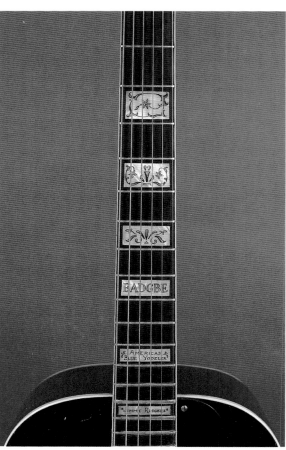

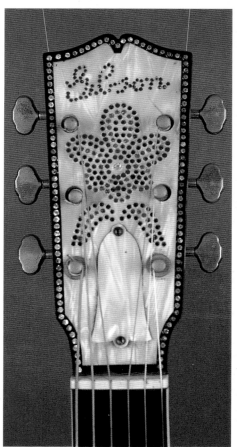

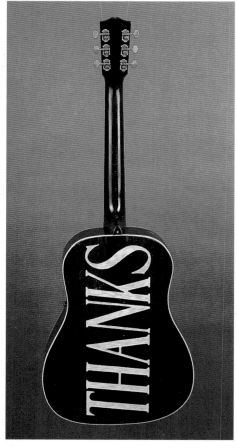

♦ Gibson double-wall custom, circa 1930 (above). One of the most unusual Gibsons ever made, this guitar combines the double walls of the HG models with the body lines of the L-5 archtop. This body does not appear on a catalog flat top model until after World War II, on the J-185. The neck is that of a Nick Lucas, with 13 frets clear of the body. The back and sides are of rosewood. The round holes around the top edge may have been an attempt to "open up" the sound of the double-wall body. This guitar has been refinished, but to its original color. The bridge is new, though it is probably the original style. The truss rod cover is not original. Roy Acuff Museum, Opryland USA/WC

♦ Gibson L-C, circa 1937 (above). The Century of Progress Exposition opened in Chicago in 1933, and Gibson named its fancy new model of that year the Century, or L-C. The L-C was discontinued in 1939. Lloyd Chiate/BM

♦ Gibson L-C, 1933 (center). This example has a custom-ordered fingerboard inlay pattern similar to that of a Bella Voce banjo. Gary Burnett/BM

◆ *Gibson Jumbo, 1934. The Jumbo, a 16-inch dreadnought with one soundhole and no inner walls, appeared in 1934, the same year Gibson's high-end archtops were advanced in width by an inch. Aside from the pearl peghead logo, the Jumbo is a rather plain guitar with mahogany back and sides. From the side, the Jumbo is easily distinguished from any other Gibson dreadnought (except the HG-24) by its almost uniform body depth: 4 3/16 inches at the neck to 4 1/2 inches at the endpin. Other dreadnoughts are as much as an inch deeper at the endpin than at the neck. Gruhn Guitars/WC*

 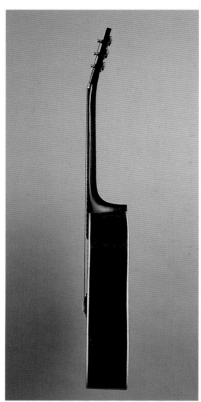

◆ *Gibson Jumbo 35, 1942 (lower left). In 1936, the Jumbo was replaced by two new dreadnoughts. The Jumbo 35, with mahogany back and sides, was the cheaper of the two, with a list price of $35. Steve Shaw/DL*

◆ *Gibson Jumbo 35, early 1940s (lower right). The J-35 was available with a natural-finish top beginning in 1940. The model was discontinued when Gibson diverted most of its production effort to World War II in 1942. Steve Shaw/DL*

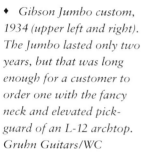

♦ Gibson Jumbo custom, 1934 (upper left and right). The Jumbo lasted only two years, but that was long enough for a customer to order one with the fancy neck and elevated pickguard of an L-12 archtop. Gruhn Guitars/WC

♦ Gibson Advanced Jumbo (center). The Advanced Jumbo with rosewood back and sides was the deluxe model of the two dreadnoughts introduced in 1936. Two years earlier, "advanced" referred to an increase in body size, but the Advanced Jumbo is the same size as the Jumbo and an inch smaller than the "advanced" archtops. In this case, the term may have referred to the increase in ornamentation. Original examples are rare, with a total of 271 made between 1937 and 1939. Some players and collectors consider the Advanced Jumbo to be the finest flat top Gibson ever made, and in response Gibson reissued the model in 1990. Gary Burnett/DL

◆ *Gibson SJ-200, 1937, custom-made for Ray Whitley. Cowboy movie star Ray Whitley recalled that he wanted a guitar with a powerful bass sound. Gibson took the body lines of the 17-inch archtops and made a flat top that was more than an inch wider than Martin's standard dreadnoughts. Although the model would first be cataloged as the Super Jumbo, the label on this inaugural instrument calls it the SJ-200. Whitley asked for a neck like that of the L-5, and he got it, complete with block fingerboard inlays and flowerpot peghead inlay. The custom-ordered engraved Western scenes did not carry over to production models—at least not Gibson production models. The concept was picked up by Gretsch in the mid-1950s on a series of Western-trimmed guitars, including the Rancher flat top. The pickguard material is that of the Super 400. The bridge has a single-piece saddle; early production models have individual saddles. The tuners are Grover Imperials, also found on the Super 400 of this period. After Gibson made this guitar for Whitley, his fellow cowboy movie stars Gene Autry and Tex Ritter also custom-ordered SJ-200s. Country Music Hall of Fame Collection/WC*

♦ Martelle Deluxe, mid-1930s (upper left and right). The distributor of the Martelle brand is unknown, but the maker is definitely Gibson. The pearloid fingerboard and peghead overlay, banjo-type tuners, and elevated pickguard are highly unusual on a distributor's model. The maple back and sides are quite unusual on a Gibson dreadnought prior to World War II. Gary Roberts/DL

♦ Recording King Ray Whitley, circa 1941 (center). This fancy non-Gibson brand flat top is as curious a model as it is a fine one. The back and sides are of rosewood—reserved for only the top Gibson-brand models. The fingerboard inlay is as attractive as and more delicate than that of any standard Gibson. The pickguard is engraved, a feature found at that time only on Gibson's SJ-200. One wonders why, if Ray Whitley was influential enough to deserve this quality model, did he not deserve a Gibson? As the man who ordered the first SJ-200, his association with Gibson had been long established. Perhaps it was the fact that his usual movie role was that of a sidekick rather than the leading man. David Sebring/WC

♦ Gibson SJ-200, late 1930s. The SJ-200 went into production in late 1937. The first catalog description listed it as the Super Jumbo, with a body width of 16 7/8 inches. By 1939 it was officially 17 inches wide, and the list price (with leather-bound case) was incorporated into the model name—Super Jumbo 200. Gibson was looser with its jumbo designation than Martin was with its dreadnought. The SJ-200 was not only larger but completely different in body shape from Gibson's round-shouldered "jumbo" dreadnoughts. Although most collectors refer to the two Gibson shapes as "round-shouldered dreadnought" for the dreadnought-shaped models and "jumbo" for the models with the circular lower bout, Gibson used "jumbo" for all 16-inch models, regardless of shape, and "super jumbo" for 17-inch guitars. SJ-200s made prior to World War II are of rosewood, except for this maple example. Postwar J-200s (the model name was shortened in the 1950s) are the opposite—maple, except for the occasional custom-ordered rosewood instrument. The back is unusual in that it is of two pieces but has no back-stripe. The bracket on the peghead, the 1930s version of a strap button, is factory original. John Miller/BM

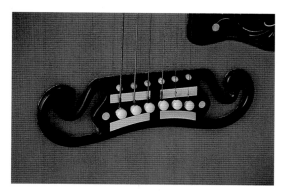

◆ SJ-200, circa 1940 (upper three). From the front, this guitar is almost identical to the previous one, except for the larger sunburst area and the string saddles. By the time this guitar was made, the individual saddle bearings no longer have brass seats. The back and sides, however, are of rosewood, which is standard for the prewar SJ-200. A total of 96 SJ-200s were made before World War II. John Miller/BM

◆ J-200N, 1953 (lower right). After World War II, the S was dropped from the model name in Gibson literature, although labels in instruments continued to say "SJ-200" through the early 1950s. The N stands for natural finish. Anonymous owner/BM

289

♦ *Gibson J-200, 1965 (above). In the 1960s Gibson apparently could not resist making some "improvements," among them a tune-o-matic bridge, which was standard equipment on Gibson's high-end electrics, and an adjustable top brace (not visible). In 1968 this particular model configuration sold 317 units, the highest yearly total of any version of the J-200 from its introduction through 1979. In 1985 the J-200 was redesigned to specs similar to those of the early postwar models. It continues today as the top model in the flat top line. Joe Nuyens/DL*

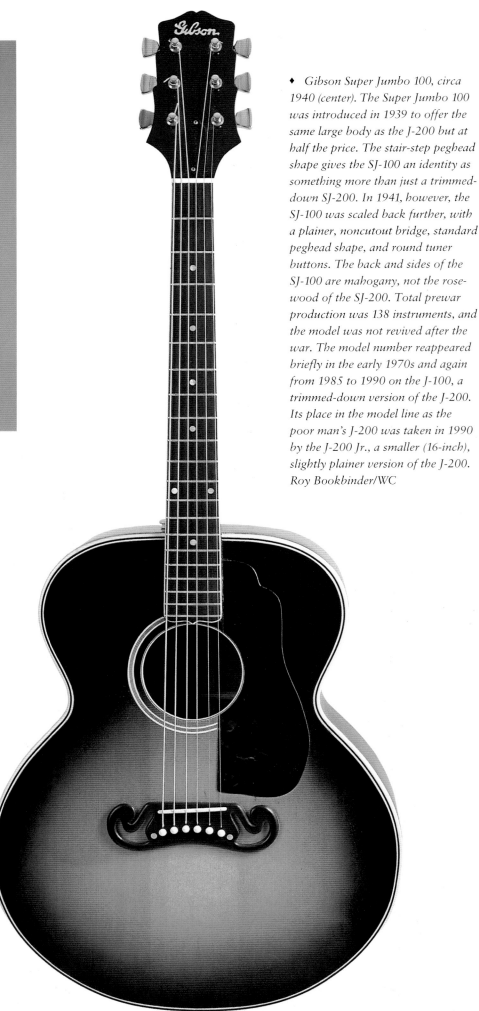

♦ *Gibson Super Jumbo 100, circa 1940 (center). The Super Jumbo 100 was introduced in 1939 to offer the same large body as the J-200 but at half the price. The stair-step peghead shape gives the SJ-100 an identity as something more than just a trimmed-down SJ-200. In 1941, however, the SJ-100 was scaled back further, with a plainer, noncutout bridge, standard peghead shape, and round tuner buttons. The back and sides of the SJ-100 are mahogany, not the rosewood of the SJ-200. Total prewar production was 138 instruments, and the model was not revived after the war. The model number reappeared briefly in the early 1970s and again from 1985 to 1990 on the J-100, a trimmed-down version of the J-200. Its place in the model line as the poor man's J-200 was taken in 1990 by the J-200 Jr., a smaller (16-inch), slightly plainer version of the J-200. Roy Bookbinder/WC*

♦ *Gibson Jumbo 55, 1940. The Jumbo 55 is the dreadnought sister of the Super Jumbo 100, complete with moustache bridge and stairstep peghead. The J-55, listing at a little more than half the price of the SJ-100, was more than twice as successful, selling a total of 311 units. Like the SJ-100, however, the J-55 was trimmed down in 1941 and did not survive the war. Its model number was revived on a square-shouldered dreadnought from 1973 to 1981. Gary Burnett/BM*

♦ *Gibson J-55, 1941. The revamped J-55 of 1941 has simpler (and cheaper to make) bridge, peghead, and tuners. The oversized dots and the stripe down the middle of the fingerboard are not standard for any Gibson-brand model, but instruments with the Cromwell brand, made by Gibson for distribution by such mail-order houses as Grossman, Richter and Phillips, and Continental, typically have this type of fingerboard ornamentation. Gruhn Guitars/WC*

♦ *Gibson Southerner Jumbo, 1942 (upper right), replaced the J-55 in late 1942, just before Gibson sharply curtailed production because of World War II. The first batch of SJs— probably no more than 40 guitars—have rosewood back and sides. A few wartime examples are maple; otherwise, they are mahogany. Wartime metal shortages caused Gibson to make some models, such as this one, with no truss rod. Gary Burnett/DL*

♦ *Gibson Southerner Jumbo, 1942 (left). This guitar is stamped with the same batch number, 910, as the other example (at upper right), meaning the bodies were made at the same time. However, the two have some significant differences that illustrate the inconsistency among Gibsons made during World War II. This guitar has a noticeably larger sunburst pattern, and it does have a truss rod. From 1942 to 1945, almost all Southerner Jumbos have a banner on the peghead with the slogan, "Only a Gibson is good enough." The banner was dropped after Epiphone launched a campaign based on the slogan, "When good enough isn't good enough." Gruhn Guitars/WC*

♦ *Gibson Country and Western, 1962 (right). The SJ was offered with a natural top in 1954 and given its own model name, the Country and Western, two years later. It was discontinued along with the SJ in 1978. Strings West Tulsa/DL*

♦ *Gibson Southerner Jumbo, 1943 (left). This early example has mahogany back and sides, no truss rod, and a curious painted black stripe running down the center seam of the front and the back. The stripe appears randomly on wartime models. The round-shouldered dreadnought held a solid position as the midline Gibson flat top from the 1930s through the 1960s. The SJ and the plainer J-45 and J-50 became the workhorse guitars of the Gibson line. The SJ switched to a square-shouldered body in 1963; the other two models followed in 1969. Popularity waned in the 1970s and the SJ was discontinued in 1978. Gibson reissued the wartime version, with rounded shoulders, optional rosewood or mahogany back and sides, and "Only a Gibson is good enough" peghead banner, in 1991. Gruhn Guitars/DL*

♦ Gibson J-45, circa 1944. The J-45 is less fancy but no less respected than the SJ. Its combination of quality and low price made it and its natural-top sister, the J-50 (introduced in 1947), among Gibson's most successful models. The J-45 was specified with mahogany back and sides, but during World War II Gibson used whatever materials were available. This example has maple back and sides. Some J-45s from the period have a mahogany top. Gary Burnett/DL

♦ Gibson CF-100, 1957 (lower left). The cutaway body style was so well received in the archtop line that in 1950 a cutaway flat top was added. The CF-100 is a small-bodied guitar, 14 1/8 inches wide, and like the smallest cutaway archtop, the 16-inch L-4C, it has a pointed cutaway shape. An electric version, the CF-100E, was also introduced in 1950. Hoss Huggins/BM

♦ J-185, 1952 (lower right). In 1951 the J-200 body shape was appropriated for a smaller 16-inch model with maple back and sides. The J-185 lasted through 1958. Though not a commercial success, it is now considered one of Gibson's best flat tops and was reissued with a 25 1/2-inch scale, rather than the 24 3/4-inch of the original, in 1990. Guitar Tracker/BM

FLAT TOP GUITARS

◆ ◆ ◆

Other Flat Top Makers

The flat top guitar withstood the challenges of archtops and resonator guitars in the 1930s and even in the age of the electric guitar, the acoustic flat top is still the guitar that most people pick up first. Martin and Gibson remain the giants of flat top guitar production, but many other companies and individuals have left their marks.

♦ *Supertone Bradley Kincaid, early 1930s (upper right). Bradley Kincaid of Berea, Kentucky, joined Chicago's radio WLS in 1927 and began a prolific recording career in 1928 that lasted into the early 1970s. This model, sold by Sears and others in the 1930s, is of better quality than the stenciled cowboy guitars of the day—meaning it is playable—but far from professional grade. Its 1933 list price of $13.50 included one of Kincaid's songbooks, valued at 50 cents. Kincaid himself preferred a Martin 000-45. W. T. Smith/WC*

♦ *Key-Kord, early 1930s (left). The four-stringed tenor guitar was touted by one manufacturer in the late 1920s as ideal for those who did not have enough time to learn the guitar. The Key-Kord, with its mechanical chorder, was apparently designed for those who had no time at all. The peghead shape suggests that this guitar was made by Regal. Roy Acuff Museum, Opryland USA/WC*

• *Cowboy guitars, 1930s to 1950s. In addition to musicians, many cowboy movie stars lent their names to guitar models. These items are more closely related to such merchandise as lunch boxes or T-shirts than to real guitars. Upper row, from left: Red Foley, Smooth Trailing, 1950s; Gene Autry, Melody Ranch, 1940s–1950s; Gene Autry, Round Up, 1930s–1940s. Lower row: The Lone Ranger, Hi-Yo Silver!, circa 1936; Roy Rogers, circa 1954; Buck Jones, Good Luck Buck Jones and Silver, 1942. Jacksonville Guitars/BM*

• *Vivi-Tone Acousti 580, 1932 (opposite lower right, and lower left and right). Lloyd Loar, Gibson's legendary acoustic engineer of the 1920s, introduced his own radical line of acoustic and electric instruments under the Vivi-Tone brand in 1932. Acoustic model specs include a bridge assembly that spans the top soundhole and connects directly to the back of the instrument, although many do not have this feature. Loar's innovations were unsuccessful and Vivi-Tone folded at the end of 1932. The frets on Vivi-Tones are too high to allow the strings to come in contact with the fingerboard, possibly to allow the player to effect a vibrato by up-and-down pressure rather than side-to-side movement. Loar intended for the bridge assembly to extend through the body and cause the back to vibrate, so he made the back of spruce and cut f-holes into it. The rims are unusually thick. Strings West Tulsa/BM*

◆ *Epiphone, circa 1930 (upper left). This small, 13¾-inch guitar was probably designed to compete with all-mahogany models such as Gibson's L-0 of 1928 or Martin's Style 17. Epiphone's flat top designs were not fully developed at this time, as indicated by the staggered bridge-pin configuration (similar to that of the Recording series archtops) and the archtop-style elevated pickguard. Gruhn Guitars/WC*

◆ *Epiphone FT 27, 1935 (upper right). In the 1930s Epiphone was a serious contender in the archtop market, but Epi's prewar flat tops offered little challenge to Gibson and Martin. The FT 27—or as this one is labeled, F. T. No. 1—is 14¾ inches wide and the smallest of three flat tops introduced in 1935. As the model name suggests, it was a $27 guitar. Gruhn Guitars/DL*

◆ *Epiphone FT 110, 1953 (lower left and right). The FT 110 was introduced just before World War II as a square-shouldered dreadnought or, in Epi's terminology, "jumbo" size. The postwar version has this non-dreadnought shape, with a thinner waist dimension and the compensated saddle standard on Epi's high-end flat tops. The maple-body FT 110 features a "tone back" design. It is not a carved back, however, but pressed plywood. Except for the exceedingly rare flat top version of the De Luxe archtop (available with or without cutaway), the FT 110 was the top model in the line until Epiphone was sold to C. M. I., Gibson's parent company, in 1957. Gruhn Guitars/DL*

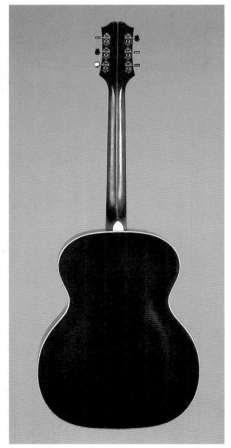

♦ *Epiphone Frontier, 1964 (above). Gibson's Epiphone flat top line, introduced in 1958, was topped by a square-shouldered dreadnought with maple back and sides. It carried the FT 110 model number and the name Frontier. In 1963 and 1964 only, it was outfitted with Western motifs on the pickguard. Lloyd Chiate/BM*

♦ *Epiphone Excellente, 1967 (right). The Excellente, or FT 120, was introduced in 1962. It is the most highly ornamented guitar in the Gibson-made Epiphone line of the 1960s, and even among Gibson-brand models, it is rivaled only by the J-200. Furthermore, the Excellente is Gibson's first postwar steel-string catalog model with rosewood back and sides. The cloud-pattern fingerboard inlay is that of Epiphone's De Luxe, the top model of Epiphone's original archtop line. With only 141 shipped from 1962 to 1970, the Excellente is one of the rarest high-quality flat tops made by Gibson during that period. Lloyd Chiate/BM*

♦ Gretsch Synchromatic X75F, circa 1947 (center). Gretsch's only serious prewar flat top was a Hawaiian model. Immediately following World War II, however, flat top versions of the fancy, large-bodied Synchromatic archtops appeared. Just as the archtops have unique "cat's-eye" soundholes, the flat tops are easily identifiable by their triangular soundholes. The Synchromatic X75F, introduced in 1947, is 16 inches wide, the smallest of the triangular-hole models and, with a list price of $79, the cheapest. It was renamed Synchromatic Sierra in 1949 but it retained the "75" on the peghead. Gruhn Guitars/WC

♦ Gretsch Rancher, 1954 (upper left and right). Gretsch ads of the late 1940s tout the Sierra flat top as being "very popular with cowboy and other singing stars." With the introduction of the Rancher in 1954, Gretsch put the cowboy association right on the guitar itself, branding the top with a G and engraving Western figures into the fingerboard inlays and pickguard. The Rancher is a descendant of Gretsch's Jumbo Synchromatic, a 17-inch flat top introduced in 1947. Gary Bohannon/DL

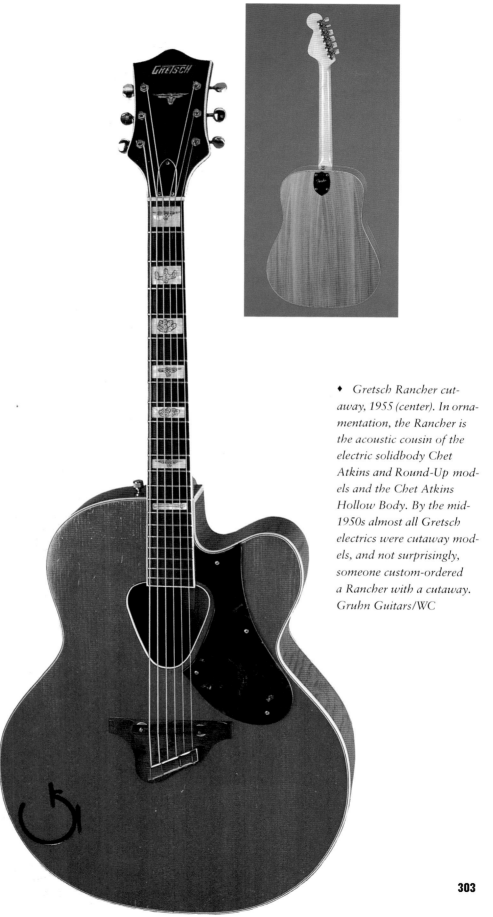

◆ Fender Wildwood III, late 1960s (upper left and right). The Fender company of Fullerton, California, revolutionized the electric guitar market in the 1950s with the first successful solidbody models. In the acoustic market, however, Fender's influence was just the opposite—negligible if not comical. Fender entered the market in 1963 with two flat tops, the larger of which was called the King, and later the Kingman. On this Kingman-size guitar, the green grain of the peghead overlay and the decal identify it as having back and sides of a colored wood known as Wildwood. Wildwood was the invention of a Scandinavian scientist who injected a chemical into basswood trees, causing the wood to turn a variety of colors, including green, orange, blue, and purple. Wildwood III is the designation for green. Fender discontinued its entire flat top line in 1971, and later Fender flat tops were made by other manufacturers. Gruhn Guitars/DL

◆ Gretsch Rancher cutaway, 1955 (center). In ornamentation, the Rancher is the acoustic cousin of the electric solidbody Chet Atkins and Round-Up models and the Chet Atkins Hollow Body. By the mid-1950s almost all Gretsch electrics were cutaway models, and not surprisingly, someone custom-ordered a Rancher with a cutaway. Gruhn Guitars/WC

♦ *D'Aquisto Flat Top De-lux, 1978 (upper left and above). Recognized as the finest living maker of acoustic archtop guitars, James D'Aquisto has also made 15 steel-string flat tops and three classical cutaway models. Aside from the scroll logo on the peghead, this 16-inch dreadnought is relatively free of ornamentation. Nevertheless, D'Aquisto added his own design touches with the oval soundhole, asymmetrical bridge, and peghead cutout. Gruhn Guitars/WC*

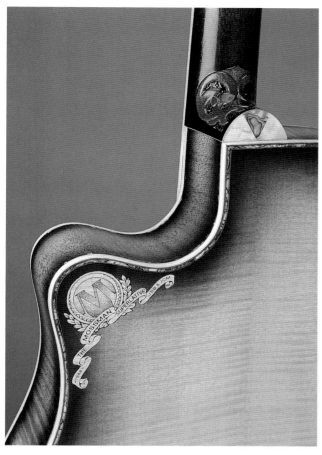

♦ Mossman Superlative custom, 1988 (opposite right and upper left and right). Few guitars from any period display the ornamentation of this instrument. Stuart Mossman began making guitars in Winfield, Kansas, in 1964. He closed his business in 1977 and sold the Mossman name to Scott Baxendale of Garland, Texas, who later sold it to John Kinsey, also of Garland. This guitar was custom-built by Baxendale for Danny Davenport, a promotion and A&R man for Warner Bros. Records. The parent company's best-known character, Bugs Bunny, resides at the fifth fret. The top ornamentation has a carved appearance but it is actually hand-painted. Around 3,500 separate pieces of pearl were used on this instrument. Danny Davenport/BM.

♦ Collings OM-3-45, 1992. Bill Collings began making flat top guitars in Houston in 1975. He moved to Austin in 1980 and by the end of the decade had established himself as one of the premier flat top makers. This guitar uses the Martin OM-45 as a starting point, with Martin-style body, pickguard, bridge, fingerboard inlay, and pearl trim. The 3 in the model name is Collings' degree of ornamentation. Bill Collings/Regan Bradshaw

FLAT TOP GUITARS
◆ ◆ ◆

Lead Belly's 12-String

There were 12-string guitars and guitarists before Lead Belly, and there are 12-strings still made today, more than 40 years after his death, but for all practical purposes the 12-string market owes its existence to one musician and one instrument. Lead Belly is single-handedly responsible for the very survival of the 12-string guitar today in American popular music—an accomplishment no other musician can claim.

Huddie (rhymes with Judy) Ledbetter was born in 1889 in Caddo parish in northwest Louisiana. He played with blues singer Blind Lemon Jefferson from around 1911 to 1913, by which time he had acquired his first 12-string guitar. In June 1918 he was imprisoned for murder in Texas. His sentence was 30 years, but he sang his way to a pardon from the governor in January 1925. Five years later, in Louisiana, he was convicted of assault with intent to murder and sentenced to 10 years in the infamous Angola penitentiary. Legend has it that Lead Belly once again sang himself out of prison, and he did record a plea for clemency in the summer of 1934. He was granted an early release in August 1934, but it came as a result of the state's effort to relieve overcrowding.

Lead Belly arrived in New York on New Year's Eve, 1934. Sean Killeen, editor of the *Lead Belly Letter*, believes that Lead Belly acquired his Stella 12-string in January 1935, and he played it on his first commercial recordings, made in April 1935 for American Record Corporation, the forerunner of Columbia. In the summer of 1944 he moved to Los Angeles, hoping to land the role of himself in a proposed Paramount movie of John Lomax's life with Bing Crosby in the starring role. He lived there off and on for about eight months, during which time, with the help of Tex Ritter, he recorded for the newly formed Capitol label. He returned to New York in 1945.

Lead Belly died in Bellevue hospital in New York in December 1949 of amyotrophic lateral sclerosis, commonly known as Lou Gehrig's disease. His wide repertoire of work songs, blues, cowboy songs, and children's songs brought him some fame during his lifetime, but it was nothing near the success of his music after his death. In 1950 the Weavers folk group had a pop hit with Lead Belly's "Goodnight Irene." They followed with another Lead Belly tune, "Rock Island Line." By the folk music boom of the late 1950s and early 1960s, he was a legend. His fingerpicking style was widely imitated, and his songs were recorded extensively.

Lead Belly was not the first to record with a 12-string, but he is the only artist to be exclusively identified with it. Moreover, his instrument, the 12-string guitar, was put into production by all the major manufacturers in the 1960s, including Martin, Gibson, Guild, Gretsch, and Kay—none of which had ever marketed a 12-string guitar before. Rickenbacker introduced an electric 12-string in 1964. The first one was given to the Beatles' George Harrison,

♦ *Stella 12-string, custom-ordered by Huddie Ledbetter, 1935. When Lead Belly ordered this guitar, the 12-string was not a new instrument, but rather an almost forgotten one. The only major makers offering 12-strings in 1935 were Regal of Chicago and Oscar Schmidt of Jersey City, New Jersey. Stella was Schmidt's low-end brand (Sovereign was the high-end), but Lead Belly's Stella is nevertheless a sturdily made instrument that can still be played without fear of it caving in. The Stella company was formed in 1935 by John Carner, who had bought Oscar Schmidt's business (except for zithers and autoharps), so this guitar, or at least its label, is not any earlier than that. Carner sold Stella to Harmony in 1940. From the label, it appears this guitar was ordered through Barth Feinberg, a New York wholesaler. The story handed down through Lead Belly's family is that he went to Jersey City to pick it up.*

who featured it on "A Hard Days Night." Harrison's influence was felt by the Byrds' Roger McGuinn, and in McGuinn's hands, the 12-string would take folk music into the electric era.

Incredibly, Harmony, which owned the Stella brand name, seemed unaware of Lead Belly's use of a Stella. Not only did the company fail to exploit the association by marketing some sort of a Lead Belly model, but it failed to see a 12-string market developing. Harmony discontinued the Stella 12-string in 1958, and Harmony offered no 12-string models whatsoever until 1964, when a cheap Stella and a Harmony-brand jumbo model were introduced.

Although the booming demand for 12-strings fell off with the decline of folk music, both acoustic and electric 12-strings continue to hold a small but significant market niche today. Were it not for Lead Belly, the 12-string guitar might well have joined the harp guitar in the category of interesting but obscure innovations.

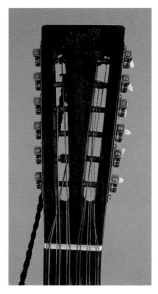

Lead Belly's guitar is 15 3/4 inches wide. The plastic pickguard is double the thickness of a standard pickguard. It may not be original to this guitar, but it appears in old photographs. Lead Belly's niece, Tiny Robinson, has preserved this guitar as Lead Belly left it, and the string sizes show that he tuned the first three courses (pairs) in unison, the fourth and fifth in octaves, and the sixth in a double-octave. Because of the heavier string gauges of Lead Belly's time and the long, 26 3/8-inch scale, he tuned four half-steps lower than standard, with the lowest string tuned to C rather than E. Queen "Tiny" Robinson/WC

BIBLIOGRAPHY

◆   ◆   ◆

Bollman, Jim, Dick Kimmel, and Doug Unger. "Vega/Fairbanks Banjos." *Pickin'* 5, no. 5 (June 1978).

Bellson, Julius. *The Gibson Story*. Kalamazoo, Mich.: Julius Bellson, 1973.

Collier, James Lincoln. *The Making of Jazz: A Comprehensive History*. Boston: Houghton Mifflin Company, 1978.

Evans, Tom, and Mary Anne Evans. *Guitars from the Renaissance to Rock*. New York: Facts on File, 1977.

Ewen, David. *Great Men of American Popular Song*. Englewood Cliffs, NJ: Prentice Hall, Inc., 1970.

Gruhn, George, and Walter Carter. *Gruhn's Guide to Vintage Guitars*. San Francisco: GPI Books, 1991.

Hartman, Robert Carl. *Guitars and Mandolins in America, Featuring the Larsons' Creations*. Rev. ed. Hoffman Estates, Ill.: Maurer and Co., 1988.

Longworth, Mike. *Martin Guitars: A History*. 3d ed. Nazareth, Penn.: Mike Longworth, 1988.

Malone, Bill C., and Judith McCullough, eds. *Stars of Country Music: Uncle Dave Macon to Johnny Rodriguez*. Urbana, Ill.: University of Illinois Press, 1975.

Pisani, Agostino. *Manuale Teorico-Pratico del Mandolinista*. 3d ed. Milano: Ulrico Hoepli, 1923.

Ramsey, Frederic Jr. "Leadbelly: A Great Long Time." *Sing Out!* 15, no. 1 (March 1965).

Siminoff, Roger. "Gibson Banjos." *Frets*. 3, no. 1 (January 1981).

Siminoff, Roger. "Gibson: The Early Years: Part I." *Pickin'* 2, no. 5 (June 1975).

Smith, Richard. *The Complete History of Rickenbacker Guitars*. Fullerton, Calif.: Centerstream Publishing, 1987.

Tsumura, Akira. *Banjos: The Tsumura Collection*. San Francisco: Kodansha International Ltd., 1984.

Turnbull, Harvey. *The Guitar from the Renaissance to the Present Day*. London: B. T. Batsford Ltd., 1974.

Webb, Robert Lloyd. *Ring the Banjar!: The Banjo in America from Folklore to Factory*. Cambridge, Mass.: The MIT Museum of the Massachusetts Institute of Technology, 1984.

Wheeler, Tom. *American Guitars: An Illustrated History*. New York: HarperCollins, 1990.

Wolfe, Darryl G. *The F-5 Journal* 1 (1987).

INDEX

◆ ◆ ◆